Soldier's Heart

SOLDIER'S HEART

Close-up Today with PTSD in Vietnam Veterans

William Schroder and Ronald Dawe

PRAEGER SECURITY INTERNATIONAL

Westport, Connecticut • London

Library of Congress Cataloging-in-Publication Data

Dawe, Ronald.
  Soldier's heart: close-up today with PTSD in Vietnam veterans / William Schroder and
  Ronald Dawe.
    p. cm.
  Includes bibliographical references.
  ISBN–13: 978–0–275–99951–3 (alk. paper)
  ISBN–10: 0–275–99951–3 (alk. paper)
1. Post-traumatic stress disorder. 2. Veterans—Mental health—United States. 3. Vietnam
War, 1961–1975—Psychological aspects. I. Schroder, William. II. Title.
RC552.P67D39 2007
616.85'21—dc22   2007016347

British Library Cataloguing in Publication Data is available.

Library of Congress Catalog Card Number: 2007016347
ISBN–13: 978–0–275–99951–3
ISBN–10: 0–275–99951–3

First published in 2007

Praeger Security International, 88 Post Road West, Westport, CT 06881
An imprint of Greenwood Publishing Group, Inc.
www.praeger.com

Printed in the United States of America

The paper used in this book complies with the
Permanent Paper Standard issued by the National
Information Standards Organization (Z39.48–1984).

10 9 8 7 6 5 4 3 2 1

This book is dedicated with love and devotion to Elizabeth Jean Jacks and Ann Dawe.

"Every gun made, every warship launched, every rocket fired signifies in a final sense a theft from those who hunger and are not fed, those who are cold and not clothed. This world in arms spends not money alone. It spends the sweat of its laborers, the genius of its scientists, the hopes of its children."

Dwight D. Eisenhower,
Speech, American Society of Newspapers, 16 April 1953

Contents

Acknowledgments

Dr. Dawe and I owe a great deal of thanks to a number of people, but without the selfless contributions of Carol Jean Sundling, Marlin Jackson, Dave Sekol, Sidney Lee, and Lance Johnson, this book would not have been possible. Also, my personal thanks and best wishes to John Neal and Peter Hilgeford, brave men and fine Americans whose life stories were courageously told but could not be included in this publication.

To Dr. Judy Kuriansky, thank you for helping bring this work to the printed page, and to Judy Mikalonis of the Andrea Hurst Agency, thanks for being a great agent.

To Byron Sacre, Jim Adams, Mike Donnelly, Bonnie Daybell, Bob Watters, Ali Mosa, and Sally Jenkins, thank you for your frank and honest criticisms. Thanks also to the many generous individuals who read and contributed their thoughts to early drafts of this manuscript: Tom Bishop, Dean Welsh, K.C. Amery, Mike Stokey, Dennis Ryan, Dave Buechel, Steve Wald, J. Kiel Gibbs, Murry Taylor, Spence Davies, Willard and Lu Gatewood, Chris and Lisa Cluett, and Jeff Nygaard. Special thanks to Sheri Short for her kindness and to Jerry Gross for his brilliance.

William Schroder

Introduction

A ragged band of prehistoric Cro-Magnon men scouts an unknown forest in search of food for their tribe. Slowly, the hunters push through the leafy underbrush, their senses tuned and alert to any movement. Vision limited to a few meters in the primeval woodland, the men maneuver stealthily so as not to alarm their quarry and fail in their quest. Soon, they hear sounds of movement in the near distance. However, these animals do not behave in the accustomed fashion, and as the hunters become more vigilant, their brains discharge even more adrenaline into their bodies.

Suddenly, the men are assailed by a terrifying clamor, and a hail of spears and stones rains down on them from every direction. In an instant, the hunting band is reduced by half, the savaged bodies of tribal confederates litter the ground, and the acrid tang of fear hovers in the air. During the first moments of the sudden attack, the men are physically and psychologically incapable of immediate response, and now, even though potent neurochemicals released into their systems enable the men to act in self-defense, eons of evolution have limited their options to three. The hunters will fight, flee, or freeze, and in seconds, each man chooses his own course of action. As the brief but deadly battle develops, the hunters—themselves now killers—wreak havoc on their assailants. The men slash, grapple, and strike the enemy. Horror all around, psychologically, each man retreats into one of the three protective options. Some will fight with unexpected bloodlust and determination. Others will turn away from the sights, sounds, and smells of human carnage to ensure they live through the day. Still others will freeze. Incapable of action, they will not defend themselves but instead psychologically shut out the overwhelming butchery.

When the fighting ends, the surviving constituents assess the damage, bind their wounds, and head for home. From the first moments of the attack, preservation of life was each man's goal, and each survivor rejoices in his durability. However, the men will bear the burden of the memories of the day's violent encounter. For some, fading body scars will provide lasting testimony to the ferocity of the battle, but an unfortunate few, psychologically wounded, will suffer the pain of combat for life.

"What's wrong with Dad? I don't understand why he does those things."
"Aunt Marion is so unhappy. Will she ever find joy?"
"The whole family was devastated when Roger took his life. Why? He had so much going for him."

Living in the shadowy interior of the brain's limbic system and invisible to the untrained eye, posttraumatic stress disorder (PTSD) reaches beyond its stricken victims negatively to influence family members and loved ones. For years, families and friends have heard bits and pieces— snippets—of wartime events the veterans faced in their lives. Grudgingly revealed, generalized, and non-specific, these anecdotes leave the veterans' loved ones yearning for more information, desperate to understand what made the veterans who they are, and if necessary for discovery, to *know* and *feel* the horrors their husbands, daughters, sons, brothers, or fathers experienced. This book examines the life portraits of five courageous veterans who suffer with PTSD and provides a roadmap to gain understanding of PTSD's insidious and often counterintuitive symptoms.

Today, an astonishing 25 percent of our brave American servicemen and women return from Iraq and Afghanistan diagnosed with "psychological problems," and our hearts ache at the evidence of their struggle to adjust to civilian life.[1] Away from the blood, gore, and bared teeth of the combat zone and once again in a safe environment among friends and family, many still experience difficult homecomings. Seemingly uncomfortable in their own skin, they abuse alcohol and other drugs, seek isolation from loved ones, and randomly and for no apparent reason, display levels of anger and even rage that frightens and confuses.

Are these the same men and women who, a year earlier, kissed their loved ones, winked, and then waved goodbye with optimistic smiles? Could combat so dramatically change someone, or does wartime service create a new, altogether different person? How? What happens? Who gets PTSD, and why? What does it look like? Can it be cured?

The answers to these questions and a great many more are found within the pages of this book. This exploration of PTSD's myriad symptoms and insidious effects will equip you to recognize the disorder in a loved one, and through understanding, take positive steps to facilitate the healing process.

To explore fully the lifelong effects of war trauma in the twentieth century, the focus necessarily must be on Vietnam veterans. Sadly, given today's course of events in Iraq and Afghanistan, 30 years from now, researchers will have another generation of combat veterans to study, but until that unhappy day, only Vietnam veterans provide a lifetime of experience with war trauma from which we can learn a great deal. Without compensation or promise of recognition, the five combat veterans featured in this book courageously agreed to share their life experiences, to re-live decades of fear, pain, bitter resentment, hope, and redemption, so others can learn, and future comrades-in-arms will not suffer so greatly the anguish of Soldier's Heart.

William Schroder
Dr. Ron Dawe

NOTE

1. JAMA, Issue 295 Vol. 9, 1 March 2006, Charles W. Hogue, MD, Jennifer Auchterlonie, MS, Charles Milliken, MD.

Prologue

In January 1973, Richard Nixon appeared on nationwide television and announced a treaty had been signed. The United States had achieved "peace with honor" in Vietnam.[1] Two months later, the last remaining combat troops were withdrawn, and America's 10,000 day war was over. Of the three million American servicemen and women who served in the war, 58,000 died, 1,800 remained missing in action, and 305,000 were wounded.[2] Few took seriously Nixon's attempts to put a positive spin on the outcome of a national tragedy. Still, an angry, disaffected, war-weary population was happy to see the bloodshed end and our troops home at last.

Soon, in cities and towns across the nation, anecdotal evidence abounded of "troubled" or "disturbed" Vietnam veterans lurking in the shadows of society, unable to adjust, unable (or unwilling) fully to reenter their communities and pursue "normal" lives. Not long after the war, Vietnam vets were frequently depicted on television and in movies as solitary, drug-addled figures who lived in the wild and clung to dark memories. As the years passed, tens of thousands displayed abnormal behavioral patterns, and their friends, families, and loved ones wondered why. The life portraits that follow give voice to a generation of Americans who faced the horrors of an ill-advised and unpopular war, and then lived with the tragic aftermath.

Before journeying through the lives of the veterans featured in this book, the reader should be aware of a few basic facts about PTSD:

1. An estimated 5.2 million American adults ages 18 to 54 have PTSD.

2. 30 percent of Vietnam veterans developed PTSD at some point after the war, and the disorder has been detected in high percentages among veterans of the Persian Gulf War and the wars in Iraq and Afghanistan.

3. Depression, alcohol or other substance abuse, or other anxiety disorders frequently co-occur with PTSD. The likelihood of treatment success is increased when these other conditions are appropriately diagnosed and treated as well.[3]

Today, the accepted criteria for a diagnosis of PTSD are:

a. The person has been exposed to a traumatic event in which both of the following have been present:

   1. The person has experienced, witnessed, or been confronted with an event or events that involve actual or threatened death or serious injury, or a threat to the physical integrity of oneself or others.

   2. The person's response involved intense fear, helplessness, or horror. Note: in children, it may be expressed instead by disorganized or agitated behavior.

b. The traumatic event is persistently re-experienced in at least one of the following ways:

   1. Recurrent and intrusive distressing recollections of the event, including images, thoughts, or perceptions. Note: in young children, repetitive play may occur in which themes or aspects of the trauma are expressed.

   2. Recurrent distressing dreams of the event. Note: in children, there may be frightening dreams without recognizable content.

   3. Acting or feeling as if the traumatic event were recurring (includes a sense of reliving the experience, illusions, hallucinations, and dissociative flashback episodes, including those that occur upon awakening or when intoxicated). Note: in children, trauma-specific reenactment may occur.

   4. Intense psychological distress at exposure to internal or external cues that symbolize or resemble an aspect of the traumatic event.

   5. Physiologic reactivity upon exposure to internal or external cues that symbolize or resemble an aspect of the traumatic event.

c. Persistent avoidance of stimuli associated with the trauma and numbing of general responsiveness (not present before the trauma), as indicated by at least three of the following:

   1. Efforts to avoid thoughts, feelings, or conversations associated with the trauma.

   2. Efforts to avoid activities, places, or people that arouse recollections of the trauma.

   3. Inability to recall an important aspect of the trauma.

   4. Markedly diminished interest or participation in significant activities.

   5. Feelings of detachment or estrangement from others.

   6. Restricted range of affect (e.g., unable to have loving feelings).

   7. Sense of foreshortened future (e.g., does not expect to have a career, marriage, children, or a normal life span).

d. Persistent symptoms of increased arousal (not present before the trauma), indicated by at least two of the following:

   1. Difficulty falling or staying asleep.

   2. Irritability or outbursts of anger.

   3. Difficulty concentrating.

   4. Hyper-vigilance.

   5. Exaggerated startle response.

e. Duration of the disturbance (symptoms in B, C, and D) is more than one month.

f. The disturbance causes clinically significant distress or impairment in social, occupational, or other important areas of functioning.[4]

The veterans featured in this book exhibit a wide array of the symptoms of PTSD. As you walk with them through their life experiences, PTSD will become more than a sterile enumeration of causes and symptoms and will change forever the way you view this debilitating disorder.

NOTES

1. White House address, 23 Jan 1973.

2. Historical Atlas of the Unites States, 23 March 2003, Matthew White. http://users.erols.com/mwhite28/20centry.htm.

3. American Psychological Association Plenary Session, 9 August 2003, United States Surgeon General Vice Admiral Richard H. Carmona, MD, MPH, FACS.

4. Diagnostic Criteria from Diagnostic and Statistical Manual for Mental Health Disorders. DSM-IV.

The Soldiers Speak

CHAPTER 1

Carol Jean Sundling
Pennsylvania
U.S. Air Force Flight Nurse

In Vietnam, I cared for Americans, Koreans, South Vietnamese soldiers, and enemy soldiers. I cared for old men, women, and children. Every one bled, had pain, loved, and wanted love. We are all children of the same Father.

Oh, my gosh, where do I begin?

After everything I went through in Vietnam, you'd think I'd not remember so vividly the events leading up to my first day in country. The whole thing was silly, and it embarrasses me to tell, but all my life I've been called a dizzy blonde. I guess this proves it.

I had leave time accrued, so in September 1970 when I received orders to ship out, I took a few days and visited friends in Hawaii. I was in uniform when my plane lifted off from San Francisco, and a handsome navy commander sat next to me. He introduced himself and suggested we pass the time with a Hawaiian drink. At that time in my life, I had no experience with alcohol, and the words *Mai Tai* had an exotic ring. An amiable, chatty guy, our difference in rank seemed not to bother the commander. He ordered a second round, and then a third. I was having a grand time and looked forward to seeing my friends in a few moments. Then, the commander told me we still had four more hours flying time. Four more hours? Where the hell were we going? What can I say? I came from a small town in central Pennsylvania and thought Hawaii just off the coast of California. Plenty of time for more Mai Tais. By the time we landed in Honolulu, I was fried.

My friends met me at the airport, shocked I'd planned a two-day visit. Civilian flights home were booked, so I went to the air force terminal to reserve space and get back to California. Tired and scared, the Mai Tai glow long since gone, now I had visions of me listed AWOL and shot as a deserter.

A corporal at the air force terminal read at my orders aloud, "Depart SEATAC: Republic of Vietnam." Then, he sighed, shook his head, leaned over the counter and tapped the paperwork with his thumb. "You're not supposed to leave CONUS, Lieutenant."

Oh my gosh, I'd already violated orders. I was doomed. The corporal motioned for me to follow him down a long hallway. In front of his supervisor's office, he shook his head again. "I don't know how much trouble you're in."

The sergeant behind the desk was the biggest, meanest looking guy I'd ever seen. He must have been in the air force his whole life, because he had stripes all the way up and down both arms. He took one look at my orders, and then bellowed, "Jesus Christ, Lieutenant! What the hell do you think you're doing? You can't be here. You're not supposed to leave CONUS!"

That was enough for me. The long flight, the alcohol, and the big sergeant were too much for my rural Pennsylvanian sensibilities. I broke down and bawled like a baby. My shoulders quaked, my chest heaved, and through a river of tears, I sobbed, "I'd be in CONUS if someone would just tell me where it is!" Then, he told me CONUS was military talk for Continental United States.

All military flights to the States full, the sergeant put my shattered dignity and me on an embassy flight through Clark Air Force Base in the Philippines, and then on to Saigon the next day.

When we landed at Ton Son Nhut, I stepped out the door of that aircraft dressed in my air force skirt and heels certain I was the greenest second lieutenant in Southeast Asia. The heat almost knocked me over. It felt like heaven and earth were on fire, and when I gasped for breath, my lungs closed against a peculiar, sweetish-sour odor that hung in the air. Certainly, Vietnam was like no other place I'd ever been.

➤ *Carol Jean's first impression of being "in country" was a forceful reminder of the vast gulf that separated her view of life before she experienced her first olfactory, auditory, visual, and tactile sensations of Vietnam.*

I checked in to Headquarters Company of the 903rd Air Medical Evacuation Squadron, and within the hour, I was on a C-130 to Cam Rahn Bay. This first flight was indicative of things to come. A dozen wounded men were strapped into litters lining the aircraft interior. My first air evacuation, and I still had on my high heels.

➤ *With no time to prepare psychologically, immediately, Carol Jean was airborne in an aircraft filled with wounded soldiers.*

We approached Phan Thiet at dusk, and with the enemy active in the area, we did an assault landing, a really scary high-overhead spiraling dive into the airfield that felt like a wild, out-of-control carnival ride, and I instinctively tightened my seatbelt and mumbled a quick prayer. On the ground, the crew scrambled into action and loaded more wounded on board. Medical personnel scurried among the injured, strapped them down, checked for bleeding and administered intravenous bottles. Scared speechless, I sat frozen in my seat and thought, oh, my gosh, Mom. I'm going to be here a whole year.

➤ *Her first exposure to combat induced traumatic stressors. In response, Carol Jean's brain released amino acids and neurotransmitters, which gave her the ability to deal with the immediate threats to her physical integrity—chemicals that transformed and damaged her brain.*

Airborne again, I looked out the little window next to my seat and saw sudden swarms of little red and green bees floating near the ground and sudden balls of bright, white light that flared up then died down again. What was all that? Everything was so strange—so foreign. Later, a member of the crew noticed me trembling, put a hand on my shoulder, and told me everything would be okay. I looked around at the injured men, heard their moans over the rush of the slipstream, and tried hard to believe him. That was my first day in Vietnam.

➤ *Repeated stressors would make the damage to Carol Jean's psyche permanent.*

* * *

Growing up in Selinsgrove, Pennsylvania, I don't remember being anything other than happy. My parents had settled in Pennsylvania after World War II, and when my sister and I came along, they moved to Selinsgrove to get the family out of the coal regions.

I was three when we started building our house there, and when I say we built it, I mean we *built* it—ourselves. Everyone in the family participated. Just a little three-bedroom ranch, and I knew people lived in bigger, fancier houses, but I thought ours the best. Dad had drawn the plans himself, and every afternoon when he came home from work, we met him at the construction site and carried bricks and mortar. Our whole family built that house together.

Once in first grade we had show and tell, and I told the story of helping my father mix cement to build a path out to a picnic area behind our house. I guess even then I didn't know when to shut up, because when I told how the bunnies came into our yard at night and made little turds in the wet concrete, the teacher stood me in the hall facing the coat rack. I was mortified, but I also felt cheated. We'd laughed about that story at home just that morning, and I'd looked forward to telling it in class.

I lived in the house *we built* until I went off to nursing school.

I'm a Pennsylvania girl all the way. Until I joined the air force, I'd never been anywhere else. I came from a close family, and when you love each other as much as we did, why leave? Mom and Dad met in France during World War II and married in England. Dad was in the 82nd Ordinance, and Mom was an Army nurse. I honestly can't think of a way to tell you how wonderful they were.

➠ *Her veteran parents modeled a strong sense of duty and service. Never guilty of abuse or neglect, they instilled in young Carol Jean the value of marriage and family.*

Dad worked for Pennsylvania Power and Light. He liked his job—his career—but music was his first love. He was a drummer and a musician in his heart and soul. Of course, there was no way to support a family doing that in Selinsgrove, so he kept his "real" job, but he played music until he died.

I still love music today. As a little girl, I remember Dad playing or singing something, and we took trips to New York, Paris, and Rome in our imaginations. Later, when my sister was older, we played Dad's records and sang and danced around the room pretending we were elephants or monkeys. I still remember the words to those songs today, although I don't sing them much anymore.

Music nurtured the spirit in my family. Dad loved jazz, and he had a collection of big, heavy records. In the evenings, he let me put them on, and together we listened to *Lady Day* by Billy Holiday, or I tapped my toes while Dad played along with Gene Krupa and Buddy Rich. All that music has stayed with me, stayed in my head. Even today, when I vacation, instead of souvenirs, I buy local music from the places I visit.

* * *

I heard a lot of noise my first night in Cam Rahn Bay but not much music. I arrived late and signed in at company headquarters, a two-story, concrete block building next to the main runway. The duty officer looked tired, but he smiled and offered to drive me to my new quarters, a corrugated steel Quonset hut with plywood partitioning. I'd had no expectations about living accommodations, so even though my little room lacked style and fresh air, I had privacy, and I was determined to make my new home as comfortable and pleasant as I could.

I lay on my bunk that night and stared at the ceiling, my mind racing. The continual *wop wop*-ing of helicopters coming and going rattled my little window, punctuated occasionally by the roar of a departing jet.

➠ *The hallmark auditory stimuli associated with the Vietnam War, the UH-1 Huey helicopter. Soon, Carol Jean paired that sound with the arrival of broken, bloody, and dying young men.*

Frightened and alone, I did then what I did in the Girl Scouts when faced with a difficult problem: I took stock. A good nurse knew how to care for people, and I didn't doubt my competence, but I thought about the flight in, my compatriots hovering in the dim light over wounded soldiers in the back of that aircraft, and I wondered whether this little blonde from Pennsylvania would hold up and do her duty. I said a prayer and asked God for courage. Sleep came, but my fluttering heart brought dreams of Buddy Rich and my dad, and I found comfort in their repeated phrases and uncluttered rhythms. A week later, I learned the other noises I heard each night were rats scurrying between the partitions in our hut.

❧ *The isolation that would become a chief characteristic of Carol Jean's life began the day she reported for duty with the 903rd Air Medical Evacuation Squadron.*

The 903rd Air Medical Evacuation Squadron consisted of 30 nurses (four female) and 120 medical technicians. Our mission was to fly out to the field, pick up wounded soldiers, and keep them alive until we got them to a treatment facility.

❧ *The medical staff consisted of 150 medical personnel but only four female flight nurses. Because of this, Carol Jean was denied the opportunity for the feminine support and intellectual understanding she needed to maintain her identity.*

The first thing a flight nurse did in Vietnam was qualify in the various aircraft the air force used for evacuation. I started with the C-130 then went to the C-7, C-118, and C-123. In those days, new nurses qualified flying live missions. Qualification consisted of mastery of all emergency systems, set-up and disassembly of medical equipment, preparing the aircraft for the wounded, loading and unloading patients, ditching and evacuation, and crash landing procedure. I learned everything while in the air from the onboard nurses who shouted instructions all day over the roar of the engines.

On the ground, I helped with the injured. After takeoff, with the patients stabilized, we went over procedure again and again. We worked 15 hours a day. During my first two weeks in country, I qualified in all four types of aircraft. I'd been on the receiving end of enemy rockets, mortars, machine gun, and rifle fire, and already I'd seen enough charred, torn, and mangled flesh to last a lifetime.

❧ *Only days into her tour, Carol Jean had been exposed to far more traumatic stressors and events than necessary to meet the requirements for a diagnosis of PTSD.*

Each night, I went back to my hooch exhausted and flopped down on my bunk. My last thought before sleep was that in a few hours, I'd do it all over again.

➤ *Experiencing the symptom of detachment from others, Carol Jean began psychologically and emotionally to isolate herself from the suffering she witnessed each day. Gradually, she succumbed to fatigue and the gruesome nature of her daily existence.*

The squadron's officer's mess hall was just down the road, but we didn't use it much. We were airborne in the mornings before it opened and rarely got back before it closed at night. The female nurses ate when we could in the guys' little common-area lounge with a kitchen and a few pots and pans. Between work and the heat, I never felt much like eating, but at least my stateside baby fat disappeared pretty fast.

The first month in Vietnam, I thought they would work me to death. It took time to toughen up and get used to the pace.

➤ *The complexity and traumatic nature of her duties in the midst of such chaos caused her brain to under-process much of the detail of these memories. These types of fragmented memories are remembered not in the neocortex but in the limbic system and present as symptoms of PTSD.*

I reported to my aircraft at dawn each morning, flew all day, and returned late at night. In the mornings, while I prepared the aircraft for the day's patients, the pilots went to briefing and came back with the mission sheet, which told us where we went that day and whom to contact. Our flight schedule was often determined by the firefights of the previous night and the wounded that needed evacuation. In addition to our scheduled sorties, we got numerous calls every day to pick up "urgents" from the medivac choppers. When those calls came, we broke off whatever we were doing and hustled out to a prearranged pick up point. We never knew what came next. We just went where called.

Not all our evacuations were under enemy fire, of course, but we treated them as though they were. In the field, we never knew where the bad guys were, so we always made assault landings, hit the brakes hard, and got the ramp down quick. I got out of the aircraft and screened patients while the technicians loaded them on board.

Usually, by the time the wounded reached us, the medics in the field had tagged them, so I crosschecked the manifest and quickly went over their injuries. This all happened fast. We didn't waste time on the ground. If we could spare the precious few seconds, we strapped the patients in before I signaled the crew chief to go. Every takeoff from a field strip was an ear-splitting, bone-jarring event. To get out of enemy small arms range quickly, the pilots applied maximum power, nosed the aircraft up, and rocketed to altitude as fast as possible.

✤ *The psychological insults exacerbated by the physiological strain on her body.*

We loaded patients according to where they got off, like in temporary warehousing, so a single patient could be dropped at his destination without moving anyone else. At the time, our C-130s were equipped with 50 litters stacked five-high down the center of the aircraft and 22 along the cabin sides. Airborne and en route, my first responsibility was to check for bleeding and make sure all the IVs were running.

There was never any time for real nursing on board evac flights, no time to spend with individual soldiers. Mostly, we were up and down—short turnarounds—get them to the hospital as quickly as possible. You see, there were too many. Too many suffering young soldiers transported in my aircraft. I was just one person—the only nurse on board—and I barely kept up with the seemingly endless stream of bloodied and broken American boys.

✤ *Carol Jean couldn't fight or flee, so the only survival strategy left to her was to freeze.*

Very quickly, it became clear to me I could not do my duty and remain the person I was—sensitive, caring, and emotionally involved. In a real shooting war with a mission to accomplish, I had no time for fooling around with any bullshit *feelings*. No time for crying or any kind of acting out.

Sometimes, as we drove to the flight line in the morning, I looked out at the sun rising over the South China Sea and thought it a promise from God, a new day—a new beginning—and I had to leave behind the events of the day before. We transported between 80 and 200 wounded a day, a continuing parade of baby-faced victims, but I couldn't allow myself to lose faith in God. He was the only person I could talk to—the only one I could get pissed off with.

✤ *Carol Jean turned to her faith for assurance that God, her only sanctuary, had not abandoned her to the evil that was Vietnam.*

I saw all the bullshit around me and wondered why He allowed it to happen, but there was never any time to ask questions, no time to talk about it. I just did what I had to. I saw all that stuff day after day and won-dered how man could be so inhumane, but that little flicker of light was always in my heart, and I clung to it. I had to have that in my heart to keep going and be the person my patients needed. I had to smile and touch them and somehow convey I cared, even though I didn't have time to do anything for them. Not enough time—never enough time—to give those young men the care they deserved. From the first moment I arrived in country, I froze inside and locked my emotions behind a wall. I put on an iron mask and kept it on every single day for 365 days. I kept everything I felt behind my mask, and I'd not realize until many years later I'd never learned how to take it off and let my emotions out.

➤ *Psychologically avoiding the stimulus associated with her life in Vietnam, Carol Jean became aware of a numbing of her prior emotional responsiveness towards human pain and suffering.*

* * *

Pissed off at God. What a joke that was. Like He had time for that, but I couldn't help myself. What else could I do? The world I found myself in was all wrong—all violence, heartbreak and sadness.

I guess it was natural I turned to Him for answers. I was born and brought up Protestant, United Church of Christ, a union of the Church of Christ and the Reform Church. Looking back over my life, having a background of faith has been my greatest strength. As a child, I always believed I had two extended families, my aunts, uncles, and cousins, and the other members of the church. All our family reunions and holiday gatherings were on the church grounds. On those occasions, we got together and ate huge meals, and I romped with my cousins while the old folks played music. You can picture it. Even if you've never lived it, you can see it in your mind—life in rural America in the 50s.

➤ *In contrast to many of her generation, Carol Jean truly had a Father Knows Best childhood. Reared to believe in a just and loving God, in her world, her immediate family extended to the members of her church.*

Once, six or seven years old, dressing for Sunday services, I got it into my head I wanted to wear my everyday shoes to church. They were in sad shape, worn, and the toes scuffed, but so white, soft, and comfortable, I couldn't resist. I put on my best white dress socks, fixed my hair just so, and put a pink ribbon in. I thought if I looked particularly nice that morning, Mother wouldn't notice the shoes.

Fat chance.

I walked into the kitchen carrying my little purse, and Mother looked me over. Her eyes got to the offending shoes, and she frowned then extended her arm and pointed toward my bedroom. I got the message. I wanted to protest, plead my case, but she just stood there, hand on hip, pointing. I knew "comfortable" wouldn't be a good enough argument. I'd have to think of something more persuasive, like a rare form of childhood arthritis. Silence in the kitchen. I thought I'd give it another minute. Maybe the phone would ring or a bird would fly in the window, Mother's attention would be diverted, and she'd forget. Then I heard the tap,

tap, tapping of her right toe on the linoleum, and I knew I'd better go change.

Mom was the disciplinarian in the family. She was such a kind person and gentle spirit. I know the little punishment she dealt hurt her far more than us kids. Occasionally, when she gave me a swat on the butt, I'd run into my bedroom, stand in front of the mirror, and pinch my rear end until it turned rosy red. Then, I'd lay on my bed with my pants down so when Mom came in to talk about what happened, she'd feel bad. When I was a little girl, I used to do silly things like that.

Mom was the cook in the family, too, and we ate midwestern. Meat and potatoes, and if we had dessert, pudding or Jell-O. Sundays after church, we feasted on ham or roast beef. I remember always having enough to eat, but if we wanted seconds, usually only potatoes or vegetables remained. One of my earliest fantasies was growing up to be 16 years old and driving our old Chrysler to the Dutch Pantry restaurant outside town, buying an entire roast beef, and taking it out in the country to eat the whole thing. I guess a child not getting everything she wants is a good thing.

* * *

Our medivac aircraft got shot at a lot. I think the enemy considered it sport. A private in the North Vietnamese army knocking a big American plane out of the sky with his old Chinese rifle would be a hero for life. Our aircraft often took enemy fire, but in back, we were usually so busy we never paid attention. Sometimes, we didn't even know the aircraft had been hit until the crew chief showed us the bullet holes. Also, tracers flying around us got to be old hat—those swarms of red and green bees I'd seen on my first day in country. After a while, we didn't even think about it.

➤ *During moments of extreme danger and stress, the brain may develop a survival strategy of dissociating or freezing out the threat to the physical integrity to self.*

Once, we'd been busy up north all day, and at 10 P.M., we deadheaded back. The navy threw a party that night, and we wanted to attend. On short final into Cam Rahn Bay airfield, the VC let go a barrage of mortar fire, and the tower diverted us around until the dust settled. When we landed, the guys on the flight line told us the navy club had taken a direct hit, and there were lots of casualties. I don't know why, probably because I knew those folks, but at that moment, I thought for the first time about my own destruction. My own charred and broken body could have been among the others in the rubble of that navy club. I didn't sleep much that night.

➤ *Carol Jean now began to have intrusive distressing thoughts of the danger she faced every day, which resulted in sleep disturbance.*

The thing was, we never talked about what we saw or how we felt on mission days. I mean, who wants to revisit and rehash a parade of mangled American boys? Sometimes we talked about how many we evacuated that day or the places we went, but we kept the conversation light. When we spoke about the Vietnamese villages we flew into, we always made our technician, Dennis, tell the story. Dennis stuttered. Getting your tongue around Vietnamese words was hard enough but impossible if you had a stammer. Is that sick humor? We laughed until we cried. Of course, today, no one would do something like that, but Dennis was a great guy and a good sport. I've frequently wondered what happened to him.

❖ *Like a great many Vietnam veterans, Carol Jean made no attempt to stay in touch with her friend, Dennis—"a great guy." Avoidance of people, places, or activities that arouse recollections of traumatic events is a symptom of PTSD and quite common in veterans.*

That fall, everyone was excited about the college football games on the Armed Forces Television Network, our only contact with the outside world. At the time, a group of army helicopter pilots was temporarily stationed at the navy compound and had built a drinking club from plywood and corrugated tin, so we became friends and watched the games with them. The army chopper pilots drank too much and walked a little on the wild side, but if you ever needed entertainment, that was the crowd to hang with.

A week before the Army/Navy game, the army pilots concocted a scheme—Operation G.O.A.T.—to kidnap the Navy mascot, and they asked another nurse and me to help. They needed a diversionary assault, and we were it.

I was skeptical. The navy compound was ringed with a high chain-link fence and guard towers with spotlights. When the big day came, Bonnie and I dressed in our shortest civilian skirts, put on makeup, and styled our hair. The army guys figured us diversion enough on our own, but we didn't believe them, so just before the officers club closed, we stopped in and got two big buckets of fried chicken.

At the appointed hour, Bonnie and I drove to the perimeter gate with our jeep-load of chicken. You can imagine it wasn't too difficult to get those guards out of the towers for a nighttime picnic with two American girls. While we did that, the army chopper pilots penetrated the wire at the side of the compound and stole the goat.

They hustled the poor little thing back to their club in a litter truck, painted GO ARMY on both sides and returned it while the navy ate chicken, made small talk, and flirted. Needless to say, the navy was pissed.

You know what? I don't even remember who won the game, but that stupid little incident stuck with me all these years. I guess those were the things I needed to do—trivial things to escape the reality of getting back on that plane and going out to work again. Silly, childish things a young soldier did to stay sane.

→ *However, no amount of planned diversion could ameliorate the damage already done to Carol Jean's brain.*

* * *

In the air, my primary responsibilities were the safety of my crew and the well-being of my patients, in that order. I always considered myself blessed to work with the greatest crew of technicians in the world. When we came out of a landing zone under rocket or mortar fire, everyone was scared, but no one showed it. No matter the situation or the consequences, they did their duty and were like brothers to me.

Of course, I never had the time to know patients individually, but very quickly, I came to know the type of men they were. During my tour in Vietnam, I cared for thousands—literally thousands—and to a man, they were courageous beyond belief, loyal, and if they expressed emotion at all, it was hope for the future and prayers for the comrades they left behind.

→ *Desperate not to identify with the wounded soldiers, Carol Jean attempts to compartmentalize her feelings towards the people she interacts with each day.*

On bad days, we stacked them like cordwood, young men with horrible wounds, and though I couldn't do much for them, I felt they were comforted just knowing they were en route to a medical facility. I think I mentioned there were only four female flight nurses in the 903rd AEF. You should have seen the look on those wounded faces when they saw a blonde American girl in their war zone. When I got off the aircraft to load patients, they lay on their litters with huge eyes, and invariably, they wanted to reach out to me. Some even asked, "Lieutenant—Ma'am. May I touch you?"

One severely wounded soldier asked whether he could smell me. On duty I never wore anything anyone could smell, of course, but I sensed the boy craved feminine contact, so as I examined his wound, I leaned over and let him breathe on my cheek for a few seconds. They wanted the skin, the touch, and the smell so badly. Not a sexual thing, just something that made them feel like home—made them feel alive—like a human being again. As a woman, I understood what they felt, and I couldn't deny them what they needed at that level.

→ *The vast numbers of dead and dying young men Carol Jean dealt with initiated the development of survivor's guilt even before she left Vietnam.*

Before we flew, patients were prepared for transport. If a boy had a major wound and the hospital technicians had time, they opened the wounded area and inserted an intravenous antibiotic drip. Then, they placed him in a bi-valve cast—a cast cut in half to prevent further injury to the wound during transport. Think of boxing groceries before taking them home. Occasionally, there was time to stop the bleeding, administer morphine, and such, but mostly, we only had time to get them on board, and then deal with their injuries the best we could.

Ground combat in Vietnam was particularly hazardous to heads, arms, and legs. Sometimes, however, we got a chest or abdominal wound, often a problem because we couldn't always determine the extent of the injury. If the medics on the ground had time, they tagged patients before transport. For example, AKA meant amputation above the knee. BKA meant below the knee. Bilateral BKA meant both legs below the knee.

One day, we got called to Quang Tri. The guys on the ground had made significant enemy contact, and the wounded were everywhere. As we touched down on our first sortie, a fleet of army litter trucks barreled onto the flight line. These trucks, similar to those in the TV series, *M.A.S.H*, carried four litters in back, and we called them "cracker boxes."

Our aircraft rolled to a stop, and I jumped off and ran to screen the wounds, check the manifest, and make sure the patients were all still alive and not bleeding. I crawled into the nearest cracker box and squatted down to check the two men on the lower litters first. The young soldier on my right, tagged AAK—amputee above the knee—had a blanket over him, but when I glanced down, it almost looked like he had two legs. Under a lot of morphine, he was awake and pretty hyper. When I looked into his face, his eyes lit up, and he smiled. I was probably the first American woman he'd seen in months. He reached out, grabbed my arm, and said, "Ma'am, I've got something I want you to see!" The tarmac overflowed with cracker boxes, and I had other patients to tend, so I told him I'd be back in a moment.

While I checked out the other three patients in the truck, the amputee called out, "Ma'am, look under my blanket. I want to show you something!" The poor kid was out of it but as excited as a child at a circus. I had to give him a moment. When I lifted his blanket, I saw what the medics had done. They'd placed IV bottles below the stump of his amputated leg. To fool him? I don't know. He was so sedated, to this day, I don't know whether he knew the extent of his injury, but he wasn't thinking about that. He wanted only to show me the Purple Heart pinned to his shirt—show this round-eyed nurse the medal his company commander had given him. I remember then saying a silent prayer, but not for him. I prayed I hid my expression of sad pity. I prayed I kept it behind my mask.

➤ *This overt effort to hide her feelings and perhaps deceive a terribly wounded soldier contributed to Carol Jean's future survivor's guilt.*

The technicians loaded the boy into the aircraft, and I turned my attention to the patient on the litter above. He looked in pretty bad shape. When I checked, I found his IV bottle full of blood on the floor under the lower litter. In the litter driver's ignorance, he had placed the IV bottle on the floor of the cracker box, and the patient's blood siphoned out of his body down to the bottle. That was the start of a busy day.

➤ *Carol Jean's personalization of other caregivers' mistakes added to her psychological distress and contributed to the severity of her PTSD later in life.*

* * *

Growing up, I never really thought about nursing. In school, I was good in math and the sciences, and I wanted to be an engineer, but that plan went out the window with the arrival of my brother, Jeffrey. Even in those days, it cost plenty to send three children to college, but the Harrisburg School of Nursing was within the family budget.

My sister, Lynne, the most spiritual person I've ever known, would have been a great health care provider. Though we're exact opposites, I love her with all my heart. A tomboy, Lynne was like the wind—free, independent, and she wanted little. Unaffected by the world around her, Lynne marched to her own drumbeat, her own thoughts, and her own conclusions.

➤ *Carol Jean admired her sister for her psychological strength and resilience— traits she perceived she lacked.*

I was very different. I worked hard, paid attention to my responsibilities, and never let anything slide. During the summer, Mom always told us to be indoors with the streetlights. At the appointed hour, when they popped on, I'd hightail it for home, but Lynne always took her sweet time. She'd walk around a tree or climb a wall and sit on it, acting nonchalant and cavalier. I'd look back at her and say, "Faster, Lynne! Come on!"

But she'd smile at me, take an extra spin around a light pole and chirp, "What's the hurry? If Mom spanks us, when it's your turn, just pretend she's swatting me, and it won't hurt."

I always obeyed my parents, did my chores, did the right thing, but nothing ever bothered Lynne. Nobody intimidated her. We had the usual sister-spats. What sisters do not? But we were never unkind to each other.

The family budget limited our vacations to camping trips in the mountains, but Lynne and I loved that more than anything. We pitched tents and dug fire pits, set up campsites with outdoor tables, chairs, and hammocks. Dad took us on long hikes and taught us how to make snake sticks. We learned about rocks and trees and plants, and we went on long and determined fossil hunts. Dad taught us how to shoot a rifle and pistol, and sometimes, he took us with him squirrel hunting, but fishing was a favorite activity, and for little girls, we were pretty good at it.

For me, another fun vacation was to Washington, D.C. We took our camping gear but occasionally stayed one night in a motel. During the day, we packed food and picnicked on the public lawns downtown.

Of course now, I know my family didn't have much money, but as a little girl, I thought us rich beyond belief. My friend's father owned a mill outside town. They had a big house with a swimming pool and nice furniture, but when I went there to play, I still felt they didn't have what I had. No one had a family like mine.

➤ *Carol Jean's wealth was derived from the close emotional bonds and impenetrable security her family provided.*

My parents got along well and always showed each other much love. Sometimes, I'd hear them in their bedroom talking about the day and what went on in our lives. Their gentle voices and kind words always made me feel warm and comfortable inside. My parents were happy with the circumstances of their lives, and they loved their children. Once, I overheard the neighbor ladies at the bridge table with my mother. "Oh, Jean, you're so lucky to be married to Henry." Could a little girl be more proud?

I had only one "best" friend in our neighborhood. Rosemary. As close to me as my sister, a spiritual bond existed between us I can't describe. We simply connected. We related. Together, we found joy in every silly thing we did. In the spring, we walked the streets and sprinkled perfumed water on all the flowers and shrubs so they smelled good. Winter nights, we dressed up and put on talent shows. Oh my gosh, Rosemary and I even smoked our first cigarettes together down by the playground. I guess it happened to a great many kids, but when Rosemary's father transferred to Virginia, and she left, I was devastated—heartbroken— and it took a long time to get over it.

➤ *Their parting represented a profound assault on Carol Jean's personal sense of safety and security because she could not influence or prevent the loss of a friend.*

After that, I didn't need another "best" friend. I didn't even need a pet. I liked the neighborhood kids, but I never needed to mix with others to find my place in the pack, and I didn't even look for another Rosemary.

➤ *A precursor of how she would deal with loss in the future. The loss of Rosemary, someone Carol Jean loved, was in itself a traumatic stressor, and her response was consciously to turn off her human necessity for an emotional bond with others and build a defense system against emotional pain.*

* * *

Prioritizing patients was big part of my job as a flight nurse. When we picked up an urgent, we took him to hospital first, and the less-severely injured rode along and waited their turn. The onboard nurse's decisions about the flight itinerary always prevailed. I set the priority and determined where and how we made our return flights. It sounds crazy, but even with a four-star general on board, my decision was the one that counted, and the pilots did what I said. From the moment the first patient was loaded until the wheels touched down at night, I was in charge of the aircraft. I know how weird that sounds, but it's the truth.

➤ *The heavy responsibility of her position placed additional stress on Carol Jean that contributed to the development of PTSD.*

I based my decisions about where to take patients on their injuries. Some medical facilities were better staffed and equipped to handle certain procedures than others. For example, kidney failures went to Third Surgical in Tan Son Nhut, and patients with severe head injuries went to Cam Rahn Bay. A boy with minor wounds might fly with us for hours while we transported higher priority patients. I thought carefully about every patient, and there were no guarantees. It was a big responsibility—scary at times—and I took it very seriously. People's lives were in my hands. As I look back on it, it's hard to believe the little blonde girl, the sprinkler of perfumed water, made those decisions, and most turned out right. Funny, it's taken me years since then to learn to trust the decisions I make in my own life.

➤ *Veterans often believe themselves under prepared or not sufficiently skilled to carry out their life or death duties, and this escalates their feelings of guilt.*

Frequently, we took patients directly from medivac helicopters—from the battlefield to our waiting aircraft. Those were usually the worst. The Dust Off medics gave the best care they could, but how is that done in an open helicopter under enemy fire?

Sometimes, the Dust Off patients were in pretty bad shape, and often there was more than one from the same outfit. You know what? Those guys never cared about themselves. They only cared about their buddies. After takeoff, if we had it, I crawled around the floor of the aircraft and gave the guys milk, but most wouldn't take any until the guy next to them had some first.

One time, we were called out after midnight to pick up two urgents at Qui Nhon. I'll never forget those two boys. One was 18, the other 19, helicopter crewmen from the same unit. One had severe head injuries, gray matter literally hung from the back of his head. He was intubated, and we were pretty sure he wouldn't make it. The other boy had severe facial injuries but was conscious. On the way to the hospital, I sat on the floor by the ventilated patient while his buddy asked over and over, "How's Mike? Is he going to make it? Tell me nurse, is he going to make it?" That boy's face was half gone, and his friend was all he cared about. I didn't know what to say to such a courageous boy.

So I lied.

Each time he asked, I said, "He's hanging in there. You're both going to be all right." When he asked me why Mike wasn't talking, I made up a medical answer the boy wouldn't understand. It was only a short flight to the hospital, but to me, it seemed forever.

➤ *Carol Jean learned to avoid dealing with trauma by lying to the injured soldiers—and to herself.*

We never lost a patient on board our aircraft. I wouldn't allow it. That stuff you see in the movies where the nurse gets on her knees and cradles the dying patient is bullshit. Severely injured patients stayed alive on board my aircraft whether they stayed alive and kept breathing or whether they stayed alive by paperwork. Anybody who says we didn't keep patients alive on paper is lying. Any other way was too complicated, too messy. Flight crews just didn't have time for all the administrative crap that went along with a dead body. Our patients never died during transport. We kept them alive until they got to their destination.

➤ *Carol Jean's later isolation and alcoholism may have been caused in part by her unrealistic belief that she never lost a patient on board the aircraft. She knew scores of her airborne patients would die quickly in the hospital.*

One night, we flew a C-130 to Dong Ha to pick up wounded South Vietnamese soldiers. A bad night for me. A newly arrived chief nurse showed up on the flight line in her blues, long stateside nails and hair neatly combed up into a bun. I was her qualification instructor, and even though she outranked me, I was responsible for training her that night *and* looking out for the safety of the crew and patients.

Halfway to Dong Ha, the pilot told us the VC had breached the perimeter at the north end of the airfield. We'd approach from the south and stop short. When the ramp went down, he wanted those patients on board fast.

We hit the ground hard, full brakes and reverse thrusters. Even before the dust settled, South Vietnamese soldiers ran out on the runway carrying scores of wounded, and my crew scrambled in the darkness to get them on board. Incredibly, that was the moment the new chief nurse told me to hold off loading patients until we'd completed screening. I couldn't believe it! I told her that snapping in the air around us was the sound of real bullets, and we needed to get the hell out of there while we still could. Unbelievably, she stuck to procedure in spite of the gunfire, ignored me and tended to a Vietnamese patient with an abdominal wound. As I watched her roll down his colostomy bag to inspect his injury, fate intervened. Certainly, somebody was looking out for us, because when the chief nurse opened that bag, a huge roundworm, an inch and a half wide, crawled out, and she almost fainted. After that, we loaded the aircraft without further delay.

I told you that was a bad night. We loaded wounded Vietnamese soldiers as fast as we could, but they kept coming. We tied them down in the middle of the cabin and stacked them like dominoes along the sides. I don't know how many we put on that aircraft. 250? 300? The air in the cabin was thick with the coppery odor of blood, and the floor so slippery we could hardly walk. When we ran out of room in the cabin, the crew chief raised the back ramp, and we strapped down more wounded there.

➤ *The olfactory is considered the most powerful of the senses related to triggering traumatic recall. Carol Jean would later be exposed to this stimulus time and again in her nursing career.*

In those days, Vietnamese women sometimes traveled to battle with their husbands like camp followers in Roman times. On this night, in the middle of a serious firefight, a crowd of hysterical Vietnamese women had formed at the back of our aircraft, screaming and moaning and tearing their hair. We were taking their husbands away, and they wanted to go along. I pitied them, but of course it was impossible. I turned my back and tried to put their cries out of mind while I strapped down the last of the injured.

Suddenly, the mob surged, and two women locked onto my legs and pulled me down onto the tarmac. They shouted and screamed what could only have been vile and profane curses. I tried to fight back, to get them off me, but there were too many, and they were unbelievably strong. As I was forced to the ground, I saw their angry faces and hate-filled eyes and choked on the sour odor of adrenaline. Mine or theirs?

They kicked and spat and tore at my hair. A mob of enraged Vietnamese women vented frustration over their shattered lives on the blonde round-eyed woman privileged enough to fly away and leave that awful place behind. I lost consciousness for a moment, and the next thing I knew, the crew chief, pistol in hand, waded through the crowd, picked me up and carried me to the flight deck. Thank God.

➤ *This incident clearly demonstrates a severe threat to Carol Jean's personal integrity. She was in danger of being killed by the very people she had been sent to Vietnam to help.*

More wounded needed evacuation from Dong Ha that night, but I told the pilot I wouldn't risk the crew's safety. We'd wait until daylight before going back. My entire life, I'd thought myself a caring person, all grace and kindness and goodness, but that was one decision I had no trouble making.

A week later, we got another urgent. There'd been a riot and shooting in a prison camp on Con Dao, an island just off the coast of Saigon. We landed hard and hot on a tiny runway lighted only by smudge pots and left the engines running while they brought out the wounded VC POWs. They weren't on litters—I doubt the prison camp had any—so we went to work on them on the floor of the aircraft.

Twelve or thirteen in all, they were VC captured somewhere and sent to that remote and isolated prison for who knew what methods of interrogation. We'd just begun strapping them down when a patient lying on his back moaned and cried out, so I examined him again for something I may have missed the first time around. In the dimmed cabin lights I saw no sign of entry, but when I turned him over, I found a huge exit wound, his back covered in blood and torn flesh. I signaled a technician to begin an intravenous transfusion.

Suddenly—I don't know why, maybe we'd taken incoming—but without my okay, the pilot applied power and began his takeoff roll. The ramp was lowered, the floor of the aircraft slick with blood and gore, and we hadn't yet had time to tie everyone down.

When the plane accelerated, my technicians, the wounded VC, and I all slid to the back of the aircraft. The pilot had initiated a full-power, maximum climb takeoff, and we scrambled for cargo straps, stanchion posts, legs and arms—anything to hang on to. The aircraft roared out over the dark South China Sea, turned north, and as things settled down in the cabin, I became furious. What the hell had we just done? What kind of insanity was that? The high brass had sent us to a tiny island in the middle of the night to take Viet Cong prisoners to a hospital in Saigon where they'd probably be killed anyway. Why? To what end? Politics? Arrogance? Stupidity? Did they care so little for our lives?

➤ *Carol Jean vented her rage and frustration on the government over the useless threats to her life. Eventually, she would turn this inward into self-destructive behavior.*

I never found out why we were sent on that mission, but as we flew home in the wee hours, it occurred to me that six months earlier, when I arrived in country, I wouldn't have complained about any mission that saved lives—ours or theirs. Goddamn it, I was a nurse! Selflessness and caring for others went to the core of my being. No sacrifice was too great if it brought comfort to someone suffering. Now, anger outweighed compassion—a dark sign something inside me had changed.

→ A change that contributed to her restricted range of affect and to her core belief about the essential decency of her character.

* * *

Another change in my life occurred in tenth grade. My father died suddenly of a ruptured aneurysm while attending our high school football game. I was a majorette, and that afternoon, the last time I saw him alive, he wished me luck and said, "Kick high enough, Honey, and your team will win."

Just 45, Daddy's death devastated the family. We'd lost the man dearest to us in the entire world—the man who took us camping and explored nature with us—the father who read us books and newspapers and taught us how to sing. I fully appreciated the strength of the love and the bond between us only after I got older, but I felt the crippling pain of loss immediately.

→ When Carol Jean lost Rosemary's companionship, she had been "devastated—heartbroken." When her father left her, she could not find words to express her feelings, but she experienced "the crippling pain of loss immediately."

Recently, Mom has talked about the influence my father had on her own life. Before their marriage, she'd been a nurse, straightforward and no nonsense. She didn't believe in outward displays of emotion, and she wasn't particularly fond of intimate physical contact. However, over the years, Daddy—Henry—taught her how to experience her emotions and express and share them with others. Laughter, kindness, and music were the tools he used to reshape her.

When Daddy died, I watched Mom change into a person I'd never seen before. She withdrew from the world. Much of the affection she showed us kids cooled, and when Dad's family visited, I felt her no longer comfortable with the hugs and kisses they showered on everybody. I thought I took these life changes in stride, but I know now those experiences gave me the survival skills I'd need later in life. The very young and very old are not good with change, rarely see it coming, and do not handle it well.

→ Carol Jean's mother dealt with her own traumatic experience by withdrawing from the world and withholding her affection. Her mother's restricted range of affect—her diminished ability to have and sustain loving feelings (a PTSD symptom)—for her father's family reinforced her own developing defensive system.

Half the county and all the relatives came to Daddy's funeral, and it was the saddest day of my life. After the service, Grandpa Schrum, a tough old German, sat me down on the porch steps and told me it was now my responsibility to care for the family and look after my mother. At 15, I wasn't clear on just how I should do this. Directed by that hard, lantern-jawed man I called Grandpa, I became imbued with a sense of purpose and familial obligation.

* * *

Every Sunday, a squadron aircraft flew to Clark Air Force Base in the Philippines to ferry wounded Korean soldiers out of the country. Now and then, I went along. Usually, we spent the night there and returned early the next morning. Sometimes, we stayed an extra day.

The guys I flew with bunked downtown at the Marlin Mansion. They knew the hotel manager, and he took good care of the Americans. As the only girl in the crew, they insisted I accompany them so they could watch out for me. When I stayed at the Marlin, I got the penthouse suite with a sunken tub for three dollars a night.

The medical crewmen who made the Clark run regularly kept Filipino lady friends there. When I went along, they took me out to party with them – four or five American servicemen, their Filipino prostitutes, and me. As time went by, I got to know some of the women pretty well, and I learned something about judging people that stayed with me all these years.

Growing up in Snyder County, Pennsylvania, I was taught women who sold themselves for money were among the lower forms of life, and the Filipino bar girls I met rattled my adolescent sensibilities. How, I wondered, could anyone stoop so low? The streets of Angeles City were *alive* with prostitutes. The place was like Babylon—an entire city of sin. I walked down *A Santo* Street stupefied by the sheer volume of flesh for sale in and out of the clubs.

That night, we had an excellent meal in the hotel restaurant, and while the guys talked flying, I got acquainted with their Filipino escorts. Shy at first, they didn't want to share information about themselves, so I told them about my own life and the little town I grew up in. They were amazed by big American farms and wanted to hear all about our new super stores—malls. Before long, they opened up to me, and for the next hour, I couldn't shut them up. Eventually, the conversation drifted to prostitution. Why do it? Simple. Unless they worked the hotels and clubs, the rent went unpaid or there wasn't food for their families. Facts of life. Not a hint of a moral dilemma for them. As the hours passed, I grew fond of the girls, and I think they liked me.

Two of them, sisters, invited me home to meet their family. The next morning, we crowded onto a Jeepny and drove to a grimy suburb of Angeles City. We walked the last few blocks, turned into a narrow alley, and arrived at their home, a tiny shack made of scrap lumber and tin. They introduced me to the old folks and a seemingly endless procession of brothers, sisters, and cousins.

The girls told the old ones I was a representative of the clothing manufacturing company they worked for on a sightseeing trip, and pressed for time, we'd just stopped a moment to pay our respects. I don't know whether those people believed their daughters' little fantasy, but I think they wanted to.

Back at the hotel, I said goodbye to the girls and rushed to my room and wept. I pictured myself living in squalor, the victim of crushing poverty, and my heart went out to them and the countless millions of others like them around the world living joyless lives, dying anonymous deaths. I was stricken with the sad reality they were just like me—living in a war zone and just trying to survive. Young and not in charge, they did what they had to. The chief differences between us were that I'd fly away in the morning—and my chances of survival were far better than theirs.

Of course, after that, I looked at the Vietnamese people differently, too. I recalled that terrible night the village women pulled me off the aircraft. They'd only the clothes on their backs and their husbands to protect them. In their eyes, I robbed them of everything they owned in life. I guess the best lessons are the hardest to learn. Vietnam taught me all human souls are the same. We all feel pain, we all bleed the same color, and we're all children of the same Father.

One day, at the Base Exchange, I ran across two young women shopping for underwear. As there were not many round-eyed girls at Cam Rahn, I spoke to them. One from Australia and the other from Canada, they'd come to the BX for much-needed feminine wear.

They worked for a charitable organization called Project Concern, assisting at a Vietnamese hospital in a village near Dalat. People from several countries—Australia, Japan, the United States, and Germany staffed their remote, makeshift hospital. The girls and I hit it off, so later, I took them to my company area, introduced them to the guys in my squadron, and we spent the afternoon together talking about them and their volunteer work.

➤ *Almost against her own judgment, Carol Jean lowered her defensive wall just enough to connect and identify with these young women.*

The enemy was quite active in their area, and as the staff was civilian and had no defenses, the VC came into the hospital at will and walked out with whatever medical equipment and supplies they wanted. Nonetheless, they considered themselves fortunate the communist troops only took *things*, and so far, no one had been harmed, but even though the VC hadn't yet killed anyone, the hospital was always short of food and medical supplies.

As time passed, everyone in the squadron became close to the two volunteers. When they came to Cam Rahn, we put them up with us or found rooms. Also, we made a project of finding the supplies they needed. We scrounged. Every 10 days or so, I put on my best civilian clothes, got in a jeep with another nurse, and visited mess sergeants and supply officers. Whether army, navy, or air force, if they were into food or supplies, they became our new best friends. In return, the girls brought us strawberries and other fresh commodities from the markets in Dalat.

Eventually, we got to know the entire Project Concern hospital staff. One weekend, half the staff came from Dalat, and we exchanged views and information on treatment procedures. We'd planned to bring the other half down the following week.

Three a.m. Sunday morning, the duty officer woke me for a phone call. The VC had overrun the hospital and killed all the Project Concern workers not with us in Cam Rahn, including, of course, the two girls I'd become such close friends with.

➤ *Once again, people Carol Jean loved had been unexpectedly and brutally taken away from her.*

The rest of that night was a blur. We awakened the visiting staff, told them what had happened, and arranged transportation back so they could pick up the pieces and bury their comrades. A horrible night, a horrible experience.

It may seem strange—sounds strange to me even to say it—but after that night, I didn't have any more contact with the Project Concern people. I knew their needs remained just as great after the attack as before. I knew they'd appreciate our friendship just as much, but I didn't want to know anything more about them. I no longer cared about helping folks who helped others. It didn't matter. I wanted to put their existence out of my mind, and I did.

➤ *A manifestation of PTSD—avoidance, a form of running.*

I knew even before I arrived, Vietnam was a man's world, but a round-eyed girl packed her own ballpark, and where my social life was concerned, I was determined to call my own plays. With so many available men, some girls went crazy over there, but that behavior didn't impress or interest me. Don't get me wrong. I wasn't a prude. I had a brief relationship with a male nurse in my squadron, but mostly it was like working with 26 older brothers. The guys showed me the ropes and protected me from everything. They wouldn't let me party with people outside our squadron—rarely let me go to the BX by myself. Most had arrived in country months before me, so when I joined the squadron, they tucked the new little blonde girl under their wing and kept me out of harm's way. They were my friends, and I knew none would ever betray me.

Trouble was, their tours of duty ended months before mine, and when they all went home, I was deeply saddened. Their leaving was like losing all my fingers. I was really alone. Everyone remaining in the squadron was junior to me, and I couldn't relate to anyone. The old cliché about how people came and went in that environment—and sometimes died —really hit home then. For me, it just didn't seem worth it to make new friends in the few months I had left.

➤ *Now, Carol Jean was more alone than ever.*

One night, I went to a party with the officers from the base hospital, the first time I'd gone anywhere since my big brothers had left. Strange to be in a room full of people and feel so alone but all the while thinking I might find just one person I could talk to. I'd never been in that situation before and wanted to make it work, so I had a few drinks and tried to enjoy myself.

➤ *Even in a room full of people, still Carol Jean felt alone and uncomfortable— another symptom of the PTSD she had developed during her months of unceasing war.*

When it was time to go home, an officer I knew offered to walk me back to my quarters. He was a major with an important staff position at the hospital, and I'd known him professionally for seven or eight months. That night, he was less talkative than usual on our stroll home, but at the time, I didn't think too much about it. Truth be told, I probably wasn't very chatty, either.

When we got to my room, I opened the door and suddenly, he pushed me inside and threw me down on my bunk. I was stunned. Violence was the last thing I expected from that major, and I screamed, "No, no, no!" but he wouldn't stop. I tried to push him off me, but he was too heavy. I begged him not to do it, but he was possessed and wouldn't listen. I fought as hard as I could but to no use. He pinned my arms, put a hand over my mouth and did his dirty business.

➤ *The final episode that destroyed Carol Jean's belief the world could be a safe and trustworthy place.*

Rape. The act every girl fears from childhood. I'd known that officer for months and liked and respected him. His sudden act of violent aggression had come as a complete surprise. Of course, I couldn't report it. How could I? A single, 22-year-old blonde living in a man's world, I'd been to a party, and I'd been drinking. I know it sounds stupid in this day and age, but I felt then as though I were to blame for the incident, that somehow I'd triggered the lust natural to all men.

When he'd finished and left, I sat alone in my room consumed with guilt, shame, and embarrassment. I remembered the biblical expression, "pride goeth before a fall," and hated myself for my hubris, for thinking I could call the plays and set the boundaries in a man's world.

➤ *The horror and violence that was Vietnam had finally found and assaulted her own person.*

So much for my last remaining emotion—arrogant self-righteousness. Now, it was out the window, too, and there was nothing I could do about it. Who the hell would buy my story? I was a lieutenant and he a major, a high-profile staff officer with influence and connections. In the air force of 1970, my complaint wouldn't even rise to the level of laughable. With nothing I could do, I kept the incident to myself for decades. I tried never to think of it again, but forever after, for me sex was tied with drinking alcohol. I couldn't have sex without drinking first.

➤ *This violent trauma neurologically paired sex and alcohol in Carol Jean's brain, which influenced subsequent behavioral patterns.*

After that, I stopped paying attention to what happened around me. I really didn't care. I flew every day. I tended to torn and mangled young boys—stop the bleeding, clear the airway, that sort of thing. I did my duty, but it was sleepwalking with a purpose. I couldn't physically disconnect from that place, so I did it mentally and emotionally.

Occasionally, I had a vague recollection of myself when I first arrived in Vietnam—a giggling little girl who laughed and blushed and was shocked by the most trivial incidents. Clearly, that person was gone forever. I'd have to conjure up another set of memories to fit the person I'd become and just forget altogether about the old Carol Jean, the small town girl who loved to fish with her father.

The night before I returned to the States, the VC tunneled under the wire at Cam Rahn and blew the ammo dump. When that ordinance went off, all hell broke loose. I ran to check on the female nurse quartered next to me, and just when I opened her door, the concussion from a huge blast shattered her window, and glass hit me in the face. I was lucky, a lot of bleeding, but my injuries were hardly more than scratches. No problem, I thought. I was going home in the morning. I'd never have to wear a flak jacket and helmet again.

They threw a party for me the next afternoon. Nice, but I'd been to plenty of going-away parties for other people, and I knew them as just another excuse to get drunk and escape for a few hours. Fine with me, but I wasn't deluded enough to believe their conviviality had anything to do with my departure.

When the wheels of that freedom bird left the runway, and we headed out over the South China Sea, everyone on board erupted in a thunderous roar. That's the only thing I remember of the flight home.

❧ *A dearth of feeling during the flight—no joy, relief, or anticipation.*

Twenty-three hours later, we were welcomed in Seattle by a light spring rain and a big crowd of war protesters shouting and carrying signs positioned so we had to walk right past them to get into the terminal building. They tossed profanities around and waved banners, but I just lowered my eyes and ignored them. I thought it funny they believed anything they said or did penetrated my armor. When we got inside, I broke off from the others, went to the airport bar, and bought myself a beer.

❧ *Home safe and secure, Carol Jean's first act was to find a bar and drink.*

* * *

My first stateside duty assignment was at Lackland Air Force Base, Texas. Don, the male nurse I'd dated in Vietnam, was already stationed there, so we hooked up and married two months later. A divorced father of six, all Don's children lived with us in our two-bedroom apartment in San Antonio. Everything considered, it was a beautiful experience. They were great kids, and I loved them very much.

❧ *From combat flight nurse to spouse and mother of six stepchildren in 60 days. Carol Jean remained in character—caregiver to the many.*

The biggest medical center in the air force, Wilford Hall provided care to members of all three branches of the service and their dependents. Also, every kind of surgery—some war related, some not—and even some of the first open-heart surgeries and kidney transplants.

For me, stateside in a post-operative ICU was really awkward after being in Vietnam. I found I no longer knew how to be a real nurse. I had become accustomed to fast, spur-of-the-moment medicine, but now, in starched uniform and cute little hat, I struggled with the adjustment to stateside duty.

❧ *Without the rush of adrenaline and other potent brain neurochemicals to keep her psychological trauma from surfacing, Carol Jean began to experience intrusive PTSD symptoms.*

When Don came back from Vietnam, he attended anesthesia school at Wilford. Nine years older than I, he was a country boy with a great sense of humor, and everybody liked him. Even crowded into a small apartment with six children, we never had a fight or even a cross word.

I'd only been at Wilford Hall a short time when I started having terrible nightmares.

✦ *Carol Jean began to exhibit a red-flag symptom of PTSD—significant sleep disturbance in the form of nightmares. Not encouraged to talk about her Vietnam traumas, this was perhaps her last chance to avoid severe PTSD, and it was lost to her.*

After each one, I woke up crying, in distress, and sought comfort, but Don only got upset with me and told me not to think about it. I was hurt he didn't understand when I tried to speak to him about Vietnam. After all, we'd shared the experience, but he never wanted to talk about it. For him, Vietnam was in the past, and he thought it ridiculous to dwell on it.

✦ *Like most people who serve in combat, Don did not develop posttraumatic stress disorder and was unable to empathize with the psychological battle raging within his wife.*

Soon, my dreams got worse, and I decided to do something about them. I couldn't sleep anyway, so I decided to work night shifts.

My nightmares consisted of a variety of intense feelings and images, but the scenes were not distinct or well framed. Submerged in a sea of mud, green and brown, red and black all smeared together, I smelled blood, gore, dirt, and leftover scotch and beer. I was trapped inside that place like inside a balloon. I'd search and search but find no way to move forward—no light on any horizon—no way out. Then, I'd wake up exhausted, soaking wet, and crying. Night after night, always the same.

✦ *Carol Jean's night terrors represented everything she had endured—too much to break down to single incidents.*

At Wilford, we worked 12-hour shifts, six or seven days a week. The war in Vietnam raged on, so we were always short handed. Looking back, I don't know how I found time to enjoy life with Don's kids, but I did. However, as the months passed, I drank more than ever. I was on automatic. Work most of the time, drink when I could, and sleep when I had to.

✦ *Carol Jean turned to alcohol to avoid the night terrors, because she had no other mechanism to numb the pain and still her fear.*

The following year, 1973, Don and I transferred to Travis Air Force Base in California, a different location, but for me a continuation of the Texas scene. Work, drink, and avoid sleep. I took a job at the Air Medical Staging Facility, a large receiving station where most of the casualties from Vietnam were sent. As many as 300 a day came in on C-141 cargo planes. We admitted them, provided care, and as soon as they could safely travel, shipped them to a military hospital as close as possible to their home of record.

➤ *With few exceptions (no bombs or bullets), her stateside work environment mirrored her tour in Vietnam. Traumatized individuals often seek out opportunities to be in environments similar to the ones in which the traumatic events were experienced.*

The irony of that assignment was not lost on me. There I was, looking at the same injuries, the same wounded boys I'd seen in Vietnam. Like one of those crazy, closed-loop Escher paintings, frequently, I wondered about the Carol Jean who now brought them out of the battle zone and put them on the airplane to send to me.

I found this work exceedingly difficult. On the battlefield, a wounded soldier thought only of his buddies and his duty. Once they hit the States, however, horrible reality set in. Away from their comrades, they were frightened and alone. Somewhere inside, I processed how painful that was for them, and it was killing me. As difficult as it was for me to face their pain and sorrow, if I tried to avoid it, I was overcome with guilt and shame. Eventually, I asked for and received a transfer to the hospital surgical intensive care unit.

Things weren't going well at home, either. I drank more, and my nightmares grew worse. At night, I was afraid to close my eyes. Afraid terrifying sleep would grab me and not let go.

➤ *Now, Carol Jean experiences a wide array of PTSD symptoms—detachment from others, foreshortened future, difficulty falling or staying asleep, inability to sustain loving feelings, difficulty concentrating, and night terrors.*

Our marriage survived because Don worked in the operating room with me, and we saw each other often. Even though I was confused and unstable, I was a good wife, and he never lost patience with me, never said an unkind word. Don was a wonderful man and a loyal and supportive husband. The problems in our marriage did not start with him. I've since wished many times in my life I had someone to love me as much as he did.

* * *

After a year at Travis, we both discharged from the air force, and Don took a job with a medical group in Richmond, Kentucky. I disliked the place from the first day. That part of the South was still racist, and I could not force myself to live among people who hated. Adding to my anxiety, we couldn't find permanent quarters, so we camped out where we could, a motel here, a rental there. No easy task with six children.

At work, Don associated with country clubbers, incredibly shallow people who believed themselves southern aristocrats, like in the old movies. Unfortunately, the showy wealth and southern snobbery soon influenced my country boy husband. I swear, every day, I read every little change in him. Now, of course, I know those observations were delusional. I was drinking and felt sorry for myself, and Don was like a deer in my headlights.

Two months, and I'd had enough. I'd made up my mind I wanted a family of my own and saw no chance of getting it with Don. Every hour of every day, I burned to start life all over again, find a new me somewhere, shed the past, and begin again, so one morning I packed my bags and left. I left him, the children I loved, everything. I'm not proud of it, but that's what happened. In my mind, it was time to move on, and I didn't even think of looking back.

➤ *Powerless to run from herself, Carol Jean did what she believed would solve her problems—she ran from her marriage and family.*

I returned to California, moved in with a friend, and took a job at a VA hospital—sick and wounded soldiers—again. Of course, you see the pattern, but at the time, I could not. I'd been a nurse eight years and had worked only two in a civilian hospital.

➤ *Compelled to seek out the same conditions that traumatized her in Vietnam—arduous flying, blood and gore, men and alcohol—Carol Jean reconstructed the only existence in which she could function.*

Also, I was pretty unstable during that period. I thought no one noticed, but on the inside, I was up one moment and down the next. Maybe the military offered an element of predictability to my otherwise screwball life. Maybe that's why I took jobs at VA hospitals. Maybe I just had a compulsion for veterans, because I'd only been in California a few weeks when I met and fell in love with a man on active duty.

Several years younger than I, Dave was a California surfer boy. We moved in together, married, and nine months later, my first child was born. During that period, I joined the active reserves and flew on weekends with the 65th Air Medical Evacuation Squadron. The reserves, my work, and the long commute didn't leave much time for personal things, but that was the whole idea. I knew I couldn't drink while pregnant, so I kept myself busy morning and night.

* * *

Taya was born in July 1976 and Cara in September 1977. Dave left the military and attended school full time, so he stayed home and played Mr. Mom. During this time, the night terrors came on me worse than ever. I became completely petrified of sleep, and even now, I don't know what kept me going.

One day, while on shift at the VA hospital, 29 high-school teenagers were killed in a bus accident on the freeway, and the injured survivors were brought to us, the closest hospital. The only one on staff with triage experience, they called me to the emergency room to receive them.

The injuries were massive, predominately head and crushing chest wounds, so there wasn't a lot of triage to do. Mostly, the patients went to ICU for immediate treatment. As the doctor and I worked feverishly with a young man whose scalp had been pulled over his face, suddenly, a powerful feeling of impending doom overwhelmed me, and I trembled uncontrollably. My hands shook, my eyes lost focus, and I remember saying out loud, "This is just like Vietnam."

✤ *Her first dissociative flashback induced by working among people who'd suffered the same massive physical trauma she was exposed to in Vietnam.*

It was the first time I'd ever compared anything stateside to anything I saw over there. Then, a strange thing happened. I thought about it a moment, and as quickly as the sensation came over me, it went away. Reflexively, I had put on my old iron mask and continued working as though nothing had happened. I worked another 36 hours without stopping.

✤ *Carol Jean stuffs this experience as quickly and efficiently as she had all the traumatic events during the war. Once again, she retreats inward.*

Dave left me in 1979. After the children were born, I passed the days taking care of my family, working nights, and trying not to let the alcohol I consumed catch up with me. Dave didn't drink at all, and he never liked that I did, but that wasn't the only problem between us. As our marriage ran slowly but inexorably downhill, we entertained ourselves by exploring our differences. He was from Southern California—I from rural Pennsylvania. He was agnostic—I from a Christian background. I earned the money in the family, but he controlled the finances. Toward the end, he tried to tell me when I could and couldn't drink, and of course, that just made me drink more.

✤ *Carol Jean self-medicated to avoid guilt feelings over her failing marriage—the same guilt she had repressed in Vietnam—and prepared to flee to escape the psychological consequences.*

After Dave moved out, I brought in a nanny to help with the children, and I continued working nights. Grandma Jen was a wonderful woman, and the kids loved her. Sometimes, on my days off, I took the girls to Sacramento to see Dave. Even though we couldn't live together, I wanted them to know their father. Dave and I had remained on friendly terms, and when we could, the kids and I visited him, and I cooked and tried to do things like a real family.

Three years later, Grandma Jen left us and moved east to tend to a seriously ill relative. We were crushed. She had become an important part of our household. The kids were devastated.

❖ *Carol Jean's support system diminishes, and she becomes more isolated.*

Her leaving meant I had to quit working nights and weekends, so I took a position with a nurse's registry—a placement service where I set my own schedule. Between the job, kids, and flying for the air force, I was busy all the time. I had no social life and wasn't interested in one. As hard as I worked, sleep became even more of a problem during this period. I couldn't escape the terrors and didn't want to close my eyes at night, so I slept an hour or so in the mornings and napped with the kids on the weekends.

❖ *Overwork in the same type of environment constantly exposed Carol Jean to external cues that symbolized aspects of her traumas.*

A year of this, and I realized a succession of babysitters for my children —strange faces coming and going—was a recipe for disaster. Something had to change. That summer, I sent the girls to Pennsylvania to stay six weeks with my mother. With them safely cared for, I worked double shifts to earn enough money to take time off to visit. I know it sounds like a makeshift, half-baked plan, but at the time, I could think of nothing else.

❖ *Psychologically and physiologically distressed, Carol Jean was unable to cope with the additional responsibility of parenting.*

When I went home to visit, I saw the positive interaction between the children and their cousins and grandmother. They glowed. For the first time in their lives, they felt they had a real family. My head may have been pretty messed up, but I was still a mother, and instinct told me what I had to do.

I quit my job, sold my house, and arranged for a transfer to an air force reserve unit on the east coast. Then, I bought a little house in Selinsgrove, a clean, healthy environment where the kids walked to school and church and Brownies.

I'd finally done the right thing. You couldn't paint a more perfect picture of Americana. My mother lived just down the street, so when I went away to reserve duty, the girls stayed with her, and everyone loved that. After all the years, I'd finally made a good choice, and I prayed we could all grow up and grow old together. Turns out, Selinsgrove *was* a blessing, my girls *would* experience stability in their lives, the decision I'd made *was* a good one, but my own personal life went downhill from there.

➤ *Carol Jean has a dual diagnosis—PTSD and alcohol dependence. In terms of her PTSD, the move was avoidance. As related to alcohol dependence, it was an attempt at a geographical cure.*

* * *

I *had* done the right thing. I'd provided a healthy, loving environment for my children, but I'd not considered my own needs. Everything around me was so different. I went from a big house to a small one, and I had a new job and a new reserve squadron. I thought if I moved back to my childhood home, I'd find friends—people I'd known growing up. I'd hoped for some kind of support system. Not the case. Most people I knew in childhood had moved from Selinsgrove, so I had no one outside my immediate family.

My reserve unit was three hours away by car, so even if I'd found time for a social life there, I couldn't form friendships with people who lived 180 miles away. In California, I'd lived in a military community, worked in military hospitals, and shared much in common with the people around me. Looking back on it now, I realize even with all those anchors, I lived a fragile existence. Now completely adrift, lonely, and uncertain of my ability to make friends, I didn't want even to take the risk.

I made more money with my reserve squadron flying five days a month than full time work on rural Pennsylvania wages, so I started flying more and took a part-time job at a nursing home my family owned.

I was pretty far gone, not in touch with reality, and held onto life by a thread. As a nurse, I knew the dangers of drugs, so I never got involved, but instead, I got drunk every day. I worked nights at the nursing home, and in the mornings after I got the girls off to school, I closed the drapes to shut the world out, curled up on the floor in my darkened living room, and drank. I'd have a couple shots of vodka, then a couple more, then more.

I always stayed indoors alone, and I kept the curtains closed. Sometimes, after morning cocktails, I napped before the girls came home from school. Sometimes, I could sleep then. In the evenings, I cooked dinner, and if I didn't have to work, I put the kids to bed, sat on my floor, and drank some more.

➤ *Carol Jean now exhibits the PTSD symptom of hypervigilance.*

Aware of my behavior and concerned, my mother and sister tried to talk to me, but I was in complete denial and wouldn't listen to anyone. One day, the chief nurse at my squadron called me in and talked to me about my drinking. That surprised me, because in my twisted mind, I thought nobody outside my family could discern I had a problem. She told me I needed help, reminded me of my flight-safety responsibilities, and suggested I do something soon. I liked and respected the chief nurse but didn't see any possibility of changing my life, so after that, I stayed clear of her and avoided crossing her path.

That winter, I had an attack—maybe anxiety, I still don't know. Perhaps my continuing gastrointestinal problems set it off. I don't remember what happened, and since I was alone, I couldn't diagnose myself. At this point, I'll just call it anxiety. Anyway, I ended up in the hospital.

➤ *Alcohol, lack of sleep, anxiety, and loneliness took their predictable path, and Carol Jean broke down.*

I'd worked with the doctor who came to see me and knew him to be a fine physician. I'd lied to the hospital nurses about the alcohol I consumed, but the doctor had analyzed my tests. He told me I had a choice: get sober or die. That's when I started AA.

The doctor's grim diagnosis scared me, but I wasn't afraid of death. Deep inside, I knew I had to end the life I lived, and if that meant dying, okay. I looked at myself isolated and drunk on the floor in my darkened living room, and I knew *that* life had to end. I lived that way not because I wanted to but because I *had* to, and that scared me. At the time, I believed I had to be a good person for God to love me, and since I didn't like anything about myself, I feared God wouldn't either.

➤ *Carol Jean begins to grasp an understanding of her compulsions since Vietnam. She believed if she stayed away from alcohol, her life would be better.*

I tried. I tried hard. The AA meetings were held in the basement of the church down the street, and I went every chance I got. During evening meetings, I took my girls with me. I stayed sober four years.

Not having alcohol in my life helped me in my relationships with family and co-workers, but the terrible nightmares continued, and I struggled to keep myself occupied. I worked, spent time with the girls, played flute in an orchestra, volunteered in the community, did my reserve duty—everything expected of a drunk trying to stay sober, but it wasn't enough. Even clean and sober, I was on the edge of life, only a step away from too little or too much. Also, I played the blame game. Hang around drunks for a while, and you discover they always have a reason or an excuse for their behavior—abused as children, suffered some great personal tragedy—something. I had no excuse. I'd grown up happy and healthy. I had no one to blame for my life but myself.

➤ *Lacking built-in excuses such as childhood physical or sexual abuse, neglect, or deprivation, Carol Jean blamed herself for the mess her life had become. In her mind, she alone was responsible for all her misery, and it never occurred to her Vietnam was the origin of her problems.*

Step four of AA requires a searching inventory of self. I did that over and over again, and each time I searched for when I started to go wrong, I always arrived back in Vietnam. I inventoried every part of my life, past to present and vice versa, but when I got to Vietnam, I could not revisit that place. I could *not* do it. When I talked to my AA sponsors about it, they told me Vietnam had nothing to do with my alcoholism. They prohibited using Vietnam as an excuse for alcoholism, and it was not discussed in meetings or private sessions.

➤ *Unfortunately for Carol Jean, the good men and women of AA did not accept service in combat as an excuse for alcoholism. That subject not discussed, Carol Jean was unable to find a safe place to give herself over to the pain of all she had witnessed.*

I wanted the AA program to work. I'd been sober long enough to know I was finally getting my brain back. I honestly wanted to complete that fourth step. I knew I could no longer shy away from the black hole in the center of my life. I really tried but could *not* do it. I was stuck.

* * *

In 1990, while working in my office at the rest home, my sister's daughter, Tara, stopped to visit and had just left to take her friends home when the phone rang. My mother said she'd heard news of an accident on the route Tara drove with her friends. Mother thought she might have had a fender-bender and suggested we drive out to make sure she was okay.

Only a half-mile from my mother's house, when we approached the accident scene, we saw police and rescue vehicles on the road ahead. Mother insisted I stop the car. She refused to go any farther and said she'd walk home. She wanted me to go up and see what happened.

It was a beautiful spring day with a bright, blue sky overhead. As I got closer I knew the car was Tara's, even though it was smashed and twisted beyond recognition. Then, starkly contrasted against the black mud, I saw four rumpled figures in the field around the wreckage.

I stopped my car and raced out to find Tara. Teams had already arrived on scene and started work on the injured teenagers. I saw someone put a white sheet over a body near a drainage ditch, but I avoided that and looked first at the injured kids—the survivors. Frantic, I ran through the mud and called Tara's name. In a moment, although it seemed an eternity, a medic stopped me. When I asked him about Tara, he lowered his eyes and frowned then signaled to follow him. When we got to where the body lay, he pulled a wallet from under the sheet and showed me a picture I.D. of my niece.

At that moment, I didn't know what anyone else said or did. In a split second, all the air around me sucked away, and I felt myself shrink into a vacuum jar. I couldn't breath, see, or hear. I felt as though I'd been hit by a train. I felt like a ghost—dead but still among the living. *Tara*. An honor student and concert violinist, a beautiful, popular girl just accepted to Penn State, now she lay dead under a bloody sheet in a muddy field. An overwhelming sense of loss consumed me.

❧ *A panic attack brought about by a sensory trigger related to the traumatic events she endured in Vietnam.*

While I stood there in mud to my ankles, somewhere in the back of my brain, I sensed the flight-for-life helicopter coming, and when I heard the *wop, wop* of the chopper blades and looked again at the body lying at my feet, instantly I was swept back to Vietnam. Shoved through a portal, 20 years in one instant, I was *really there*, and I was alone. Then, something else happened. All the frenetic activity around me slowed. My vision sharpened, and my head cleared.

❧ *Severe dissociative flashback brought about by the distinctive sound of the helicopter approaching.*

From that moment on, I functioned like a well-oiled machine. I went to my mother's house and told her that her granddaughter was not coming home. Lynne was out of town, so I made arrangements to get her home before she learned of her daughter's death. I called Tara's father and gave him the terrible news. I picked up Tara's sister and my own two girls from school. I took care of the important things first then handled all the messy details after. For weeks, Tara's death crippled the entire family, but I remained on automatic—sleepwalking with a purpose—until she was in the ground and the dust had settled.

❧ *Now in total avoidance mode, Carol Jean could not tolerate being close to anyone for fear that person would be violently taken away from her.*

Two months later, I started drinking again. I don't remember much about that period in my life. Everyone begged me to get help. I'd heard that old saw before, but I suppose, drunk as I was, I must have considered my girls, because I went to the doctor, and he admitted me to a rehabilitation clinic where I stayed for a month. I talked to the counselors there about the accident that had triggered my relapse and told them about the Vietnam flashback. They encouraged me not to ignore my feelings about the war, the first time a medical practitioner had suggested my problems may have been service related, and I was hopeful. I really thought I might be on the path of something. However, when I got home and back into AA, Vietnam was still a forbidden topic. Another dead end.

* * *

For the first time in years, I found a friend and started dating. Older than I, Jim had been a friend of my father's. He was a kind and patient man, and I liked and respected him. At first, we were just companions. We went to movies, concerts, and shared dinners. When our friendship became something more, I found I couldn't be intimate. Just the thought of having sex with a man made my skin crawl, and dark feelings of shame washed over me. I wanted a complete relationship with Jim, wanted to please him. I wanted something of what other women had in life, but for me, sex, intimacy—whatever you want to call it—wasn't possible without booze. I needed to anesthetize the dark feelings that washed over me at the prospect of a man touching me.

�》 *The trauma of Carol Jean's rape in Vietnam rendered her unable to be physically intimate or have loving feelings. These are avoidance symptoms.*

Of course, the relationship was doomed. I tried, but it ended with a broken heart and another failed recovery. Sneaking drinks around the house quickly escalated into full-time drinking. This time, my children organized the family intervention.

"Mom, we love you, and we want you get help now."

"Mom, we don't want you to die."

That same day, I entered a second rehab.

Also 30 days, the second inpatient treatment center looked like the first—nice facility, friendly, competent counselors, packaged program. I sailed through it and stayed clean for a year, but when I relapsed, I drank for a day or two, and then stopped for a week, month, or even two months before relapsing again for a few days. On many occasions, I had a few drinks at home, went to an AA meeting, and then came home and had a few more. At the time, I really thought I fooled everyone. I knew my behavior was wrong, and I knew what I needed to do. I just couldn't understand why I could not do it.

➤ *Carol Jean had fallen back to her use of deception to continue to self-medicate and avoid dealing with her feelings.*

In 1995, I retired from the reserves, and both my daughters went away to college. Except for work at the nursing home, I remained entirely isolated and joyless. Relapses into alcohol became more frequent, and I stayed off the wagon for longer periods before the next stretch of sobriety. I drank often and to excess, my drink of choice vodka chased with wine. I drank to get drunk. One day faded into another, and while I looked fine on the outside, inside I was screaming.

In 1998, my family sold the nursing home, and the new owners didn't want to keep me on. That place had been in our family for years, and my girls had been practically raised there. The day I packed my desk and moved out, another big part of my life disappeared in smoke.

After that, I really isolated. I never left the house. I kept the curtains drawn and never answered the telephone. Jolting stabs of paranoia consumed me. The night terrors got worse, and I had frequent intense flashbacks. Sometimes, I actually smelled Vietnam or tasted it. Thinking I must be crazy scared me. Over and over, my mind told me I had nothing to fear, but my body was beyond my control. I panicked when the phone rang or a loud noise sounded on the television. Adrenaline rushed through my veins, my hair stood on end, and I became suddenly short of breath—all entirely involuntary reactions. I had no idea what went on inside me.

➤ *More symptoms emerge. Nightmares become night terrors, the olfactory sensations sharpen, and Carol Jean develops a super-exaggerated startle response. Her brain is in a constant state of preparedness for danger not there, and the flood of neurochemicals pumped into her neocortex causes even more damage to her nervous system.*

One day, I thought if I changed environments for a while, I could get a handle on my situation, so I decided to visit an old friend in North Carolina. It was pleasant country, and I enjoyed the new surroundings, but on the third day, my daughter called sobbing and hysterical from her dorm room in college and told me her boyfriend of two years had drowned in a boating accident on the Susquehanna River.

It was the last straw for me. Immediately, I opened a bottle of vodka and got obliterated. I don't remember well what happened next, but apparently I passed out while standing on my friend's backyard patio, bruised myself badly and lacerated my face and arms. My friend wanted me to go to a hospital, but I only wanted to get home, so I patched myself up, cut my visit short, and headed back to Pennsylvania.

En route, I stopped in Washington, D.C., to change planes, but I was so out of it. I missed my flight and bunked that night in a hotel near the airport. The next day, I guzzled bloody marys in the bar while waiting for my flight. I couldn't drink them fast enough. At the departure gate, just before my flight boarded, I dropped my purse, and everything spilled out. An airport policeman came over to help, and when he smelled alcohol on my breath, arrested me for public drunkenness and put me in detention until sober enough for another flight.

Don't ask me why, because to this day I don't know—maybe it was the grace of God—but while in detention at the airport, I phoned a woman I'd met years earlier, a counselor at the VA hospital. She answered on the second ring and told me she'd waited a long time for my call. Then she told me I'd be okay. "You have posttraumatic stress disorder, and you can get help."

➤ *The beginning of the end of Carol Jean's nightmare.*

At home that night, I called Lynne and asked her to take me to the VA hospital. Moments later, she and my brother arrived to find me unconscious on my kitchen floor, and they called an ambulance.

I was admitted into the psycho ward, where the doctor studied my chart and then did a brief examination. When finished, he looked at me and asked whether I'd ever been sexually assaulted. I didn't answer him right away, but I didn't have to. My expression told him everything he needed to know. A week of recovery in the hospital, and then I was assigned to inpatient PTSD treatment.

Night and day, I prayed they'd found the answer that had so long eluded me. For 30 years, I'd thought my problems were not merely alcohol related—but I knew how not to drink—and it wasn't only the rape. I'd put that in my emotional lockbox with all my other baggage. Something else was wrong inside me, and I had never been able to put my finger on it.

Finally in the PTSD ward, I was alcohol free but still a sick girl. I had trouble organizing thoughts. I stuttered. I had difficultly brushing my teeth. I couldn't dial a telephone or tie my shoes. I couldn't replace the battery in my watch. I couldn't follow through with anything. I couldn't focus. All this notwithstanding, I was happy to root out the source of my problem. Now, I could attack it and finally change my life. Every day, I looked at the sign that hung in the hospital entry hall: *Not all wounds are visible.*

➤ *Experiencing physiological and psychological collapse as a result of the massive PTSD-induced neurochemicals secretion and copious amounts of alcohol, Carol Jean's system was no longer able to process effectively. Difficulty concentrating, a symptom of PTSD, accounts for her cognitive, manipular, and spatial impediments.*

First, the counselors convinced me I wasn't crazy or just a hopeless drunk. They told me what happened to me was not just in my mind. It was real, and they had the means to treat it. At last, I saw a path out of the darkness.

That was seven years ago. Since then, I've attended twice-weekly PTSD counseling sessions, and my life is coming back to me. The Veterans Administration classified me 100 percent disabled, because I can't work a real job anymore. A few things I can't do at all, and a great many I can't do well. I can't multi-task—cook and listen to the radio at the same time—and I struggle to focus on the kind of detailed activities that used to come naturally to me. I have to make lists or I forget things like paying bills or grocery shopping. However, I sleep better now, and when I have nightmares, I have mechanisms to deal with them.

➤ *Severe and persistent symptoms of the brain damage caused by the traumatic stress Carol Jean endured during her lifetime.*

Now, I can revisit my experience in Vietnam. The counselors have taught me to face that time in my past—to dig it out and come to terms with it. For so long, it had seemed unreal to me, as though it never really happened. I had talked myself into believing it was not part of my life, and I never wanted to face the fact that the Carol Jean who went to Vietnam was not the Carol Jean who came away from there. After being in war, I couldn't be that old person anymore, and I had never dealt honestly with the new me. The old Carol Jean, the silly little blonde from Pennsylvania who went to amusement parks, football games, and movies, left me 30 years ago, but now I'm beginning to identify once again with the young girl I was before I went to war. I can hear her voice. Sometimes, I can even feel her feelings.

Today, I am clean, healthy, and can find joy in my life. Not every day is great. I still have bad times, but my world is steadily more livable. I'm not running anymore, and I'm not hiding. For the first time in three decades, I've learned to allow myself to feel again. PTSD counseling and therapy have permitted me to start over, and this time, I can love myself.

I owe my life to my family, the dedicated, selfless people at the Veterans Administration, and the love and support of my brother veterans. More than ever before, I have hope for the future and faith in my loving God.

—Carol Jean Sundling

➤ *Carol Jean Sundling, sprinkler of perfumed water, majorette, nurse, wife, and mother, led a life of pain, substance abuse, guilt, and avoidance induced by wounds received while in service to her country. At last treated by caring professionals who understood how the traumas she suffered affected her brain and her psychological well-being, she was allowed to take back her self-respect and reconnect with the open, trusting person she had been before she went to war. Carol Jean Sundling spent decades tending the wounds of thousands of young Americans. Now, she tends her own.*

CHAPTER 2

Marlin Jackson
Oregon
U.S. Marine Corps

✈ *The human brain does not fully develop until approximately age 25. For 17-year-old Marlin Jackson, nearly one-third of his psychological maturation, both cognitive and emotional, was influenced by the events of one terrible night in 1966. The psyche of a young man—a boy not old enough to buy beer or vote—was transformed forever in four hellish hours. 240 minutes of adrenaline-soaked fear and bloody slaughter redirected the remainder of Private Marlin Jackson's life. Whatever future fate might have had in store for Marlin was incontrovertibly altered on a horseshoe-shaped rock overlooking the Laotian border. Here, he and a ragtag collection of diminutive tribal warriors came face-to-face and hand-to-hand with the North Vietnamese army.*

What's in my future? I'd like to remodel my little bunker here – carpet, tile, new cabinets, that sort of thing. I'll get around to it some day, but no hurry. As far as the rest of my life is concerned, I'd be happy to find a way back into this world. If somebody told me how, I'd give it another go, but I've tried, and at this point, I'm not optimistic. I thought I treasured solitude, but in reality, I've never been alone. I've lived with that fucking war inside my head twenty-four seven for thirty years.

Dad and I sat on the front porch one night in 1965, my old Studebaker parked on the front lawn. Sixteen years old and a high school dropout, I'd spent the previous year on the road pumping gas and bussing dishes. I was always an independent bastard, one of those pups no one could control. I would never work in an office, never wear a tie. I had no skills and no thought of going back to school. At that point in my young life, my prospects were dim and my options limited. Dad studied my beat-up Studebaker, looked out at the night sky, and then came out with it. "Marlin, just what in hell do you want in life?"

Like I should know. I'd given thought to the military. My parents were for it, but I wasn't sure. I knew only one thing. "Dad, I want to get out there and see what the hell this world's all about."

The next day, I went to the recruiting office and interviewed with the air force, army, and navy. The flyboys wouldn't talk to me because I didn't have a high school diploma. The army and navy said they'd give me this training and I'd travel to exotic foreign places—tried to make me believe I was a prince or duke or someone they couldn't get along without. No go. I wasn't comfortable with them laying it on that thick.

The following day, I went back to the recruiting center and strolled into the marine corps recruiting office. A huge gunnery sergeant sat behind a metal desk, head down, staring at his paperwork. Three minutes passed before he finally looked up and growled, "What the fuck do you want?"

How does a 128-pound 16-year-old answer that? Suddenly, I felt naked and vulnerable in the big sergeant's presence. I must have smiled, because he frowned. Not good. Then, I decided to try assertiveness. A tough little guy not afraid to work the system might impress him. I straightened up and looked him in the eye. "What have you got to offer me?"

Immediately, his frown turned into a scowl. A black carpet of big, bushy eyebrows covered his forehead, his voice was a low rumble, like bowling balls loose in the back of a truck. "Not a God damned thing! My beloved marine corps will give you only what we want you to fucking have."

Talk I understood. I liked this sales pitch! I asked him about enlisting, and he told me my parents had to sign. The next morning, I was back with Mom and Dad to do the paperwork.

* * *

Three days later, my parents said goodbye to me at the airport, and I was off to San Diego for boot camp. In those days, marine corps basic training lasted 13 weeks. Later, when they needed more live bodies in Vietnam, they cut the program to eight.

Even now, people talk about the tough marine corps training, but for me, boot camp was no problem. Small but in good physical condition, the running and training didn't bother me. Several in our unit couldn't take it and washed out, but I didn't have any trouble. At 5:30, they played reveille, and we fell out for P.T. and the morning run. Then, we had chow and attended classes all day—basic infantry tactics, marksmanship, first aid, and map reading. Evenings were for weapons drills, taking care of personal gear, and writing home.

There was a lot said about Vietnam in boot camp. Everywhere, you heard tough talk about how the badass marines over there killed Cong and ate snake. Seven weeks through boot, things changed when our D.I. learned his brother had been killed. That sobered everybody. Some guys still bragged occasionally about going to Vietnam and killing everything in sight but not around that D.I.

➢ *Marlin's first lesson in death from the war. Learning of the soldier's death, a vicarious threat to Marlin's own physical integrity, was a traumatic stressor.*

I suppose I talked tough, too. After 13 weeks in the corps, I couldn't get my chest out far enough. Just 17, I was a marine and proud of it. Damned right, man!

After boot, I went to five weeks of advanced infantry training and learned the specifics of weaponry. I think I fired every weapon in the marine corps inventory except tank-mounted cannons. Every marine is an infantryman first, and marksmanship is the biggest thing in the corps. If you can't qualify on the rifle range, you're out. We also studied map reading, small unit tactics, patrols, ambushes, and booby traps. No problems with the training, but I just wanted to get out and see the world, walk among men, and let my uniform do the talking.

As a marine recruit, I didn't watch TV or read the newspapers. All the information I needed I got from the corps. At 17 years old, the marine corps was my mother, father, and all my sisters and brothers put together. The corps fed and clothed me, provided me with a home and brother marines I trusted. No way could I look objectively at a geopolitical situation like Vietnam. I believed it my duty to secure the blessings of freedom for millions of South Vietnamese threatened by northern Communists. It was a privilege to be an American fighting man in the war against global totalitarianism.

Now, I look back and shake my head at that naïve kid. Now, nobody could feed me that same propaganda. Of course, now I understand a soldier needs propaganda to believe he's doing the right thing and his cause is just. He needs the portrait of righteousness painted for him, and he needs to believe it. Fortunately for governments, soldiers almost always want to believe. They want to believe the small unit tactics they learned will keep them out of an enemy ambush. They want to believe every time they fire their weapon, something will fall down dead. If any part of that is false, then all the rest could be false as well, and a soldier refuses to believe that.

After advanced infantry training, I was transferred to Twenty-Nine Palms, California, and assigned to an artillery unit. As a young, green marine, I got all the flunky jobs. I made beds, emptied buttcans, and stood watch twice a week in a little duty hut checking people in and out of the headquarters building. Fortunately, that only lasted a month, and then I received orders to report to the Seventh Communications Battalion. I was to be a radioman.

At last, I was on my way to my permanent MOS. Fucking cool. I remembered in every war movie I'd ever seen the radioman stuck close to the platoon leader or company commander and kept his composure under fire. A high priority target for the enemy? Sure, but what the hell —that was the movies. As the weeks flew by, I learned to operate and repair every piece of marine corps radio equipment. I climbed poles, strung wire, learned combat communication procedure, and in just a few months, went from artillery flunky to radioman in an infantry company. The best time of my life; I was a real marine, God dammit!

❧ *Marlin was physically prepared and trained for the war in Vietnam. He was also psychologically indoctrinated for combat by his culture and marine corps training. However, regardless of his training and youthful optimism, Marlin's brain would react negatively to the coming traumas, and he would develop PTSD*

Summer of 1966, Seventh Communication Battalion received orders for deployment to Vietnam. Within 24 hours, five communications companies loaded gear and convoyed to San Diego. After two days to get everything stowed aboard the Navy LST, Litchfield County, we shoved off.

The first days of the voyage, everybody was sick. LSTs are flat-bottomed boats, and the ocean swells were murder. We got a break when we stopped in Hawaii for three days of provisioning, and then another 10 in Guam for repairs. You know what the hell there is to do on Guam? Nothing. I spent all my time drinking beer in the Navy club. 10 wasted days, but I had a chance to acclimatize to the unbelievable Southeast Asian heat and humidity.

On the way from Guam to Vietnam, all the FNG marines underwent the ceremony of the Knights of the Golden Dragon, a navy tradition to celebrate the first crossing of the international dateline. The navy guys made us crawl through a trough full of garbage they'd saved up for days, and they shaved our heads. The marines, however, got a little of their own back. That afternoon, we locked the skipper and several of the officers in their own mess hall. All in fun, of course, but a big deal for us and a welcome break from the monotony of the voyage.

When we finally arrived in country, we laid off the coast of Chu Lai for a night before we landed. I sat with a buddy on the bow of the boat and watched flares, explosions, and tracers light up the dark sky over the hills beyond the coastline. My buddy and I looked at that shit and thought, wow, a real war zone. To us, it looked like the *Sands of Iwo Jima*.

The next day, the LST motored up to a sand ramp, the bow doors opened, and we assaulted the beach with full field gear—but no ammunition. I felt like a God damned idiot. What the hell was going on? Did they think we needed more practice? When I hit the beach, I saw a navy guy sitting on a little bulldozer wearing shorts, sandals, a straw hat, and sunglasses drinking beer with a Vietnamese girl on his lap. As we stormed the beach, he waved and lifted his beer can, a salute to the FNGs, Vietnam style. The girl waved too, and when she smiled, I saw an ugly row of teeth stained black as tar. Later, I learned Vietnamese women chewed betel nut as an appetite suppressant and because they believed it prevented tooth decay. The downside (for me, anyway) was the black teeth.

What the fuck? That whole scene was too unreal. I wouldn't have been surprised if the navy guy had tossed me a football or the Vietnamese chick spread a picnic blanket. I felt like a fool lying in the sand with an empty weapon, but apparently, the guy next to me hadn't caught on by then, because he looked up from beneath his helmet and said, "Who's that dude, and where'd the war go? I know it was here just last night."

The first moment I set foot on Vietnamese soil, I experienced the endless dichotomy that was the Vietnam War. Things were never entirely what they appeared, and you never knew what to expect next or what reality would unfold before you.

➤ *Marlin's first encounter with the absurdity of the war he was about to fight caused him unease and anxiety as the underpinning of his beliefs regarding the war eroded. Then, anxiety-induced stress released the neurochemicals that conditioned his brain for survival. Marlin's hypervigilance began on his first day in Vietnam.*

Later, they marched us in the hot sun up the hill past division headquarters to a cleared area at the north end of the airstrip. GP tents were going up when we arrived, but we dug our own latrines, and in the days that followed, built bunkers, put in a helipad, and finished setting up the place. That hilltop was the home of Seventh Comm for the duration of the war—but not for me.

Somebody pegged me to go division headquarters and stand watch in the communications bunker. When I reported in, they sat me in front of a bank of radios and told me to write down all the transmissions from the units in the field. I couldn't believe it! What a bunch of crap. 12 hours in a hole in the ground listening to other people fight the war. Two weeks of that, and I'd had enough. Sitting in a rear area facing all those damn radios was too much like sitting in high school. I went to the gunny in charge and told him I had to get out of there. He said my only other choice was a line unit, and I said fine. The next day, when I reported for duty, the gunny pointed to a jeep and told me to get in and get the hell out of there. I had been re-assigned to Seventh Marines.

Paperwork? Look, the corps didn't always bother with written orders. I was loaned out to two dozen different grunt outfits during my first tour, and I don't recall once receiving written orders. When an outfit needed a radioman, it was, Jackson, you're with so and so now. Move out.

My first field assignment was with the 3/5 Marines on Operation Jackson. I checked in for briefing at the Southeast end of the airstrip, where I was assigned to a line company and picked up the frequencies and codes. When I reported to my new lieutenant and told him I was his radioman, he looked at me, shook his head, and then asked me how old I was. In his eyes, I was child *and* a FNG. I heard him mumble something under his breath, and then he told me to get some sleep.

That night, I asked the guys in my platoon a thousand questions. My first assignment to a line company, finally, I was with men who'd been in combat, and like a damned sponge, I couldn't get information fast enough. In my book, anyone who'd been in the field a month was an old-timer, and I listened to every word anyone said. Typical FNG—nervous, excited, and no clue what he got himself into.

➤ *Marlin's brain began to prepare him for the immediate reality of combat. Quickly, he became super-alert, obsessed with absorbing all the protective skills and reactions that would serve him under fire.*

As the outsider in the tent, I tried to remember my place in the pecking order, but I know I must have been a pain in the ass. Those marines were a close-knit group and didn't know me from Adam. I understood their standoffishness, and I didn't resent it. Hell, ordinarily, I closed up around strangers, too. Nonetheless, they welcomed the teenage FNG into the unit and made me feel I belonged. I always remembered that experience, and later in my tours in Vietnam, I was always supportive of FNGs.

➤ *Human beings are by nature social animals. For eons in our early evolution, we were not the top predator on the food chain, and the necessity to form groups for survival was paramount. This need has not diminished, and Marlin's fear abated when he was welcomed into the group. He most certainly would not have survived in Vietnam without the support of his comrades.*

I already told you radiomen shadowed the officer in charge. At first, I was concerned about that. You still hear talk about bad officers in Vietnam, but my first platoon leader was a calm, purposeful, mission-oriented, serious-minded, no-nonsense marine who wouldn't stand for any bullshit.

We convoyed out the next morning and set up around a village called Bong Song. Our job was to sweep the area and kill every bad guy we saw. Turns out, there wasn't much going on. We sent out patrols, set up ambushes, and now and then took some incoming fire, but nothing intense. A good, five-day warming up exercise for me, the lieutenant called it "an easy break-in." On the third day, I took rifle fire over my head—what a surprise, Charley took a shot at the radioman—and I first heard the crumping sound of incoming mortars. A good week, I learned a lot and hardly got my hands dirty. I thought at the time combat wasn't anything like I'd imagined. Of course, I had no idea what I'd get into later.

* * *

You keep asking about my other life, so I guess I'll tell you. It's why boot camp—the tough marine corps thing—didn't bother me. I'll put it this way. I grew up tough, and I never, ever took shit from anyone.

I was born in Portland, Oregon, and as a young boy, my family lived on a chicken farm just outside town. Later, we moved in closer but still lived in the country. We had a dinky little house nestled in the trees, and I shared rooms in the attic with my two brothers. Six children in our family—three boys and three girls, and I was the youngest boy. Now, only an older brother and one sister are still alive. My oldest sister was murdered in the late 60s, and another died a few years ago. My oldest brother committed suicide in the late 90s.

My old man worked as a custodian for the Portland school district. Dad was pretty stiff on the discipline, but he was fair and a good man. Ours was a tightly knit family, and we never fought among ourselves. Everyone worked. The girls babysat when they could, and my brothers and I picked crops on the weekends. When I was a little older, I pumped gas at the neighborhood service station. Throughout our childhood, we all worked long days and thought nothing of it.

❖ *Early childhood practices and values much like the ones Marlin would later experience and embrace in the Marine Corps.*

Every year, Dad put in a huge garden and grew enough vegetables to feed us and the neighbors. Also, we raised chickens and rabbits. We really didn't have much in the way of material things, but we always had enough food to eat, and most of the time, a little pocket change. In my book, I had a great life, and I never felt I lacked anything. Trouble was, I was the black sheep of the family. Always off in the woods by myself, sometimes I stayed gone days, and then showed up with crawdads or game fish that Mom cooked for supper. Something about being on my own in the wilderness attracted me. I didn't need buddies. If no one was around, I happily wandered off by myself and stayed gone as long as I wanted.

However, things changed. I turned 15, and the woods behind our house became too small for me. I needed broader horizons, so I learned to hotwire one of our old cars, and man, I drove that thing all over the county. At the time, Dad pretended he didn't know, but years later, he told me he kept track of the odometer mileage. The same was true with his whiskey bottle. When I stole some, to cover the theft, I replaced it with tea. Dad never said anything about that, either, but years later, he let me taste tea-flavored Jack Daniels. I guess I was as big a fool as any other teenager.

All my brothers and sisters were talented. One brother played the violin, another the trombone, and my oldest sister played the lap steel guitar and sang. Also, I had a brother who was good in drama. When my sister, Thuvia, was 13, she found a way to cut a record of Dad's favorite song. Just a floppy little slice of black vinyl that sounded like she'd recorded it in a phone booth, but Dad kept it until the day he died. Unfortunately, the family talent skipped me. Like every other teenage boy, I tried the drums, and then the guitar, but I'm better at listening to music than playing it.

My high school career was less than spectacular—in fact, you could say less than below average. I was a James Dean wanna-be. I wore Levis, T-shirts, and black engineer boots, and I combed my hair in a ducktail like the great man himself. I suppose all that dressing up didn't mean much, because no matter who I tried to look like, I just couldn't force myself to attend classes. I'd get off the school bus, throw my books in my locker, and then leave. Once in a while I went to class, but mostly I just wandered around the countryside while everyone else sat inside the school building. I didn't think myself stupid, I just didn't go to class. In fact, I didn't finish ninth grade. For me, school was like being in prison. I want you to understand, just because I didn't like school doesn't mean I was a dumb troublemaker. I never harmed anyone or made a spectacle of myself. I just couldn't sit in a classroom. Otherwise, I was an ordinary guy.

✦ *Had Marlin grown up in the 1990s, most likely he would have been diagnosed with Attention-Deficit/Hyperactivity Disorder and treated with stimulants. Successfully treated, he may have finished school and had more choices regarding his future. Perhaps, he may have avoided Vietnam altogether.*

A few months into ninth grade, the principal called me into his office and expelled me. My parents, upset and not sure how to handle the situation, knew I wasn't a bad kid, just a loner—"an independent bastard," my father had said—who wouldn't do anything he didn't want to. Ultimately, they sent me to northern Nevada to live with my Uncle Donald and Aunt Pauline. Nice folks, they were kind to take me, and I never gave them any trouble, but after just a few months at the local high school, I saw that wouldn't work, either. Not wanting to cause those good people grief, one day, I packed a bag and hit the highway.

I bummed around for the next year, pumping gas and bussing dishes. Kids my age didn't do drugs then, but I partied and drank a lot of beer. Look, you just need to know, I never caused anybody any trouble. I marched to my own drumbeat, that's all. How did I square that with joining the marine corps? I'll tell you how. You see, I never really minded being told what to do. I just couldn't stand being told what *not* to do. Think about it. The corps gave me a rifle and told me go kill people. As long as I did that, I did most anything else I wanted. Made perfect sense to me.

* * *

When I returned from the Bong Song assignment, I reported to Seventh Comm, and they sent me right out with another grunt outfit for a month of night patrols, LPs and Ops. Then, I went with another after that. I did a lot of night patrols with units south of Chu Lai. Usually, I went with a squad, maybe seven or eight guys, to see what trouble we could find. Generally, we worked in hilly terrain with thick vegetation, but now and then, we patrolled the flatlands and rice paddies. We stayed off the trails because the whole area was littered with booby traps, and after we moved two or three miles without coming across anything, we set up ambushes along suspected enemy re-supply routes and waited. As radio operator, I kept the folks back in camp up to speed on where we were and what we did. When we stopped and set up for ambush, I keyed the mike a couple times to let CP know we were in quiet mode.

Night patrol was humping the bush for hours and finding nothing, hanging out and waiting half the night, and then suddenly, when we least expected it, we were in the middle of the shit diving for cover. First we saw the muzzles flash, and then watched green tracers come belly-high right at us. Of course, everybody hits the deck and returns fire, and as long as it lasts, it really is like the *Sands of Iwo Jima*. In the middle of all that shit, my job was to radio our coordinates and ask for fire support, and that was when I got serious and made sure I did everything right. If I didn't send accurate messages quickly, I could really fuck us up. Early on, I learned to carry my handset wrapped up in my helmet so the microphone dangled next to my ear. That left my hands free for my M-16, and even in the middle of a gunfight, I could hear when someone contacted us.

➤ *Marlin's deep sense of responsibility for his duties added to his susceptibility to stress and made him more vulnerable when a major traumatic event occurred.*

Generally, the heavy metal took the fight out of the bad guys, and they broke contact. Then, just as quickly as it had begun, my ears still ringing with the echo of gunfire, it was over, and I would look around to see whether anyone had been hit. After that, it was a matter of getting my adrenaline under control.

➤ *He reports the unexpected surreal nighttime visual stressors as intensely stimulating. Marlin experienced enough traumas in these firefights to produce an acute stress reaction.*

That was pretty much my life for the remainder of my first tour. During my last month in country, I'd surrendered all my illusions about the war and saving anyone from Communism. I only wanted to do my job and hope everyone went home alive.

I moved around a lot that year but occasionally returned two or three times to the same infantry unit. After a while, I got to know some of the guys, and they always said hello and asked me where I'd been. Even for a loner like me, it was good to see a friendly face now and then. Trouble was, sometimes I went back to a unit and some of the guys I'd known weren't there anymore. Better not to think about them.

One more thing. Before my first tour ended, I was loaned out to 1st Recon Battalion to accompany a three-man team to a Montagnard village. Called Montagnards by the French troops that occupied the area in the 1800s, they were a primitive, tribal people that had lived for centuries in the hills between Cambodia, Laos, and Vietnam. Small, but surprisingly strong, hard living and an uncertain food supply had turned their skin and hair a musty, reddish-brown. Like indigenous peoples in many other nations, the Montagnards were socially isolated and perpetually at war with their lowland neighbors. During the American occupation, the U.S. used the Montagnards to spy on communist forces and interdict their operations in the hill country.

In the late afternoon, we choppered in to a tiny village at the top of a huge, horseshoe-shaped rock in the foothills next to the Laotian border. Half the village was built on one end of the horseshoe, and a narrow trail led around the curve to the other half. Standing on one tip of the rock, you looked across a deep canyon to the other tip. Besides the trail, the only way to get to the other side of the village was to climb down a vertical wall of rock, cross the canyon, and climb up the other side.

The Montagnards lived underground in trenches and bunkers, and everyone over the age of 12, including the women and girls, went on patrols and conducted hit and run operations in the area. Clearly, somebody's government had supplied them, because in addition to their usual weapons—spears, knives, and crossbows—they carried a mix of American and Chinese Communist automatic and semi-automatic rifles. I don't know what those people had been promised to induce them to live in that remote and isolated spot. The western mountains were littered with NVA flags, and they were completely surrounded by bad guys.

Our recon team was sent there to observe NVA activity in the area and report back. Because of the remote location and heavy concentration of enemy troops, in addition to our personal weapons, we brought a .50

caliber machine gun and a BC scope. The only Americans within miles, we were more than a little spooked, and from the first moment we arrived, looked forward to getting out of there as soon as possible.

On the second day, I hiked the trail to the other half of the village and met the headman. He wore a uniform with no insignia, so I figured him for somebody's hired assassin. He spoke a little English and made me understand he wanted us to come to his bunker for dinner and conversation. That night, the four of us hiked the trail again and brought C rations to add to the stewpot and a carton of American cigarettes for the headman. After dinner, I played checkers with his young son while the man told us about his people.

They'd been on that hilltop just over a month, but recently, the enemy had moved heavy concentrations of new troops in, and they didn't know how much longer they could hold out. I asked him where they planned to go next, and he shrugged and pointed to the sky. I never found out whether he meant only God knew or whether that was their next destination. An interesting evening; I saw a side of life few get to witness, and it was the first time I ever ate dog stew.

Below the village, across a wide valley, an NVA trail led to a river that flowed from the western mountains. The enemy portaged supplies, weapons, and ammunition through the passes, and then floated them down the river. Two big boulders sat on either side of the trail where it made a bend, and then doubled back on itself. As the days went by, we saw so much enemy activity on that trail, we radioed base and received permission to shoot.

First, we bracketed the two boulders with our .50 and calculated the 10-digit coordinates halfway between. Then, when we saw troops moving, we waited until the right moment and put a six-round burst into them. Surprised at being shot at in their own backyard, nine times out of ten, they ran back the way they came, and we only had to swivel our .50 a notch and put down 20 to 30 rounds to get every one. A nice little system, and for a while, we had a hell of kill ratio.

We stayed in that Montagnard village 25 days before the NVA finally got sick of it and hit us two nights in a row. I was God damned amazed. What those bastards did wasn't humanly possible. From the floor of canyon below us, those sons-of-bitches actually scaled the rock walls of the hill that village sat on. The bastards crawled up the side of the cliff, their weapons at sling arms, and when they reached flat ground were right in front of us lobbing grenades, screaming like banshees, and coming at us. Dug in, we had cover and concealment, so we just hunkered down and picked them off. I don't know how many of those poor fuckers stood up at the edge of that cliff, got hit, and then fell over backwards. We were up half the night until they gave it up and things finally quieted down.

➤ *Even though in imminent danger of being killed or wounded, his empathy for his enemy was evident. The huge number of NVA Marlin and his teammates killed were indirect threats to his own physical integrity and a traumatic stressor.*

The following night, they came after us with an attitude. Apparently they'd had enough of us and our Montagnard friends, because they opened up with an 82 mm mortar and tried to dismantle our hilltop stone by stone. Between incoming rounds, I looked across the valley and spotted the enemy mortar crew on a little rock outcropping. I put a burst of .50 on them and took them out, but their buddies obviously had orders to follow the mortars in, because when the tube went quiet, the shit really hit the fan.

➤ *That night and the following morning, Marlin Jackson met both Criterion A conditions for PTSD. He witnessed and experienced numerous events involving actual or threatened death or serious injury, or a threat to the physical integrity of self or others.*

Within seconds, the God damned NVA came at us from all directions. We called for artillery and told them to keep tossing it in until we said to stop. Four hours of the most intense, close combat I'd ever experienced, they crested the hill five at a time and came at us, and we clicked off just as many rounds as it took to drop them. The firefight lasted half the night, and who knows how much ammo we put through that .50. The next morning, when the sun topped the eastern foothills, we stuck our heads up and took a look around. Everything around us had been shot to shit, and I mean everything. All the sandbags in front of us were torn up, and even the machine gun tripod had nicks in it. Later, the Montagnard headman reported he lost a few people, but no American even got a scratch.

➤ *To permit Marlin to react in accordance to the threat, Marlin's brain pumped large doses of neurochemicals throughout his neocortex. However, the chemicals that motivated him into self-protective action had an immediate and deleterious effect on his still-developing brain.*

When the clouds lowered, I took a couple Montagnards with me and patrolled the perimeter. As we came across dead NVA, we tossed their bodies over the edge of the cliff. I wondered how many more already lay on the floor of the canyon. For all I knew, there could have been a carpet of dead gooks down there, but one thing was certain: I really didn't give a crap.

➤ *The threat to Marlin's physical integrity was reinforced when the lull in enemy activity and weather conditions made it possible to assess the battle damage.*

Fear for one's own life and witnessing loss of life in others traumatizes. This holds whether the maimed and slain are friend or foe, even when cognitively it is vehemently denied. After this battle, and even for the rest of his life, Marlin would not or could not acknowledge how the deaths of so many of the enemy affected him.

Too hot for a recon team, for us, that was the end of the Montagnard village, so we called in a chopper and got lifted out. I never found out what happened to the villagers. No matter where they went next, I was sure they'd be in the middle of some shit somewhere. I always wondered what happened to the boy I played checkers with, a kid already wounded three times in their never-ending war. The Montagnards were the best fighters I saw in Vietnam, and later, when I heard what happened to them after the U.S. pullout, I was sick. For years, I was ashamed and embarrassed by my government's broken promises and the way we abandoned those wretched people.

➪ *Betrayal of the Montagnards for whom Marlin cared so deeply reduced his psychological defenses against his own perceived betrayal by the government in later years.*

Fall came, and one evening, headquarters ordered me to take the next hop to Da Nang to work with a military police unit. Fine with me. I packed my things, and as I walked out to the airstrip, suddenly, my legs collapsed beneath me, and I crashed to the ground. Then, just as suddenly, all my muscles contracted at once and curled me into a tight little ball. I couldn't move, couldn't unlock, and couldn't straighten out. Alone in the dark on the tarmac, I had no idea what the hell had happened. The pain was so intense I nearly blacked out, but I willed myself to stay conscious. I dripped sweat and at the same time froze my ass off. Next thing I knew, I'd been rushed to a field hospital and pitched into a big cooler. I mean that literally—just like a God damned meat locker. After several hours, slowly, my body returned to normal, and they released me the next morning. I never learned what caused that little episode, but it really knocked me down.

➪ *A Malaria attack further weakened Marlin physically and reduced his overall psychological resiliency.*

When I arrived in Da Nang, corpsmen put me on light duty, and I stayed in my bunk for days under a dozen blankets. For a week after, my joints felt like someone had taken a ball peen hammer to them. I was so stiff and sore, I could hardly move.

Ten days later, after morning chow, the CO called me into his office and asked whether I had a sister in Sacramento. I told him my sister lived in Fresno. "Close enough," he said and handed me a telegraph from the

Red Cross. "Go pack your bag. She's dead, and you're going on emergency leave."

➤ *Emotional shock and assault do not always manifest in the form of belly-high, green tracers from a tree line. Indeed, they can come in the relative peace and safety of a commander's office.*

My sister was 26 when she was murdered and eight years older than I. As a child, I always looked up to Thuvia. Dad's favorite, he named her Thuvia after the character in the Edgar Rice Burroughs science fiction book, *Maid of Mars*. A pretty girl with a kind heart and gentle nature, what I remember most about Thuvia was her big smile.

I didn't then know how she died, so during the journey home, I assumed a car accident or some other twist of fate had ended her life, and I hoped she hadn't suffered. When I got off the plane in Portland, Dad and my oldest brother met me at the airport. I asked them what had happened to Thuvia, and instead of telling me, Dad handed me a newspaper.

All there in black and white—big, splashy headlines and all the gory details. Someone had stalked her, put lewd correspondence in her mailbox, and once broke into her apartment and stole her undergarments. Thuvia had reported him to the police, but nothing was done. I guess the asshole finally snapped. He must have been one crazy motherfucker, because he stabbed her in her bathtub—stabbed her nine times with three different knives, garroted her, and then beat her body to a pulp.

I read through the entire article as we walked to the parking lot. Then, I'll always remember this, I handed the newspaper to Dad and said, "So, how's everybody else?" That was it. The whole grisly, shocking, brutal murder of my sister just bounced right off me.

➤ *A classic PTSD symptom. Marlin numbed his pain before he even felt it. Then, he dismissed the horror of his sister's brutal murder as easily as the deaths of the NVA soldiers he killed during the battle on the rock.*

Dad and my brother were speechless at my casual, nonchalant reaction. To this day, I still feel bad about that, because I know they never got over the shock of my cold-blooded imperturbability.

I hope you don't judge me too harshly. Understand, that was all the emotion I had in me. I was still at war, and to me, the death of yet another human wasn't such a big deal. At that moment, I remember thinking it was fine with me if nobody ever again mentioned her name. In my book, we were still among the living, and Thuvia was not.

➤ *Entrenched in the survival mode that had served him well in combat, Marlin could neither fight nor flee the awful fact of his sister's murder, a major traumatic event in what was to become a long list for this 18-year old marine.*

That night, the family went to the funeral home to view the body. I admit the mortician had a tough assignment with Thuvia's mutilated corpse, but even so, he'd done a damned lousy job. She looked terrible. Mother didn't even recognize her, and that's what set me off. I saw her expression of shock and pain when she looked in that casket, and the blood boiled in my veins. I slipped out of the chapel, tracked down the asshole funeral home operators and backed them into their office, ready to kill them on the spot. I don't remember exactly what I told them. It doesn't matter now. But if my sister hadn't come in and pulled me out of there, I'd have done it, and there would have been three caskets in that viewing room.

➤ *Uncontrollable fury and misdirected anger became the coping mechanisms Marlin employed to deal with his PTSD, integral ingredients in Marlin's internal bag of distorted interpersonal relationship skills.*

Welcome home from Vietnam. I was 18 years old.

I don't remember much more about my time at home. Mostly, I sat in bars and drove my old Studebaker around the countryside.

➤ *The external element Marlin used to cope with pain. Completely unaware of the deleterious effects of self-medication with alcohol, he quickly learned to pair drinking alcohol with numbing emotional pain.*

I'd been on leave three weeks when I got orders back to Vietnam to finish my tour. The thought of losing another child was too much for Mom, and she had a breakdown that put her in the hospital. I don't know what happened—maybe someone in the family called a politician, because revised orders came in the mail assigning me to Camp Pendleton.

At Pendleton, I was attached to an artillery outfit and trained as a forward observer. In my spare time, I found myself teaching the infantry guys about staying alive in Vietnam. Aware of their own imminent departure for America's least favorite war zone, they were like children, eager to hear any story I had to tell. I wouldn't have talked to just anyone about that shit, but they were brother marines, and I knew what they were in for. I never forgot the kindness I'd received a year earlier, and I wanted to help. If anything I said saved even one life, I'd have talked myself blue in the face.

➤ *In contradiction to Marlin's overall restricted range of affect, he always had feelings of closeness to fellow combatants. As with the Montagnards, Marlin had immense empathy for the plight of these young marines.*

The year at Pendleton passed before I knew it. I'd grooved a routine. I worked in the field with the grunts during the day, and then came home and partied at night. The best time of my life, but also when I started really drinking. I drank everything I got my hands on, and I drank only to get drunk. I guess subconsciously I figured if I murdered enough brain cells, I'd forget the events of my first 18 years on this planet.

During the day, I stayed squared away and did my job, but when liberty call came, I got drunk and chased women until dawn. Sometimes, I walked out of a bar, sniffed the night air, and then woke up the next morning in my own bed with no memory of anything that happened in between. Daytime, I walked and talked marine, but at night, I was a drunken zombie fool.

During that year at Pendleton, I experienced the first symptoms of what I'd later learn was PTSD. Five nights a week I spent in varying states of half-sleep, drifting back and forth between consciousness and oblivion. I jumped at the slightest noise in the barracks, and then lay for hours reliving shootouts. I went over in my mind how I could have done things differently and saved a life instead of taking it. I saw dead people—Americans and Vietnamese—a big hole in the chest here and a missing limb there. I saw every detail. Firefights came back to me in much greater detail and starker contrast than when I lived them. I watched men get hit and go down. I watched other guys get hit and spin one direction while body parts flew off in another. I watched myself lift a dead marine, wrap him in a poncho liner, and throw him on a chopper, and I remembered every little smell in the air around me and how dust from the rotor wash packed my nostrils and cut my eyes. Also during that period, I started feeling guilty about the guys still over there. After a while, I only slept when drunk enough to pass out the moment my head hit the pillow.

I spent my nineteenth birthday alone and unconscious in a roadside bar.

❧ *Now, as Marlin experienced the sequelae of PTSD symptoms, he applied his self-destructive coping mechanism and became a functional alcoholic. His difficulty sleeping, hypervigilance, nightmares, intrusive thoughts, and flashbacks combined to make his days and nights a torturous reliving of his hellish traumatic experiences.*

The week after the 1968 Tet offensive, my artillery battery joined the 3rd Battalion, 27th Marines. All the trained and experienced marine infantrymen were already in Vietnam, so 3rd Battalion was patched together with mechanics, electricians, cooks, Remington raiders, engineers—whoever in hell they could find that walked and chewed gum at the same time. It was called the Bastard Battalion, and the corps threw every kind of REMF and POGE imaginable into that one unit and gave everybody orders for Vietnam—except me. Feeling like a major dickhead, I went to the CO's office and asked why.

"It's in your record, Jackson. You're not to be shipped back because you've already served one tour, and your mother's health is questionable." Of course, I never knew that little piece of horseshit was in my file, and I was mad as hell. The CO made a couple phone calls, and then told me if I signed a waiver, I could go over with the battalion. I knew Mom wouldn't like it, but I'd trained with those guys for months, and bastard battalion or not, I wanted to go where they went.

❥ *In spite of the nightmares, flashbacks, and other symptoms, Marlin positioned himself to be re-traumatized all over again.*

I never will forget the day we shipped out of El Toro Marine Air Station. Hundreds of marines reclined on their packs all over the tarmac. Some read while others snoozed. At the edges, guys played goodbye-kissy-face with their wives or girlfriends. The Bastard Battalion. Still-wet-behind-the-ears-pea-green-support-troops going over to fight like Real Marines. I wondered how many would make it back. Ironically, even though one of the youngest, I was among the most experienced. I knew the God damned terror in store for those guys, and I knew the dread. I looked out across that staging area and prayed this time, I could do something to help even one guy come back alive.

❥ *Marlin's entire identity was that of a marine. His ability to have empathetic feelings for other humans extended only to others of his kind.*

* * *

Third Battalion, 27th Marines landed in Da Nang in February 1968. When they opened the doors, the late afternoon furnace blast and unforgettable stench of Southeast Asia hit me, and I said to myself, "God damn, Marlin, you dumb bastard, you're back in 'Nam." Naturally, when we landed, the airstrip was rocketed, so we scrambled for the flight line bunkers until it let up. An hour later, they formed us up and trucked us all night to our TAOR.

Third Battalion consisted of four infantry companies, an artillery battery, and a headquarters company. I was the artillery radio operator scout, a job I qualified for, as I was trained and experienced in artillery, infantry, radio operations, and forward observing. Another marine, Brettman, and I were assigned to M Company as forward observers. Mike Company, a typical infantry line unit, operated south of Da Nang between the airbase and the Korean troops in the Arizona Valley. Our TAOR extended out to the South China Sea, and then back west to Highway 1.

Battalion moved the four companies around the TAOR according to a monthly rotation schedule. One company was assigned perimeter guard for a week and ran patrols and ambushes around the CP, while the other three companies went to the field. Of the three companies in the field, one patrolled out of a little village we called Capville. Another company worked out of the Tu Cau Bridge on the Song Vinh Dien River next to Highway 1. The last company operated in the Desert Area, which bordered Forbidden Lake. After a week, the companies rotated. That left each company in the bush three weeks and in CP one.

Those days were an endless series of squad and platoon-sized patrols on round-the-clock sweeps to locate and kill the enemy. The only sleep a marine got was during breaks, when he fell back on his pack and closed his eyes a few minutes.

✦ *The fatigue that Marlin experienced served to further erode his ability to withstand the almost continuous psychological stress created by the physical demands of the mission.*

Endless combat patrols anywhere were bad enough, but our area was the most heavily mined and booby-trapped place in Vietnam. Every day, we lost men and vehicles to those damned mines. 30 years later, I learned the brass at MACV couldn't figure out why the marines lost so many men. They figured the bastard battalion must be screwing up, so they sent an officer to check us out. Two weeks later, the investigator confirmed the inordinate mining and booby-trapping of our area and stated that of all the marine units, 3/27 was most qualified to locate and neutralize these weapons, because so many of our "bastards" were engineers. He wrote that any other infantry outfit would have sustained far more casualties.

Not only was our whole God damned TAOR littered with land mines and booby traps, the God damned NVA outnumbered us 30 to 1. We never knew when some asshole would stick his head in the air and shoot at us. Even the leper colony run by French missionaries out in the Riviera area was full of gooks. They came and went like they owned the place, and everybody knew about it, but the brass wouldn't allow us to go in there and take them out.

And it didn't make any difference where you were in our TAOR. One day, sitting at CP drinking beer with a buddy, a shootout started just outside the perimeter. Middle of the God damned day, just outside our wire. Can you believe it? My buddy and I stood up on a berm to get a look, and one second later, he collapsed beside me deader than hell. You couldn't go anywhere to get out of harm's way in our area. There wasn't any safe place. The whole fucking area sucked.

✦ *Fear of death and dismemberment was a constant and unavoidable companion for Marlin during this tour. He was in fight, flight, or freeze mode the entire time, his brain flooded with neurochemicals in a struggle to prolong his ability to function and survive his daily dose of terror.*

Three days after we moved in, we went out on a company-sized night patrol through the Riviera to the Desert Area. It was pitch-black, and no one could see shit, so we slogged through it, each man hanging onto the belt of the man in front. When we finally reached the sand, we spread out and stopped. The CO called Brettman, our lieutenant, and me forward and told us to call in an illumination round so he could eyeball the terrain and locate our position on the map. The lieutenant politely reminded him an illumination round bursting directly overhead was dangerous, because after the round went off, the spent canister falls to the ground. The CO wanted it fired anyway, so I called it in and dived for a hole.

Thirty seconds later, the round whistled over our heads and popped. The canister landed harmlessly between two grunts, so no damage there, but the illumination lit us up like the fourth of July. I mean, we were a company of frigging marines wearing green fatigues lying in white sand. That CO had made one major error in judgment, but we were lucky, and nothing came of it. After he'd been in country a while, he wised up pretty fast, so Brettman and I turned our attention to keeping our lieutenants alive. No easy task in that environment.

A few nights later, we went on patrol and hadn't gone a hundred yards outside the CP when the poor sucker in front of me tripped a booby-trap that killed him instantly and wounded the guy in front of him. Two hours after that, we walked into an enemy ambush. I mean, we were moving silent and slow off the trail, and in a heartbeat, bullets started flying everywhere. One of our guys got the shit shot out of him, and we called the medivac chopper to get him the hell out of there. During the next hour, our corpsman patched up another half dozen. In that one night, patrolling outside our own CP, we sustained nine casualties. I told you there was no safe place in our area of operation.

My fucking second tour in Vietnam started out tough and got worse.

➽ *The inability to feel safe, even for one day, has a devastating effect on a soldier's ability to remain resilient in the face of unremitting traumatic stressors. In this environment, the brain is constantly on guard, hypervigilant.*

The Bastard Battalion took a lot of casualties in a short time. Replacements came in steady, but they were green, too, and we couldn't go half a day without mixing it up with the bad guys. I don't know the ratio of enemy soldiers killed compared to our own losses. We didn't think much about body counts—on either side. I only know anytime I looked around Mike Company, I saw a whole bunch of new faces.

Jerry Mickelovitch was a good guy and fine marine, but he had a thing about authority figures, and sometimes, he went too far or said too much. One day, he did something with a cigarette butt our platoon sergeant didn't like, and gunny made him dig a three-foot hole in the sand and bury it. Then, he made him dig it up again. I think Mickelovitch popped off, because then, the gunny sent him on night perimeter guard. We got hit pretty hard that night and as things got tense, we fired flares to see if Charley tried to penetrate our wire. At the same moment Mickelovitch stuck his head up to get a look around, a gook rocket came in and landed right in front of him. Shrapnel cut an artery, and the gunny carried him to a jeep and hauled him away. When the shooting stopped, Brettman and I went to the battalion aid station to check on him, but he was already dead. The corpsmen gave us his personal possessions to take back to the lieutenant. I never will forget his watch completely covered in dried blood. I knew eventually his wife back in the States would get it, so I took it back to my hooch and cleaned it up.

Gunny felt bad for months about giving Mickelovitch that extra guard duty—said it was his fault the boy died. That poor fucker cried in his beer and whimpered in his sleep for the rest of his tour. I know damned well he wished he'd have been the one killed. He probably still does.

Seventh Marines kicked off Operation Allen Brook May 4th, 1968. Go Noi Island wasn't really an island—more like a peninsula between two rivers, and it was thick with gooks. Intelligence reported a reinforced regiment of NVA and three VC battalions had moved in and were playing hell with the big American base in Da Nang. Brass made the decision to clean them out, and India Company of the 3/27 was attached to 7th for the operation.

I don't care what anyone says. Somebody should have foreseen the pile of shit the marines walked into on Go Noi. The NVA were well armed, trained, disciplined, and dug in deep. When our guys went in, they ran into serious trouble right away, and it took the brass a while to get their thumbs out of their asses and figure out how much reinforcement they needed and how to bring it in. A few days later, India Company led a battalion-sized advance near the village of Le Bac, when who knows what size enemy force hit them. Difficult terrain and heavy enemy fire checked the flanking movements of the two companies in support, and that left India in the center, alone and pinned down.

The NVA decimated those poor bastards. The enemy was so deeply dug in, even air and artillery support was of little help. The marines fought like tigers and died like soldiers. A machine gunner with India, Robert Burke, put Audie Murphy to shame that day. His squad was pinned down in the middle of the heaviest shit, and taking casualties right and left. Burke grabbed an M-60 and charged the enemy single-handed—and then did it over and over again. I don't know how many bunkers he knocked out before the gooks finally got him, but he was awarded the Medal of Honor for what he did that day.

Mike Company joined Operation Allen Brook on the morning of the 17th. We'd been running security at the POW camp south of Da Nang when we got called to Go Noi to participate in our first large scale operation. We were already pretty well blooded patrolling our own TAOR, and I remember sitting in the LZ waiting to fly in. I looked around at all those haunted faces around me and again wondered how many would not come back.

➤ *Marlin looked at the other soldiers as if gazing in a mirror—thinking of his own mortality as much as his comrades'.*

The chopper pilot that flew us in did some kind of circus-act approach, because the LZ was hot as hell. All I saw out the back of the helicopter were bodies strewn everywhere on the ground, and as we touched down, bloody bandages kicked up by the rotor wash flew all over the place.

➤ *Marlin knew that at any moment, he could be transformed from detached observer to one of the maimed, mutilated, and dying marines on the ground.*

We hit the ground running and set up a quick perimeter in the elephant grass. I went out thirty meters and dropped—you guessed it—right beside a couple dead marines. Then, I looked up and saw a gunny from India Company bandaged and walking around in a daze, tears streaming from his eyes. What the hell was that idiot doing? Bullets flew all over the place. I pulled him down beside me and heard him mumble, "Where's my company? What happened to my men?" Right then, I told myself we were all fucked. That place was going to be hell.

In an hour, we fought out from the LZ and dug in near a riverbed. As quickly as they could, our corpsmen set up a makeshift M.A.S.H. unit to take casualties. Somebody found the FO from India Company wounded and bleeding in no man's land and dragged him back. When they brought him in, I heard him say the guys up front were low on ammo and water. Brettman had the radio on his back, so I asked the lieutenant if I could go forward and take them the shit they needed. He said, "Okay," so I threw ammo belts around my neck, stuffed grenades in my pockets, and hung bandoliers around my waist. Then, I grabbed two G.I. cans of water and headed out.

Trouble was, I didn't know exactly where I was going. The whole place was covered in elephant grass eight feet high, so I followed the sound of gunfire until I finally made to the line. I mean, it didn't take long for those poor India Company bastards to relieve me of that water and ammo. On my way back for more, I saw a couple wounded guys laying in the grass all bandaged up, so I threw one over my shoulder and dragged the other by the belt until I got them back to the aid station.

I guess I made eight or ten trips back to the line carrying supplies in and injured out. I really don't know for sure how many. On one trip, I grabbed a wounded marine, started back, and got lost in the grass. Hell, man, it was 120 degrees that day, and I was probably half out of my mind with heat exhaustion. You try it sometime.

❖ *Marlin may have begun to experience survivor guilt at this time and continued to place himself in harm's way as a means of assuaging his growing sense of isolation from the mortality of the other marines in his unit.*

Anyway, I tried to get oriented and in a few minutes came across another wounded man. That fucker was really hurt. I must have been the first to find him, because he had a chest wound, and he hadn't been tended to. I threw him on my shoulder, belt-looped the other guy, took the best bearing I could, and moved out. A few minutes later, I came out of the grass onto a dry riverbed. I looked left and saw our guys in position 50 or 60 meters up river—close, but there was no cover between them and me. The wounded marine on my shoulder wasn't getting any healthier, and I didn't want to risk getting turned around in the grass again, so I stepped out onto the riverbed and ran.

What's that? You think I made a great target? No shit, man. Carrying one guy, dragging another, gooks firing at me from all sides, and my own people shooting past me trying to give me cover. I ran like a maniac and dived into a hole just inside our lines. Corpsmen pulled the two wounded marines into the aid station. I never found out what happened to those guys or whether they made it out. I hope they did.

For most of the day, Kilo Company deployed in front of us, but they'd taken some heavy hits, and when the line shifted, we found ourselves in the middle of the shit. Now, Mike Company and what remained of Kilo Company threw lead at NVA troops less than 40 meters from our perimeter. About that time, a lieutenant dropped into our hole and asked whether any of us had been to India Company's line and knew how to get there. Brettman still had the radio, so I said fuck it and volunteered to take him. No one position seemed any safer than another in that God forsaken place, so for the rest of the day, I ferried ammo and water up to India's line and wounded soldiers back.

After that, things got pretty messy. Two of our squads went forward to help Kilo Company and got ambushed along the way. I was out there in the middle of it when it happened and saw wounded marines wherever I turned. The God dammed gooks were so dug in, no one could get at them. They'd reinforced their bunkers with railroad ties and rails and packed dirt on the roofs. The only way to get them out was with napalm or a direct hit by heavy artillery. Soon, both India and Kilo companies were pinned down. Nobody could pull out of the front line. Everywhere

I looked, marines fought for their lives. Finally, the battalion commander ordered the rest of Mike Company forward to try and help them pull back.

Our guys put covering fire but didn't make much progress. Every time we got up and started moving, we took fire and had to hit the deck again. I remember lying in the grass with my head on a dead guy's legs—the radioman from Kilo Company. The company CO lay next to me and asked me to hand him the guy's handset. When he reached for it, he rustled the grass slightly and instantly took two rounds. A corpsman got up to help, but the CO hollered at him to stay put. He said the gooks had snipers in the grass with periscopes. Periscopes. Can you believe it? That was some shit. In a moment, I heard a *thunk,* and behind me a marine went to his knees. Another *thunk,* and the guy next to me keeled over. Then, another guy tried to move to a different spot and got nailed. By the time we figured out what was going on, we were already fucked.

➤ *Certainly here, as much as any other time, Marlin must have had serious feelings of helplessness and impending doom.*

The CO now out of action, a lieutenant called for napalm, and that little radio message scared the hell out of me. Napalm was risky in close combat. 15 minutes later, the air force was overhead. Their first strike was on target, but when they came around for a second pass, I heard the FAC scream into the radio for them to abort. We all saw the jet come down for another run, and everyone stood up and waved arms and hollered, "Don't drop. Don't drop!" No good. They put it right on top of us. Jesus Christ, we were in the middle of a God damned firestorm. I was lucky—it only burned the hair off my face, arms and neck. The next day, however, we pulled out the charred bodies of seven marines.

After the napalm strikes, we hoped things would calm down, but that didn't happen. The enemy kept at us. A long time passed, and we were in a serious shootout, and I wasn't sure how much longer we could hold on. Sometime later, Mike Company's artillery battery ran out of ammunition and had nothing left except smoke canisters, so the lieutenant told them to throw that. It turned out to be a good thing, because when the smoke came in, we took advantage of the screen, grabbed as many of the wounded as we could, and got the hell out of there. Kilo Company put covering fire over our heads, and we ran right at them. Finally back inside friendly lines, the shooting mostly over and the wounded tended to, I took off my helmet and collapsed. That's how I finished my first day on Operation Allen Brook.

Three or four days later, Mike Company did an assault on Le Bac II. The continuous fighting since day one had thinned out Kilo and Lima companies. We'd been in reserve, but now, they told us to drop packs and move up. Déjà vu all over again, the gooks dug in solid, Brettman on the radio, and me carrying water and ammo to the line and dragging wounded back.

That day, my buddy Richard advanced with a squad on a pagoda sitting between two hedgerows. They took their time moving in, but when they got close, the gooks inside the pagoda opened up and killed three marines with the initial burst. Richard's guys hit the deck, returned fire, and for a couple hours, had a hell of a shootout. Each time I came back to the line for more wounded, I looked over and saw them trying to advance on that pagoda.

Richard was a little nuts, and he had a temper. I guess he'd taken enough gook nonsense because he ignored the fact they were in a gunfight and got up and charged. He dodged bullets until he made it to the door and threw in three grenades as fast as he could. When the dust settled, he got inside and discovered the enemy had been using the pagoda as a command headquarters. They'd built an underground bunker inside, and when Richard saw that, he went in and shot everything that moved. He killed every motherfucker in there, and he didn't come out until he was done. You didn't want to mess with Richard when he lost his temper.

The day before they pulled us out of Allen Brook, battalion sent tanks in to put direct fire on the gook bunkers in Le Bac. By the time they arrived on scene, the whole area looked like the surface of the moon. There was nothing left above ground. We'd called in so much artillery, the place was literally a wasteland. The bodies of the marines killed the day before still lay where they'd fallen. Now with tank cover, we were able to police them up and bag them. No fun. I told you how hot it was. Do I need to tell you what those poor bastards looked like after 24 hours?

➤ *How was Marlin's experience policing the charred remains of soldiers different from a firefighter or ambulance driver whose duties often require such activities? His was an environment that at any moment could render him the victim, which made the threat to his own physical integrity much more immediate and traumatic.*

That nasty but necessary job done, midmorning we kicked back to enjoy a little quiet time, when suddenly the shit hit the fan again. Middle of the day! I couldn't believe the mortar and machine gun fire. Our tanks opened up in response, and for the next hour, we had quite a little war. I saw Richard fire his M-16 from behind one of the tanks, so I went over to see what he was up to. To this day, I don't know why that tank commander opened the hatch and stuck his head out, but when he did, he took a .50 right in the chest. One second later, an RPG slammed into the turret and blew Richard and me 20 feet away. Dazed, I looked up and saw Richard take off to do his John Wayne impersonation again. When I got my wits about me, I started working my way through the bush parallel to a little trail and hadn't gone 50 meters when I ran right into a gook bunker. The problem was, they saw me the same time I saw them.

Instantly, bullets flew all around me from no more than 15 meters away. I hit the deck, returned fire, and started working up through the low scrub. I don't know how long I fired and moved—could have been two minutes, could have been ten—but finally I worked my way to the gook front door, only to discover I'd run out of ammo and had no grenades. I had no choice but to break contact and retrace my steps back up the trail. In a few moments, I came upon one of our tanks, shouted up at the driver, and he threw me a couple bandoliers of ammo and four grenades. Going back, I moved quickly because I knew the route and what to expect.

Same thing again. I exchanged fire and moved until I was where I needed to be, pulled the pin on a grenade and got ready to throw it. Just then, I saw two bloody hands reach out from the aperture of the bunker. Now, I stood with a live grenade in my hand, my M-16 under my arm and a shot-up gook in front of me who wanted to surrender.

➸ *Marlin doesn't speak of just shooting the enemy soldier—a far easier remedy to the situation.*

What the hell kind of crap was that? I looked around on the ground for the God dammed grenade pin but couldn't find it, so I secured the handle with gauze from my B-1 first aid unit. Just then, I saw another marine up the trail, got his attention, and he covered me while I tied the gook's hands and blindfolded him. My prisoner secure, we searched the bunker and found thousands of rounds of ammo, crates of grenades, and a shitload of plastique explosive. No wonder that gook wanted to surrender. If I'd tossed a grenade in there, both of us would have been blown to smithereens. I ask you, after everything I'd been through, wouldn't that have been a hell of a thing?

The next day, the choppers came in and flew us out of there. In two weeks, Third Battalion had 318 killed or wounded. I was awarded the Silver Star for hauling wounded marines around on my back, and as a unit, in Operation Allen Brook, the marines of 3/27 received the Medal of Honor, two Navy Crosses, and 15 Silver Stars. So much for the "bastard battalion."

I spent the rest of my tour back in our TAOR doing the same old thing —patrols, sweeps, search and destroy. Nothing big, but I got to drop the hammer on a few more gooks before I left country.

➸ *A symptom of Marlin's postwar PTSD and one of the many psychological wounds he suffered—feelings of detachment and estrangement from others— is vividly illustrated in Marlin's description of the remainder of his second tour in Vietnam.*

At the end of summer, the 27th transferred back to the States. They sent all the first-tour people to other units in Vietnam, but the second-tour marines went home with the regiment. Richard and Brettman were first-tour. They got sent off somewhere, and I never knew what happened to them. A few years ago, I tried to look them up but didn't find them. I sure hope they made it out and are living the good life somewhere.

➤ *This statement hints at Marlin's future inability to bond with people and speaks to another PTSD symptom—restricted range of affect or the inability to have loving feelings. The capacity to block feelings for—even ignore the existence of—dear ones is common for combat veterans suffering with PTSD.*

Let me tell you something about my time in Vietnam. During my first tour, I discovered anytime you're in combat—in a shootout—anytime guys get wounded and killed all around you—when you've got that going, it sucks. My first tour was one thing, but that second tour with 3/27 was just plain fucking bad. If you've never seen the inside of another human being, you may not understand. Even after all these years, I can close my eyes right now and see a buddy walking in front of me step on a booby trap. A white flash fills my vision, and he comes apart in the middle of it. You want to learn about human anatomy close up? Join the marines and go to war.

* * *

When I arrived home, I had only six months left in the corps. They offered early outs for second tour guys, so I grabbed one. I might have stayed in, made a career of the corps, but they were winding down, and I figured a big force reduction was just around the corner. April Fools Day 1969, I processed out, packed my bags, and hit the road. I had a seven-year-old Pontiac, and I needed to get something out of my system, so I headed east.

➤ *Had Marlin not been traumatized by his experience in Vietnam, he may have realized his service record and his decorations for valor would have marked him for retention by the corps. Instead, Marlin presented with another PTSD symptom—sense of foreshortened future. Marlin's subconscious, his PTSD, told him he wouldn't have a long-term career.*

I landed in Plano, Texas, and hooked up with a young lady I had written to while in Vietnam. She was my brother's friend and believed writing to a soldier boy in combat her civic duty, so that's how we got to know each other, but until I arrived in Plano, we'd never actually met. Joyce was Oklahoma Cherokee. We liked each other, hooked up, and I took her traveling for a few months.

En route to Oregon to see my folks, I worked a couple odd jobs, but I had no desire to stay in one place long enough to find anything good.

Joyce and I stayed on the road three months, and by the time I got her back home, she was pregnant. Deathly afraid of her parents, Joyce didn't want me to say anything about her condition, but I couldn't figure how she'd hide something like that. The truth would have to come out sooner or later, so I told her parents. The afternoon I faced them, her father, a big truck driver with a bad disposition, should have killed me, but as it turned out, he took the news pretty well, but Joyce's mother didn't. She went seven kinds of crazy on me, and I split. For a while, I thought I'd come back when she cooled off, but other things happened, and it just didn't work.

➻ *Marlin's PTSD induced feelings of estrangement, and his inability to have loving feelings were now solidly reinforced in a nonviolent, familial fashion.*

On the Texas-Oklahoma border, as Joyce and her unborn child faded from my rearview mirror, my old car blew up and died. How symbolic is that? The whole God dammed world was laughing at me. I pulled off the road, threw my keys on the floor, and said, "Fuck it." Then, I grabbed my sea bag and walked away. I left all my old uniforms, records, souvenirs, and memories—everything I owned—in that car.

Alone and unencumbered, I hitchhiked to Portland and took a job pumping gas. I stayed with my folks, and that was okay, but the rest of it wasn't too good. I bought a go-fast car, got 18 speeding tickets in nine months, and lost my driver's license three times. I was free, 22, and wild as an alley cat.

I stuck around Portland a year, but already at that tender age, my job history was suspect. After a short while, I quit the service station to apprentice as a Volkswagen mechanic, but the people there were total assholes, so I left town and went to Seattle to take a job degassing tugs and barges at a marine maintenance facility.

➻ *A reflection of Marlin's PTSD, irritability and outbursts of anger.*

I did some other stuff as well, but I can't really remember everything that happened during that period.

Back in Portland, I got word from Texas that Joyce gave birth to a baby boy. I tried to phone her a few times, but that was an impassable minefield. Her mother had her so jacked up about me, I figured no way would things ever get better between us. I hated the fact I had a son and couldn't get near him, but if I'd sniffed around her grandson, Joyce's mother would have shot me.

Spring came in Seattle, and I'd seen enough rain to last a lifetime and way too many hippies, so between work shifts, I made a high-speed run to Montana to see what that place was about and discovered a wild country full of misfits like me. Just what I'd looked for. I liked it so much, I packed up and moved.

I settled in Kalispell, but Montana was wide-open country, and I traveled all over the state. The highways were littered with trucker bars, cowboy bars, logger bars, even a few damned hippie bars, and I became a familiar face in every one. To feed myself, I took a nightshift job at a plywood plant shoving veneer into a dryer.

Good times in Montana ended the night before Richard Nixon arrived in Kalispell to dedicate the Libby Dam. I got wasted, rear-ended a car on the highway, then bounced off and hit another head-on. All this happened in front of the Libby Airport. The President was expected in a few hours, and there must have been 200 security guys there. A good thing, because it took a bunch of them and a dozen firemen a half hour to cut me out of the wreckage. That little fuck-up cost me my car and 23 days in jail for driving under the influence.

When they let me out, I thought I should make myself scarce, so I hitchhiked west to Washington hoping to bunk with relatives until I got on my feet again. I have to tell you, thumbing my sorry ass through the Pacific Northwest in wintertime with nothing but a Levi jacket was bullshit. I felt none too good about myself just then.

➤ *Marlin had lost his sense of self-efficacy. No longer a battle-hardened marine, he self-medicated his PTSD symptoms with alcohol and believed himself just another shiftless drunk.*

In Seattle, I dunged out horse stables a while, and then found a job pumping gas. Remember, I quit school in ninth grade and joined the marines at 17. I didn't have skills I could apply outside a war zone. Hell, I didn't even know what I wanted out of life. Anyway, I had never envisioned myself living to a ripe old age, so what difference did it make what I did in advance of an early grave?

➤ *A good example of the cognitions associated with the symptom of foreshortened future—a cardinal symptom of PTSD.*

I stayed in Washington a few months but got pissed at my boss at the gas station, quit, and moved back to Portland. Even then, the God damned Vietnam War was on my mind all the time. I couldn't get it out of my head, and my propensity for violent behavior darkened my already unhappy life. Everyone's heard of the lone wolf. Well, I was a lone wolf with an attitude, and it shames me to say it, but I was always on the lookout for trouble. Anytime anything happened, I was right in the middle of it. What I thought at the time was fearlessness, of course, I now know was anger. I needed the real world to be as violent as the world inside my head. Stupid? Yeah, I admit it, and I paid the price. My self-esteem was in the toilet for years. I can't tell you how many televisions I hocked to pay bail bondsmen.

Summer of 1970, I got involved big time with drugs. Name the substance, and I abused it. I smoked marijuana, snorted mescaline, consumed large quantities of speed, swallowed Quaaludes like jelly beans, did four-way windowpane—all the usual stuff. I always said I never met a chemical I didn't like, but somehow, even in a drug-induced stupor, I was clever enough to draw the line at needles. Oh yeah, when I did drugs, I drank five times as much alcohol.

➤ *Marlin needed a mechanism to escape the flashbacks and intrusive thoughts. Alcohol no longer enough, he found drugs.*

One night, I got into a hell of a fight in front of a rock and roll bar. Three big dudes, and the argument was about some girl I'd spoken to inside. They approached me in the parking lot with all kinds of threats, and I told them I had things to do, put up or shut up. The first guy made a move, but I went past him and put the other two down right away. Then, I grabbed the first guy, threw him to the asphalt and worked him over pretty good. I guess I wigged out, because I really kicked the living shit out of that poor bastard. Then he did something stupid. To get away, he crawled under my car. In two seconds, I was behind the wheel starting the engine. I slammed into reverse and hit the gas pedal. Lucky for me, his friends dragged him out, or I would have squashed him like a bug. The next morning, I looked at myself in the mirror and said, "Marlin, what the hell are you doing?" After that incident, I slowed down on the drugs a little.

About then, I met the woman who would become my wife. I'd seen Kitty around town but never had the chance to speak to her. One day, I pulled into the gas station and saw her car in a stall. She wore a miniskirt and sweater, and she was very pissed off about something and cussed the attendant up one side and down the other. The girl had spirit! I don't remember exactly what I said to her, what corny line I came up with, but it worked. Kitty was tall and good-looking with a great sense of humor, and we were instantly attracted to one another. A short time after we met, we moved in together. Not a party girl or night clubber, Kitty was a nurse, serious minded and levelheaded. I'm sure she believed I would settle down, and she could make a future with me, but she never said anything, nagged, or complained about my wild ways.

Two and a half years after I returned from Vietnam, I still caroused and took odd jobs to get by day to day. Sometimes, I worked as long as three or four months, but then something happened to piss me off, and I'd give the boss the finger and get on down the road. Sometimes, I just got bored with what I did. I couldn't help it. I was driven, compelled to keep moving. The first 10 years Kitty and I were together, we moved 16 times.

Even after Kitty and I became a couple, I still went out and partied all night long. During our first months together, I drove a delivery truck all over Oregon, and even though I worked long hours, when my shift ended, I closed the bars every night. Three months after we moved in together, Kitty told me she was pregnant. Three years later, under pressure from her parents, we married.

I will never know why Kitty stayed with me. As a nurse, she always found work everywhere we went, and God bless her, she tried to make a normal home life for our children, but I wouldn't have any of it. For the next 10 years, I uprooted the family and dragged them along while I chased one dead-end job after another. I laid pipe in ditches, pumped gas, poured concrete, drove trucks, built houses, packed hod, worked in a precision cast shop, built campers on an assembly line, welded on the Union Pacific Railroad, and climbed poles for a cable construction outfit. I played every role in life you could think of except husband and father.

✦ *His PTSD-driven compulsion to keep moving, not to become a target. Even the allure of family life could not break through Marlin's defenses and symptomology. That he doesn't speak much about his children or their lives indicates , whether drunk or drugged, he was unavailable to his family and to himself. Notwithstanding a loving wife and children, he could not attain a sense of connection to other humans.*

At Kitty's urging, we moved to New Mexico and bought a double-wide mobile home on a couple acres on the east side of the Sandia Mountains. She went to work at the local hospital, and I drove trucks for a highway construction outfit. Later, I hauled bulk concrete as far away as the Oklahoma panhandle.

Then, I hauled propane around New Mexico for a while. It was a good job, and I had a new truck and tanker and a good route. I liked my customers and co-workers but could not find a way to get along with the boss's asshole son. The guy was a dickhead plain and simple—a king-shit daddy's boy. He harassed all the drivers but always picked on me more than the others. One day, when I came off a run, he was jacked up over something and threatened me—told me how powerful he was and what he could do to me. I had never been late with a load and never failed to make any delivery, and I kept my truck in top condition. He had nothing on me, but he just couldn't resist browbeating somebody. That day, I told him to go fuck himself, and if he didn't like it, we could take it out behind the warehouse. Naturally, that was the end of that job.

I don't know where the time went. Drunk and stoned all the time, the 70s and 80s are a blur to me. I was on a track headed downhill, and I couldn't get off. I tried a few times to get training and land a real job. I attended a slot machine repair course in Reno, but when I finished, I went right back to Montana, grabbed a chain saw, and went out and cut fire-wood for a living. No way could I see myself indoors working on those goddamned slot machines for the rest of my life.

Back in Kalispell, I built a room for myself in our basement and called it my bunker. My refuge—the place I went to feel safe. Nobody came into my bunker without permission. Oftentimes, Kitty or one of the kids came down and tried to get my attention, but I never gave them much of a chance. Kitty tried for years to get me to talk, and one time—drunk as usual—I opened up to her.

Down in my bunker, I paced the floor and blabbed like I hadn't in years. During this, I stopped once to gauge her expression, to see whether what I said made any sense to her. She sat in a corner chair, her hands in her lap, and looked at me without blinking. Even in my alcoholic fog, I immediately recognized the look of contempt on her face and apparent disgust for my self-pity. That was it. I shut up and until now, never spoke about my feelings and thoughts to anyone ever again. My decades of bad behavior poisoned, and then shut down any sympathy Kitty might have felt, even if she'd understood what went on inside me. That's the thing you have to understand. Almost nobody—certainly nobody I ever found —understood anything about posttraumatic stress.

➤ *Marlin let his psychological guard down in this moment, and unfortunately for him, his wife was so shocked by his breakdown she was unable to respond with empathy. This defining moment—this turning point—was missed, and forever after, Marlin suffered alone with his PTSD.*

In time, my obsession with staying mobile finally got the best of my long-suffering wife. To this day, I don't know how she put up with me as long as she did. All those years together, and still I spent most of my time in bars, our frequent arguments and fights at home driving me further away. After 20 years of marriage, I still staggered in at three in the morning and passed out on the bed. The only time Kitty and I spent together were the morning moments before we headed out for work, and I rarely saw my children. For me, spending time with my family was an aberration. Drinking and carousing was standard business.

Try to picture 25 years of wasted life. Compelled by forces I could neither control nor understand, as far as I was concerned, I was alone in the world.

➤ *By any a standard, Marlin's level of estrangement from others is extreme and hard for most people to understand. Bereft of human closeness and support, his isolation made his symptoms even more pronounced and debilitating.*

I'd always had nightmares, but they got worse every year, especially one recurring dream. Manning a .50 caliber machine gun, I had a jam, and then I bolted upright in bed and shouted, "Feed me! Feed me!" Something else happened over there I haven't told you about, but I was in the middle of the shit, and I screamed, "Feed me! Feed me!" and I looked over at my loader, and he had taken a round right between his running lights. That's my most favorite fucking get-me-up-in-the-middle-of-the-night entertainment. A couple others come back to me all the time, too—mostly just good shootouts where I lost buddies. You don't need to hear anymore of that shit.

Also, I had regular flashbacks that grew worse as the years went by. For me, they were more like space walks. Once, I worked for a cable TV company in Boise, Idaho. While driving my pickup from one job site to another in downtown traffic, something strange happened. I drove along, blinked, and suddenly, I looked out onto the street and had no idea where I was. Totally confused and scared almost to tears, I didn't know what town I was in, what I was doing in that truck, where I was going—nothing. I'd been dropped into a parallel universe, where everyday familiar things are suddenly completely foreign. I looked around but found nothing I recognized, so I drove onto the sidewalk and managed to get it stopped.

I sat in the cab of the pickup ready to explode, and I had no idea what to do or where to go. Also, I had no sense of time, and I couldn't tell how long the spell lasted. It's amazing no one called the police on me. As frightened as I'd ever been in my life and completely clueless as to who I was or what the hell I was doing, the cops would have taken me to the nearest loony bin and wrapped me in rubber. I've taken those little space walks on numerous occasions over the past years and still have no control over them.

❧ *Perhaps the most frightening and devastating of PTSD's symptoms is the dissociative flashback. During an episode, the individual may be totally unaware of his current surroundings and see, hear, feel, and smell the same sensations experienced during the actual traumatic event. There can be total loss of control, and the individual may act out as if he were actually reengaged in the moment of the trauma. Marlin must have been completely overwhelmed by the unexpected and bizarre experience.*

Something else that sends me into that other world is certain odors. I don't know where it comes from or why, but I'll get a whiff of something, and I am instantly transported back to the bush. I mean, I'm there—living it again. I see every detail going on around me. Sounds do it, too. Even today, when I hear a helicopter, I'm compelled to get up, walk outside, and look around for that fucker, and then follow it until it disappears over the horizon.

➤ *Auditory and olfactory stimuli are powerful triggers that can induce spontane-ous PTSD symptoms.*

Kitty had been on me for years to go to the VA, but I didn't believe they could cure anything wrong with me. A couple years after I left the service, I went to a veteran center and saw a doctor, but in the 70s, when you talked to the government about compulsive behavior, nightmares, and anger, basically they just wanted you to go away. After that, I stayed away from those VA fuckers. In 1990, in Boise, when I had my first real break-down, Kitty told me to get help or she would leave me. I'd gotten into a bar fight—not too unusual for me—but that time, I really smashed in a guy's head. Lucky for both of us, the cops stopped me before I killed him. That night, I experienced a total raging whiteout.

➤ *This whiteout was a re-experiencing symptom of PTSD—physiological reac-tivity on exposure to internal or external cues that symbolize or resemble an aspect of the traumatic event. More than mere rage, this was how Marlin reacted many times in combat.*

I was 1,000 percent going to kill that guy. I turned suddenly from a human being into a monster, a predator out for the kill. Scared out of my wits, the next morning, I went to the VA, and the doctor prescribed medication.

He talked to me about PTSD, and it made sense to me, but beyond the drugs, I don't think he knew what else to do about it. By then, of course I knew something was dreadfully wrong with me. For Christ's sake, man, my life had become an evil joke. I lost count of the times I'd been arrested, I couldn't keep a job, and my wife and kids were strangers. I went back to the VA clinic every month or so, but as scared as I was, I wasn't really listening, because then I was drinking *and* taking medica-tion, so I stayed pretty fucked up most of the time. A couple years of that, and I still had breakdowns. Just more of the same, I'm not going to tell you about it.

➤ *Marlin's reluctance to share the details of many of his experiences may be in part a subconscious attempt to block the emergence of symptoms. Most likely, he believed his actions so far out of the range of normal human experi-ence that he might be considered an inhuman monster and further isolated from humanity.*

The VA sent me to a doctor in Salt Lake City, and an ex-hippie chick put me in a little room for an hour and told me what a great guy I was. When I started talking, the look on her face was the same Kitty had given me when I'd opened up to her. I looked across the table, saw that broad's expression, and thought, Jesus Christ, I might just as well talk to the fuck-ing door. I got up, got the hell out of there, and never went back.

I also tried group therapy for a while but didn't like that at all. I tried but couldn't force myself to listen to those rear-area, poge, motherfucking weenie bastards who went to Vietnam and sat around some CP shuffling papers and drinking beer. After everything I'd been through, I had no tolerance for pukes whining about how bad they had it over there.

❧ *Marlin had affection only for soldiers whom he judged his equals in harm's way. He had never truly learned to be close to others before he became a marine and only developed an intense bond with the men with whom he faced death.*

Shortly after I began group, I guess I emitted Kitty-looks of my own, because someone said something about it, I reacted, and they asked me not to come back.

No counseling ever helped me one God damned bit. I don't know whether that was because I moved around so much and didn't stick with it, or it was just me, but none of those VA fuckers ever did me any good. I already told you things got worse for me as the years went by. My marriage was in the toilet, my kids had grown up right under my nose, and I was pissed off at myself because nothing I did made anything better.

Toward the end of my marriage, suicide was always on my mind. Once, my teenage son came into my bunker just in time to wrestle away a rifle I'd pointed at my head. Nice, huh? I'm still ashamed of that. The only good that came out of that little incident was the court ordered me to see another shrink. Kitty went with me to the veteran center, and we were there only two minutes when the lady counselor started talking about PTSD and wanted to set me up with more therapy. I told her I'd already been through that, but she said it was for my own good and wouldn't take no for an answer. She begged me not to give up, to try one more time. I refused.

❧ *Marlin's refusal to go back to therapy was the PTSD symptom of avoidance. Bringing up old, painful memories in previous therapy had done him no good, and he did not wish to do so again.*

Kitty and I broke up six years ago, and it damned near killed me. When she left, I lost the only thing that ever meant anything to me. The only woman I ever really loved was gone from my life forever. I don't blame her. I put her through hell for over two decades. Amazing she stuck as long as she did. Now, I think back about all the ways she could have lived her life, and I feel rotten about the way things turned out. We don't talk much. She lives in New Mexico, and I hear she has a boyfriend. Her leaving was no more than I deserved, but I was low for months, stayed drunk night and day, and cried in my beer.

One morning while I sat hung over and alone in my little apartment, I saw my 9-millimeter sitting on the nightstand and on impulse picked it up, jacked a round into the chamber, jammed the barrel against my right temple, and pulled the trigger. Click. It didn't go off. I took a look, saw I hadn't fully inserted the clip, and laughed out loud. Two fucking tours in Vietnam, and now I couldn't even load a fucking pistol. I threw it down and laughed at myself until I cried.

➤ *Marlin's downward spiral continued, and his symptoms worsened. His marriage eventually failed, and suicide became a viable option.*

* * *

I've lived in Oregon two years now. This little house is my shelter, and except for volunteer work with the American Legion, I rarely go out. I have diabetes and take insulin daily. They tell me the diabetes is Agent Orange related. I don't really know. Doesn't matter much anymore. Recently, they told me I have tumors on my lungs. The doctors are going in next month to cut them out and see whether they're malignant.

➤ *Marlin's nonchalance at the prospect of his perhaps-imminent death speaks to his continued symptom of a foreshortened future. He never believed he would reach old age, and his disease validates this for him. Marlin was most honest when he stated, "Doesn't matter much anymore."*

My children are grown now and have families of their own. Me a grandpa—it doesn't seem possible. I've tried to explain my life to them, and I hope they understand. They tell me growing up the way they did wasn't a big deal for them, but I can't believe that. I just pray they don't hate me for who I am. Until the day I die, I will regret that my children grew up without a father. I never thought I'd live this long. Hopefully, I can be a better grandparent than parent.

I guess you could say I've slowed down some. Hell, everybody does sometime. I do my drinking at home now, but I haven't cut back. If I drink enough before I lie down in bed, I get at least some sleep each night. I've made a few casual friends at the American Legion, but I still won't get close to another human. I can't. I can't get close to anybody.

What's in my future? I'd like to remodel my little bunker here—carpet, tile, new cabinets, that sort of thing. I'll get around to it some day, but I'm in no hurry. As far as the rest of my life is concerned, I'd be happy to find a way back into this world. If somebody told me how, I'd be willing to give it another go, but I've been there, done that, and at this point, I'm not optimistic. I thought I never minded solitude, but in reality, I've never been alone. I've lived with that fucking war inside my head 24/7 for 30 years.

I am damned proud of being a marine, proud of my service, and I'd do it all over again in a second. My only regret is not that the war fucked up my life but what it did to the lives of my family and loved ones. I failed as a husband and father because I could not get that stinking, fucking war out of my head. The Beaver Cleaver family is storybook shit—I know that —but I could have been a hell of lot more than I was. So, you figure it out. I'll say it again to make sure you understand. I'm proud of every moment of the service that ruined my life. I just try not to think about it.

—Marlin Jackson

CHAPTER 3

Dave Sekol
Missouri
U.S. Navy

➤ *Scientific studies concerned with the development and prevalence of PTSD in Vietnam veterans suggest 15 to 30 percent of men and 8 to 27 percent of women veterans develop symptoms of PTSD. What makes this minority more vulnerable to the development of an acute or chronic stress related disorder? For many, the answer may lie in individual quality-of-life experiences before exposed to the traumas of combat—events that predisposed them to the development of combat-related PTSD. Unfortunately for Dave Sekol, his childhood trauma was followed by unimaginably revolting and terrifying wartime experiences. Dave was "set up" for PTSD.*

The Naval facility at Yokosuka was a huge, steel-gray city of ships' superstructures as far as the eye could see. At the front gates, I hailed a base taxi and asked the Japanese driver to take me to my boat, the LST, Vernon County. We drove the winding streets past the base hospital down to the yards where hundreds of ships were moored. Before me, aircraft carriers, destroyers, destroyer escorts, and mine sweepers underwent repair or re-supply in preparation for returning to service in the waters off Vietnam. The cab driver stopped in front of the USS Oklahoma, a destroyer. Once again, I told him I was looking for the LST, Vernon County, but playing the inscrutable Japanese, he pretended he didn't understand.

It was a nice day with plenty to look at, so I didn't press the issue. I paid him, tossed my duffel bag over my shoulder, and started walking. For 15 minutes, I passed massive piers dwarfed by the U.S. Navy's great ships, the pride of Pacific fleet, tied alongside. Although as roughhewn and cynical as a young man could be, even I was awestruck by the sheer might of the world's most powerful and sophisticated navy.

I reached the end of the last pier, turned the corner, beheld the Vernon County, and stopped in my tracks. Compared to the boats I'd just passed, that LST was a sick joke. A big, ugly rust bucket, to me it looked like a Mickey Mouse boat. It occurred to me a prankish colony of cartoon elves had tacked a superstructure onto a river barge and called it Vernon County. At dockside, grim-faced, sweat-soaked sailors scraped and painted the hull, losing their battle against decades of corrosion and decay. I looked at that tub and thought, oh, my God. That's my home for the next three years.

The Navy came into my life while I was still in high school, when my brother Rob joined in 1965. The Vietnam War was underway but not reported much in any media I ever looked at. For me and a great many of America's youth, service in the military simply meant living away from home, bridging the gap between adolescence and adulthood, and picking up a few job skills along the way. Rob trained in nuclear electronics and was assigned to a destroyer escort in the north Pacific. He lived in comfortable surroundings and rarely got his hands dirty, so the whole war thing never hit my radar screen. When Rob came home on leave, at night in our room, he showed me his uniforms and gave me coins from the various countries he'd visited. To my young eyes, the navy had transformed him from older brother to grown man. More importantly, he had escaped our severe and abusive father and now lived on his own among the world of men. This alone impressed and excited me.

During my last year in high school, my father informed me there'd be no college unless I paid for it myself, so I told him, "Fine, I'll join the army."

That did it. Dad never needed much provocation to blow up, but that time, he really exploded. His face turned red, his cheeks quivered, and his lips curled into a snarl. "I'll blow your head off with my own shotgun before I see you in the army. There's a war on, and I'll be damned if you'll go over there and get your ass shot off. A wounded kid is a chain around his parents' ankles. Your choices are limited to the air force or navy."

Good old Dad. Always the thoughtful one.

Living with my father was like being kenneled with General Patton. Steely-eyed and inflexible, he rarely showed affection toward his children. He had been in an army anti-aircraft unit during WWII, and I think he brought the war home with him, because he never let go of his tough, army sergeant persona. Prone to fits of violent anger, when Dad looked at me, gritted his teeth, and curled his lips, I knew I was in trouble. I swear to you, when very angry, he growled like a wolf.

A salesman of automotive chemicals, Dad was on the road every day calling on clients, but he went on overnights and left us in peace only once or twice a month. Unlike some abusive fathers, Dad didn't need booze to jumpstart his rages. Never much of a drinker, he kept booze in the house, but he only drank on holidays, family reunions, or other special occasions, and he measured and marked the liquor bottles.

Dad was 33 when I was born. Growing up, I always thought him old school. My friends had younger, hipper parents, and their young lives were vastly different from mine. When they complained of trouble with their folks, they spoke of a day or two of restriction or a cut in allowance—mere inconveniences compared to what my father considered punishment.

Dad had different, more direct procedures for apportioning discipline. I was nine the first time I was caught smoking. My friend's father discovered us rolling homemade cigarettes in our tree house, so he herded us into his basement game room, gave us each a Dutch Master and made us smoke until we were as green as those cigars. In those days, dads did things like that. They figured make the kid sick, and he would give up the notion of smoking forever, or at least until he reached the ripe old age of 12 or 13. Our childhood punishment thus dispensed, still queasy, I walked home unaware my friend's father had called Dad and told him of the incident. When I walked in the door, my father went nuclear.

Like so many countless times before, his belt came off, and in a blind fury, he chased me down and whipped me. If I moved, covered, or did anything to protect myself from the stinging leather strap, he swung harder and hit whatever body part was available. Relentlessly and unmercifully, like a Roman guard beating down a slave, he went for the back, arms, legs, and head. That day, the lash cut into exposed flesh, and his fury grew even as his strength waned, until finally spent and breathless, his canine growls caught in his throat.

➤ *Since 1980, a great deal of research has been conducted into what clinicians term Complex Trauma or Disorders of Extreme Stress Not Otherwise Specified (DESNOS). These disorders are related to trauma associated with early childhood and adolescent abuse and neglect that contributes to or causes chronic stress related dysfunction in individuals.*

Dad's temper and penchant for violent retribution was not directed at me alone. His beatings of my brother were criminal. He was far worse on Rob than me. Sometimes, I came home from school to the crack of the belt, Rob howling in his room, and our father screaming threats at his first-born child. On those days, I slipped quickly out the door and hid. Later, when I found the courage and risked coming home, I always heard Rob in his room playing his clarinet until late into the night.

➤ *As a boy of nine, Dave had already met the first criterion necessary for a diagnosis of PTSD: he had experienced and witnessed events that involved actual or threatened serious injury or threat to the physical integrity of self or others, and his response involved intense fear, helplessness, or horror.*

As I got older, I discovered that if I ran from my father, I could escape the worst of his anger. By age 10, I had already become too fast for him, and one afternoon, when he came after me, I ran out the back door, jumped hedgerows and raced across neighbors' lawns until I was two blocks away. 10 minutes more zigzagging through the tombstones in the cemetery at the end of our street, feeling fairly safe and out of arm's reach, I glanced over my shoulder and saw Dad tangled in a wooden fence, outraged and shaking his fist at the sky. Needless to say, on that day, I stayed away until late in the evening—until I was sure he'd cooled down. Rob and I never knew what would set Dad off, so we learned caution, and when we could, gave him plenty of room.

➤ *Dave developed his principal self-defense mechanism early, and in one form or another, for decades, it remained his primary survival tool. Dave learned to escape.*

At 17, I went to a church festival with a classmate. Judy came from a large Catholic family and had been a friend since elementary school. Together, we strolled the arcade past silly little carnival games until we came to the baseball toss. More to feed my adolescent ego than anything else, I put down a dime, wound up, fired, and won a stuffed dog. Hey, my first trophy. I didn't really want the damned thing, so to insure Judy remembered my athletic prowess, I gave it to her.

Months later, as my parents and I entered church for Sunday services, Judy's mother said hello and thanked me for giving the furry dog to her daughter. After services, when we got home, Dad exploded in fury. "What the hell are you doing giving something to that girl!" spilled from his angry lips while he reached for his belt. I ran, but he followed me out of the house and soon cornered me in the back of the garage. When I tried to work my way around him, he grabbed our old wooden stepladder off a hook on the wall and crashed it into my face. Bang! Bang! My ears rang from the powerful blows, the back of my head vibrated, and I felt my knees weaken.

➤ *Brutal corporeal punishment had a lasting impact on Dave's cognitive world-view and on his defenses against being re-victimized.*

"YOU'VE DONE IT, THIS TIME, BUSTER! I TOLD YOU GIRLS ARE NOTHING BUT TROUBLE!" Pinned into the corner and helpless, I crouched low and shut my ears to his screams about diseases, and I don't know what all. The man was as crazy as any rabid animal. Just then, I reached up, put my hand to my broken nose and felt warm blood run into my sleeve. Panic. I must have blacked out for a moment, because I don't remember where I found the strength, but somehow, I shoved him off me, and then I ran.

➤ *Studies of combat veterans with PTSD that also looked for the sequelae of symptoms of DESNOS found individuals diagnosed with DESNOS were at least twice as likely to develop PTSD as those without a history of complex trauma. These studies also indicate that the earlier in life the abuse begins and the longer the duration of the abuse, the more likely the person is to be predisposed to PTSD later in life.*

Battered, bloody, and sick to my stomach, I had nowhere else to go in my condition, so I ran all the way to the church. The priest bathed my wounds and told me I could stay there that night, but I had to return home the following day. The next morning, petrified at what awaited me, I took my time walking home and thought the situation through. I assumed the priest had telephoned my parents and told them where I'd spent the night. Not good. Shame was not in Father's character, and I prayed he was immune to embarrassment by neighborhood clergy. However, I guessed the priest had taken the opportunity to rub Dad's nose in something, and I knew the old man would not be happy to see me.

20 minutes later, I took a deep breath, put my hand on the back door latch and immediately heard him snarl, "Get your ass in here!"

I stopped and held the door shut with my knee. "I'm not coming in. You're nuts." Silence in the kitchen. Had he calmed down?

"Come inside, Davey, and we'll forget any of this ever happened. I promise."

God, I wanted to believe him. I wanted to believe the leopard had changed his spots, but something inside me told me that only happened in fairy tales. Slowly, hesitantly, I opened the door into the kitchen and peeked in just in time to see Dad pick up a chair and swing it at my head. He missed. The chair hit the wall, the windows rattled, and Mother's knick-knack shelf crashed to the floor. Blinded by rage, he swung the chair again, but this time I was ready for him. I stepped to the side, brought my arms up fast and ripped the chair from his hands. Then I nailed him. I hit him hard, and he went to his knees. I stood over him a moment, waiting to see whether he wanted more. Seconds later, his butt hit the floor, and he flopped against the kitchen cabinets. I threw the chair to the other side of the room and left the house. Can you believe it? All that over a stuffed dog. I was 17 years old.

My entire childhood was not dominated by violent abuse. In all other ways, ours was a normal family, and we lived a normal life. Our home in Champion, Ohio, the last one on the road, was almost in the country. Fifty acres of woodlands bordered us on two sides and made for long summers exploring with the neighborhood kids (hiding from our parents), slaying great beasts (trapping muskrats), and defending ourselves against imaginary bloodthirsty foes from the vantage point of our impenetrable fort (keeping girls out of our tree house).

Our family lived in a modest, midwestern ranch home with a basement. My sister, Bev, close to my own age, occupied one bedroom, and I shared the other with my brother. As a boy, I enjoyed always being around other people, even my siblings. Mother often misinterpreted my natural gregariousness as mischievousness and sometimes accused me of being a "difficult child." Never harsh or unkind, I believe her occasional criticisms sprang from years of worrying whether I'd "turn out okay."

"Why can't you be a good student, Davey, like your sister?"

"Davey, why are you always the last one in for dinner?"

"Good children don't behave that way, son."

➵ *Dave mentions no attempt by his mother to mitigate the violence of his father's furious whippings. He does not recall her being harsh or unkind, but neither does he describe a nurturing, supportive maternal figure when he speaks of her. Instead, the development of a strong, positive, and resilient self-image was stymied by his mother's verbal abuse of his ego.*

Just after they married, Mom must have cast a magic spell over my father. She was 105 pounds of American motherhood in her cotton print housedress, with her hair washed and curled every week, yet somehow, she applied the juju necessary to maintain control over her unstable husband. Whether frightened of what she would do if he stepped over the line or afraid of what she'd not do, Dad always treated my mother well. They had occasional spats over the years, but generally, I think they liked and respected each other and enjoyed a successful marriage. Mother is 86 now and lives in Ohio, and my brother watches over her.

All my neighborhood friends attended the public school just down the road, but my parents were devout, church-going Catholics and insisted I go to the parochial school, a 20-minute bus ride from our house. Typical of Catholic schools in those days, a student was sent in shame and disgrace to the principal's office for the tiniest infractions—combing hair, chewing gum, talking in class.

I can't say I cared much for school. Perhaps I would have fared better in the public system, but apart from the restrictive Catholic environment that suffocated young souls, diminished spirits, and frowned upon independence, to this day, I have fond memories of Sister Mary Richard-Ann, my second grade teacher. One of the few truly nice nuns in my school, she always tried to give every student the attention and direction he needed. For her, corporal punishment was never the first solution to any problem. Sister Mary had more temperate, caring, and in my view, effective ways of getting what she wanted from a student. Other teachers routinely sent me to the principal's office for a ruler across the knuckles, where Sister Rachel was always careful to make sure the metal strip at the edge made good contact, but Sister Mary's kind spirit and gentle nature reflected her love for the Lord and all his children. As an eight-year-old, I daydreamed occasionally about luxuriating forever in the safety and comfort of her voluminous robes.

➤ *In the absence of a strong and protective maternal object to rely on, Dave shifted his need for security onto Sister Mary. Unfortunately, she would be the last positive parental role model Dave would have.*

Years later, despite my protestations, my parents demanded I also attend the local Catholic high school. Sister Marys are few and far between in the world of nuns, and I dreaded four more years of a system that rewarded conformity and stifled creativity.

Not that I was so creative. Even the Catholics can't be blamed for inhibiting in a boy something that never existed. If I described my teenage self, considering all aspects of life at a parochial school in a small, midwestern town, the term that would come up more than any other would be "average." Hey, considering *all* aspects, that's not bad. For years, my father hammered into my head my mediocrity and utter lack of promise. Not so crudely direct as my father, the Catholics attained conformity among boys with labels such as insignificant, unworthy, and undeserving. Given that, you can see I had a big hill to climb just to get to "average."

Looking back, I suppose my Catholic high school was not so different from Champion's public school. We had a group that typically got good grades, participated in student government, and were seen at all school functions. The jocks were right under them on the social ladder, and sometimes, there was leakage between the two groups. Occasionally, a jock was pretty enough to pass as intelligent and get bumped up a rung, and now and then, a student government geek made the swim or track team.

My group hung out in the parking lot, smoked cigarettes, shot the shit, and fooled around. Not too different from elementary school, for me, high school went along day-to-day, while I walked the razor's edge between war and peace at home. Around school, my homeroom class was like the animal house. Irreverent and intolerant, my buddies and I were scornful of authority, and nobody on the faculty wanted to deal with us. When we were spoken of, it was in conjunction with deep sighs and resignation to the unpleasant reality that every school had "that element."

In my senior year, Warren Rogers, the center on the football team, and I desperately wanted to get out of Kennedy High and attend public school, so we concocted a scheme to get expelled. Every week, we took turns picking fights with one another. Fighting on school property was strictly forbidden, and to make it look good, Warren and I really beat the crap out of each other. Looking back on it, I can think of less physically

demanding schemes to get expelled, but at that time in my life, considering the potential reward, taking a few licks and rolling around in the dust
with a buddy wasn't a big thing. We tried out our plan a half-dozen times,
but when marched to the principal's office, instead of sending us home
for the semester, he issued another kind of punishment. The Monsignor
kept a three-foot length of heavy stair handrail in his office, and when
he wound up and swung it, even the center on the football team flew halfway across the room. Smarter than he looked, the old priest knew what
we were up to, and out of spite, he refused to follow school policy and
expel us.

➤ *Dave Sekol's worldview was further confused and darkened by his educational
experiences in Catholic school. When he ran afoul of the administration, the
consequences were similar to those he received from his father.*

Getting caught with alcohol on campus meant eternal excommunica-
tion, so my buddies and I drank nights and weekends. We 17-year-olds
terrorized the country bars and pool halls and whooped it up all over
the county. I don't know whether bartenders thought us old enough to
be in their honkytonks or whether they considered our money as good
as the next man's and just didn't care. Whatever the case, I spent many
nights drinking dime drafts with the farmers and refining my touch on
the shuffleboard and billiard tables.

➤ *The only respite from the cold brutality of his home and school was to escape
into drinking alcohol and acting out.*

Something about rural Ohio in the 60s drew teenagers away from town
—probably still does. Maybe it was the air, but more likely, I believe it was
the sensation of privacy, the freedom so treasured by young people. A
park in the country with a pavilion and a keg of beer on a picnic table.
You didn't need anything else. Yeah, man. That was living.

Water balloon and stick fights among teenagers were about the most
serious crimes in Champion, Ohio, and the only law in our county was
an old man who served for years as constable. He drove an ancient green
Chevy, and if your own car had any guts, you could easily outrun him.
One night, I loaded a bunch of beer-drinking buddies in my old Rambler,
and we went lawn bombing—driving up and down sidewalks and across
lawns crashing hedges and flowerbeds. Just at the wrong moment, the old
constable appeared out of nowhere, turned on his red lights and pulled
me over.

He asked me for my license, and then ignoring their smirks and rude
whispers, shined his flashlight on my friends. Then, he tipped his hat
back and looked at me like I'd just run over the postman. His hands
shook, and a hurt, sad look dulled his eyes. Then, something strange

happened to me. I felt suddenly sorry for the man and filled with remorse for my adolescent misdemeanors. At that moment, I couldn't stand the thought of disappointing that sad old man by pleading guilty to his silent accusations, so I lied. I told him the car's steering failed, and I lost control. Of course, he knew that was nonsense, but he pretended to buy the story and let us go on our way. For weeks after, I felt as though I'd let us both down.

➤ *Despite his father's brutality and his mother's lack of shelter from it, Dave had developed a cognitive schema based on traditional absolutes of right and wrong. Accordingly, he felt bad about being perceived as a liar by the old constable. This set of core beliefs would a become a major factor in his future attempts to justify the horror he endured in Vietnam.*

All that was a long time ago. Another time and another place. Now and then, I receive invitations to attend high school reunions in Champion, Ohio, and though I frequently long for that simpler time, I never reply.

* * *

Before my senior year ended, I went to the navy recruiting center and enlisted. I knew I'd never have the opportunity to attend a civilian school, so I asked for computer training, the coming thing in those days. Two months after graduation, when I left for the service, my parents took me to the train station in Warren, Ohio. Not a tearful goodbye scene like you see in movies. Dad stood impatiently on the platform while Mom waved and smiled as I hopped on the train and left them in a cloud of smoke.

Six hours later, I stood in line with hundreds of guys in the big induction center in Cleveland. My brother had briefed me on what to expect when I joined the navy, and I had an idea what was in store, so I relaxed and let it flow. After the swearing in, they pulled 10 of us from the line and told us were going to San Diego. Cool. I had no problem with basic training in San Diego. Fun in the southern California sun—a hell of a lot better than Alaska or Greenland.

I'd learned to type in high school, and Rob told me if I played my cards right, it could be a ticket to skate. The navy had a job they reserved for screw-ups and guys too uncoordinated to march and chew gum at the same time. Battalion yeoman, the job for me. Work indoors, shuffle papers, and keep the hands clean while those other dumb bastards busted butt on the training field.

Two days into basic, we stood in formation while the chief petty officer read from a list of available volunteer jobs. "Battalion yeoman. This one's a bitch. Long hours and a lot of crap to go with them. Who wants it?" My hand shot into the air so fast, the other trainees thought me nuts. Fine. They humped ass while I rode around base on a bicycle carrying paperwork from one office to another. Thanks, Rob.

After basic, the navy offered three levels of advanced training, A, B, and C schools. I went to an A school at the Naval Training Center in Great Lakes, Illinois—five months of electronics and radar training. The main thing I remember about that was how damned cold it was in Illinois. Nevertheless, the training was first rate, and I was still happy I no longer lived at home. I was never known as an overachiever in any school, but at least the navy had no priests or nuns, and unlike my tempestuous, unstable father, the navy instructors treated me like a man.

Radar school had a reputation for being tough, and for good reason. However, I found the training stimulating and challenging and the instructors and facilities excellent. We worked 12-hour days learning to operate and repair the broad array of radar equipment used on all the boats in the fleet. Seriously challenged for the first time, I tuned up, found focus, and did well. I worked hard, the weeks melted into months, and before I knew it, it was time for final examinations. One hundred twenty trainees had enrolled, and only 60 graduated. I finished at the top of my class.

In 1970, nobody wanted to go to Vietnam, so after graduation, everyone requested duty in Europe or the Mediterranean. When my orders came through assigning me to an LST in Yokosuka, Japan, I thought I'd had another stroke of luck. I'd never heard of an LST. Could duty on one be as sweet as battalion yeoman? I didn't really care. I only saw that one magic word—*Japan*. The following week, I shipped out without much fanfare. A 20 hour flight with 150 seamen, each thanking God he wasn't going to Vietnam.

* * *

The Naval facility at Yokosuka was a huge, steel-gray city of ships' superstructures as far as the eye could see. At the front gates, I hailed a base taxi and asked the Japanese driver to take me to my boat, the LST, *Vernon County*. We drove the winding streets past the base hospital down to the yards where hundreds of ships were moored. Before me, aircraft carriers, destroyers, destroyer escorts, and mine sweepers underwent repair or re-supply in preparation for returning to service in the waters off Vietnam. The cab driver stopped in front of the USS Oklahoma, a destroyer. Once again, I told him I was looking for the LST, *Vernon County*, but playing the inscrutable Japanese, he pretended he didn't understand.

It was a nice day with plenty to look at, so I didn't press the issue. I paid him, tossed my duffel bag over my shoulder, and started walking. For 15 minutes, I passed massive piers dwarfed by the U.S. Navy's great ships, the pride of Pacific fleet, tied alongside. Although as roughhewn and cynical as a young man could be, even I was awestruck by the sheer might of the world's most powerful and sophisticated navy.

I reached the end of the last pier, turned the corner, beheld the *Vernon County*, and stopped in my tracks. Compared to the boats I'd just passed, that LST was a sick joke. A big, ugly rust bucket, to me it looked like a Mickey Mouse boat. It occurred to me that a prankish colony of cartoon elves had tacked a superstructure onto a river barge and called it Vernon County. At dockside, grim-faced, sweat-soaked sailors scraped and painted the hull, losing their battle against decades of corrosion and decay. I looked at that tub and thought, oh, my God. That's my home for the next three years."

LST is short for Landing Ship Tank, and the navy had hundreds in its fleet. First built and launched during WWII, LSTs are as versatile as they are ugly. The messy evacuation from Dunkirk in 1940 demonstrated to the allies the need for a shallow draft landing craft to carry men, military equipment, and vehicles to and from the battlefields of Europe, and later, the Pacific. During WWII, many LSTs were used as mobile equipment repair facilities, complete with blacksmiths and machine and electrical shops. Also, equipped as hospital ships, surgeons aboard LSTs treated tens of thousands of wounded men during the invasion of Europe. A few LSTs in the Pacific were even modified to serve as mini aircraft carriers to launch and recover small observation planes.

My boat was 400 feet long with a 55 foot beam. Flat-bottomed and fitted with two 14-foot clamshell doors at the bow, the *Vernon County* carried tanks, artillery, vehicles, and troops—whatever anybody needed transported. As shuttles for on-board personnel, the LST carried three 40-foot open boats made of plywood.

In the Mekong River in Vietnam, the standard joke was that LST meant *Large Slow Target*, but the boat was not without offensive muscle. Armed with three three-inch cannons that fired 60 13-pound exploding projectiles a minute to a range of five miles, the *Vernon County* could hit hard. Also, two fifty caliber machine gun turrets were mounted on either side of the boat. Big, ugly, but not entirely toothless and ready to do just about anything, the *Vernon County* reminded me of half the girls in my high school, and for the next three years, I spent six to nine months at a time aboard her patrolling the rivers in Vietnam.

➤ *Dave was on board a boat designed for past wars, doing duty for which the navy had not trained him. His ship, the "Large Slow Target," became a floating stage on which terrifying and gruesome plays were presented with mind-numbing regularity.*

Cruising the Mekong River in the delta region of Vietnam was like being in an ocean, except the water was flat, shit-brown, and relatively shallow. People don't realize the Mekong starts somewhere in Tibet and runs 1,000 miles through China, Burma, Laos, Cambodia, and Vietnam before it reaches the delta and spills out into the South China Sea. For end-less miles, the banks are lined with thick vegetation, perfect cover and concealment for Charley to take potshots at us. Big, slow targets in hostile waters, navy LSTs bobbed around the river like overstuffed shooting gal-lery turkeys.

Often, our missions took us up the river all the way to Saigon. Other times, we anchored and remained on station to re-supply the swift boats, serve as mother ship for Seal teams returning from shore operations, and refuel the navy helicopters working the area.

Because LSTs were so big and slow, the skippers constantly watched for threats from the shore. To protect against swimmers, when patrolling the river, LSTs frequently steamed in crossing patterns and big circles. Not unlike WWII kamikaze pilots, Vietnamese suicide swimmers strapped mines on their backs and swam out hoping to land a big prize. When in areas of known enemy activity, the best protection against a sneak attack was to keep the boat moving and the deck guards on constant alert.

➤ *The proactive defenses against suicide swimmers were sensory assaults, which deprived Dave of the regenerative sleep he needed to remain focused and sane.*

Onboard battle berthing was a utilitarian precaution against sustaining massive casualties from a mine explosion. When the skipper ordered bat-tle berthing, crewmen temporarily changed quarters to balance skill lev-els throughout the boat. Until the threat was deemed gone, an engineer, a radar man, a quartermaster, and a couple deck people bunked together in each compartment. If the boat hit a mine and a compartment was destroyed, all the ship's gunners, for example, or all the engineers, wouldn't be wiped out in one attack.

Once, en route to Bangkok, we were diverted back to station in the Mekong. A swimmer had hit the boat that had relieved us, and because it was not at battle berthing, all but one of the operations personnel had been killed in the explosion. I guess, in one sense, sailors on LSTs in Viet-nam faced the same conditions as foot soldiers on the ground. There were no front lines, and everyone remained constantly on guard.

➤ *The first sign of PTSD: Persistent symptoms of increased arousal—hypervigi-lance—which includes difficulty falling or staying asleep and an exaggerated startle response because of the constant threat to physical integrity.*

At anchor in the river, a radar operator wasn't needed, so all kinds of duties fell to me: ammunition loading party, paint and chip detail, deck watch, and anything else needed done on the boat. Crewmen rotated small boat detail so everyone stayed proficient with his M-16, and now and then, my turn came to go out on patrol. Like police cars on the prowl, the small boats cast off in the morning and cruised the river all day in search of anything suspicious. When we came across a sampan, we flagged it down, pulled alongside, and checked it out. In those days, the locals were required to carry identity papers everywhere they went, so first, we made sure everyone on board was legal, and then we asked where they'd been and what they did that day. Anything could happen when we stopped a sampan in mid-river, and we were always hyper-alert for sudden moves or apparent attempts to conceal anything.

Once, working the river with two boats, we'd encountered heavy traffic all day and interrogated scores of damned Vietnamese. The day done, we were just headed in when the other boat crew behind us decided to check one more sampan. We watched them maneuver alongside a tiny outrigger upriver, and in seconds, we saw a muzzle flash, and the words "shots fired" jumped out of our radio.

During the war, VC tax collectors routinely toured the peasant villages and levied a "freedom tax" in the form or rice of other food. Then, they transported the goods by river to enemy base camps on shore. If we saw the same face on the river too often, or if someone had in his possession more supplies than he could account for, we were generally correct in assuming him a tax collector. That afternoon, the other boat crew stopped a sampan carrying just such a character. In the two minutes it took us to come alongside, the situation had deteriorated, and everyone was locked and loaded and ready for anything.

Faced with capture and unnerved by the burst of M-16 fire he'd taken across his bow, the VC tax collector had gone to pieces under questioning and caused all kinds of trouble. He stood up in his boat and wailed and moaned, gnashed his teeth, tore at his hair, and wrung his hands. Two other men behaved themselves at the bow of the sampan, and a teenage girl sat on a thwart bench.

I'm not sure what happened next. To this day, I can't picture exactly how it went down, but in the confusion, the girl reached for something inside the basket on her lap. Bad move. Big mistake. Everyone in the sampan had been told a dozen times not to move, but the little dummy stuck her hand into that basket, and that was all it took for our guys to let go with M-16s on full automatic.

✦ *Under constant threat of death, American soldiers became conditioned to react instinctively to any perceived peril. Dave experienced many traumatic events in which he was an active participant, such as the violent death of another person.*

I'd say it was over in a heartbeat, but I'll spare you the bad pun. When the smoke cleared—and I mean that literally—seconds passed before the usual afternoon river noises supplanted the ring of rifle fire in my ears. More seconds passed, then the tax collector collapsed in a heap on the deck of his boat. This time, his wailing and moaning was not an act. I looked down at the girl sprawled on her back, her long black hair trailing downstream with the current. A huge, blood-soaked hole occupied the space that had been her chest.

The officer in charge of the other boat whistled under his breath and said to no one, "Oh, man, we really messed up this time. We killed a child."

I don't need to tell you the tension was high on those boats hovering out there in the middle of the Mekong River. Three Vietnamese, eight navy guys, and just then, nobody could tell the difference between right and wrong, good and evil. A standoff. Tragedy looked preservation of self right in the eye, and for a moment, the earth stood still.

Suddenly, our boatswain's mate cursed at the sky, stepped up on the gunwale, and then jumped into the sampan and pulled the girl's lifeless hand out of the basket, her fingers still curled around a live grenade. No one spoke. No one needed to. That girl-child had been ready to blow herself and everyone around her out of the water. What a war.

That was the thing about working the small boats. Every time we stopped a sampan, we could never tell who was who or what the hell they were up to. If we didn't pay attention, someone went home in a box. Motoring back to the LST that afternoon, I remember thinking it lucky that girl had her hand on a grenade instead of an onion or a banana. Even in Vietnam, sailors couldn't get away with wasting innocent teenage girls. As it was, somebody probably got a medal.

Later, under interrogation, the tax collector we captured told us the VC operated a P.O.W. camp near the Bodai River on the southern tip of Vietnam. It was so far back in the jungle that until then, nobody knew it was there. A few days later, Special Forces troops raided the camp and rescued 20 American captives. I'll say it again just to make sure you get it. We just never knew what we'd find when we went out in the small boats.

Dead body patrol. Another thing entirely. At least I called it dead body patrol. The navy had a more sanitized, non-specific name for it, but I like to stick closer to the truth. Every few days, after a firefight somewhere along the shore, they medivaced the wounded soldiers out first, and then the helicopters brought the KIAs to us in cargo nets. On those days, my crew stood in a circle on the deck of the LST, and when the helicopters hovered down and the nets opened, we disentangled the bodies and lay them out for assembly and when possible, identification.

In old war movies you've probably seen someone jerk the dog tags from around a dead soldier's neck, wedge one between his front teeth, and then jam his jaw shut. Not a pretty picture, I know, but a necessity. If the tags were left on the chain hanging around the guy's neck, by the time the GRO team got to him, the guy might not have a neck, the tags would be gone, and there'd be no way to identify him.

After the choppers dumped their ghastly cargo on the deck, my crew laid the bodies out, and then used pliers to yank the dog tags from their teeth. Then, we completed a form and placed the dog tag and the paperwork in a pouch attached to the body bag. The bodies identified, we then zipped them into the bags, carried them down to the refrigerated porta-morgues on the tank deck, and laid them out like silverware in a drawer. Later, we took them into Saigon for shipment back to the States.

Because I was a radar operator with nothing else to do on the river, I drew that godforsaken duty every time, and I mean *every time*. Raw meat in the hot sun. Do it for months on end, and after a while, it gets to you.

Sometimes, the choppers dropped the bodies of American soldiers held captive by the VC. During that period of the war, the enemy liked to quarter their prisoners alive as a warning to other westerners occupying their homeland. They cut off the arms first, one at a time, and then if the poor kid was still alive, they went for the legs. Sometimes, when the VC wanted a prisoner to talk and not die right away, they just opened the abdominal cavity and let the guy's guts fall out in front of him. That was damned ugly business, I'll tell you. We'd get a load of previously captured KIA on deck, sort through the gore, and someone would say, "I've got a body, who's got a head?"

"Anybody need an arm?"

"Left or right?"

"Do you care?"

Sometimes, a KIA had his entire face shot away, teeth and all, and in the absence of dog tags, we just did the best we could identifying the pieces. On bad days, the helicopters brought in as many as 10 in every load. For months, I stood out on that deck in the hot sun and dreaded the sound of incoming helicopters. One day towards the end of my third tour, I decided I wouldn't do it anymore. I simply would not—could not—face it even one more time, and when I was called for dead body patrol that afternoon, I told my chief I wouldn't go. The executive officer stood me against a wall and threatened me with everything but the firing squad, but still I refused. After 10 minutes of calling me every name he could think of, he backed off. I don't know why. Maybe he saw something in my eyes that told him not to push me further. Want to hear something funny? To this day, the sound of rotor blades whopping in the sky gives me the willies, and I think of that executive officer.

➤ *In later years, Dave's PTSD symptoms would be triggered by the sounds and smells forever encoded in his limbic system from those ghastly days carrying out "Dead Body Patrol."*

It won't surprise you that now and then, the VC took a few shots at our LST. When that happened, everyone went to general quarters while our bridge personnel made contact with marine spotters on the ground. If we knew where the bad guys were, the quartermaster took a fix, and we turned loose with our 3-inch guns. Sometimes, we'd find out later we had nailed as many as 300 VC, when all we'd set out to do was silence a couple shooters onshore behind a log. For the deck crew and guards, their biggest worry was snipers along the riverbank. No one ever knew when bullets would fly across the gunwales. If a man up top had no weapon, he simply dropped to the deck and waited for the gunners to take care of things.

Here's something that will surprise you. The *Vernon County* had a special compartment below the cargo hold reserved for the interrogation of VC prisoners. Yeah. That's what they called it when our side did the torturing. A small, windowless room with steel walls and a hatch in the ceiling, entry and exit was gained via a circular iron staircase. In the beginning, the ARVNs who conducted the interrogations picked me to stand guard because someone told them I had a security clearance. As time went by, I remained their guard of choice because I never interfered, and they knew I kept my mouth shut.

My guard post was the empty compartment above the cell, and my job was to prevent anyone from coming within earshot during prisoner questioning. Sometimes, in the evenings, unpleasant noises within the interrogation chamber penetrated the iron walls, and the guys on deck watch peeked in. Their interest never went beyond mild curiosity and idle speculation, however, because mostly, they didn't really want to know. A look or hand signal from me was enough, and the deck hatch remained closed for the rest of the evening.

My vantage point for observing the activities in the chamber was through the smaller of the two ceiling hatches. The South Vietnamese interrogators frequently asked me for things—fresh water, rags, trash bags they'd grown accustomed to my leaving the hatch ajar. I was the fly on the wall we've all wanted to be at one time or another.

➤ *Events that can initiate a traumatic response in a person can be active, where the potential harm is directed at the individual himself, or it may be passive, as when one witnesses the violent destruction of another human being. In this situation, Dave was unable to flee the sights, sounds, and smells of the brutality inflicted on the VC prisoners. As a result, he was exposed to numerous traumatic stressors with the potential to trigger PTSD symptoms from several of his senses.*

Prisoners were brought in almost every day, and the ARVNs always tried to get as much information as they could before shipping them off to a prison camp. They underwent more interrogation there, of course, but information gleaned immediately after capture was the freshestand was occasionally even reliable.

I don't know how the ARVNs decided which prisoners to interrogate, but when they got their hands on someone they wanted information from, the routine was more or less the same each time. Vietnamese dressed in military uniforms with no insignia or rank brought the prisoner in, bound, gagged, and blindfolded. It was unlikely any of those VC had ever been on a boat bigger than the family sampan, so I doubt they even knew where they were. All the unknowns. Without exception, that's what most terrified those poor bastards, and during interrogations, the dank air in the cell was thick with the stink of adrenaline and ammonia.

Next, they strapped the prisoner into a wooden chair next to a small table, removed his blindfold, and a South Vietnamese army officer with a swagger stick strode down the iron staircase, circled the prisoner a half dozen times, and then suddenly shouted demands. I didn't speak the language, but I'd witnessed enough interrogations to know they always asked about the number of enemy troops, their location, that sort of thing. If the prisoner wasn't immediately cooperative, the other Vietnamese guys in the cell whacked him, slowly at first, but then they picked up the pace while the officer repeated the demands. This went on for the better part of an hour.

Usually, the nose broke first, and the blood flowed like an open faucet. Sometimes, they missed by a few inches, cracked the jaw, and pieces of teeth bounced on the floor like little BBs. The interrogators were pros, and all business. Beginning a session, they avoided the prisoner's soft spots, knowing they risked rupturing a spleen or puncturing a bladder, and then they wouldn't have anything left to work with.

If the initial velvet-glove techniques failed and the guy still refused to talk, the officer in charge of the interrogation leaned into man's line of sight and spoke softly for several moments. I never heard what he said, of course, but I'd seen the tactic many times, and I guessed he appealed to the prisoner's love of family, gods, or ancestors, or whatever the hell those people believed in. Interesting guy, that officer. He went from demon of destruction to trusted uncle and comrade and back again sometimes in split seconds. I swear I thought that bastard could sell me a car any time he wanted.

➻ *The character deficiencies of Dave's father had predisposed Dave to being vulnerable to becoming traumatized more easily when under the authority of this officer, since he and Dave' father shared similar volatile personalities.*

The interrogation team rarely wasted much time with the sugar and honey approach. The officer in charge had a short fuse, and if he didn't get what he wanted right away, he stood back, lit up a smoke, and turned his dogs loose. Then, the situation in the cell changed very quickly. The men in faux army uniforms went to work on the prisoner as though he was a side of beef they wanted to take apart cord by cord. I mean they just wailed on him. No other way to say it, they simply beat the crap out of the guy.

By then, the prisoner, kept conscious by submerging his face in a pail of water, must have known his life was over. Even if he held onto some crazy notion his captors eventually would release him, he must have known he would never recover from the injuries he sustained during questioning. Now and then, however, one of those VC bastards was tougher than he looked, and no amount of punishment made him talk. I knew what came next in those interrogations, and when that time arrived, I often found myself peering through the hatch and willing the poor bastard to talk, to say anything, to end the nightmare and allow the men in the cell to send him to VC heaven or Nirvana or wherever the hell they went.

Sometimes, the sessions went on for hours. Sometimes, the prisoner was so stubborn, the team had to break for chow or bring in fresh interrogators. When the officer in charge deemed phase two of the interrogation had failed to produce the information he wanted, he ordered the portable hand-cranked generator brought in. Then, the interrogators went through an elaborate set-up procedure, made certain the prisoner got a good look at the machine, its output wires tipped with alligator clips. Next, they attached the clips to the guy's nipples (or some other part of his body) and spun the wheel. The harder they cranked, the more juice came out, and the more the guy talked. Forty-five seconds of that, and you couldn't get the prisoner to shut up. I'm no doctor, and I can't tell you exactly what happens, but I've seen just a moment of that procedure fry enough brain cells to turn the strongest man into a drooling, babbling lump of meat.

The generator was not the only extreme method used during these sessions, but I'll not go into any more details. I'll not tell, and you don't need to know. It's enough to say the South Vietnamese were every bit as capable of ruthlessness as their Communist cousins. I never saw American officers actually participate in the interrogations, but somebody from our side usually stood by. When things got rough, the Americans faced the wall while the Vietnamese interrogators applied their most persuasive techniques. I can only tell you, you got a lot of screaming before the questioning ended and what was left of the prisoner was taken away. Then, the team broke out the fire hoses and cleaned up.

How glad I was those luckless bastards had been captured instead of me. Hey, both sides used uncomfortable methods to extract information from prisoners, but as far as I know, our side never sliced guys to ribbons or removed body parts just for the fun of it. Looking back on it now, I was probably good for that job because I'd already been hardened before I arrived in Vietnam. My experiences growing up had conditioned me not to be overly sensitive about that kind of thing. So they beat the hell out of their prisoners. So what? Big deal. Any way you looked at it, it was all a pile of shit.

➤ *Dave's belief that he had been hardened by his childhood was false. The exact opposite was true. Dave's brain had become malleable and more prone to developing a stress disorder.*

Occasionally, when not patrolling the river, the skipper held a beer call. To get around the no drinking aboard rule, they lowered the small boats over the side suspended from cables. Then, according to watch rotation, sailors lined up, stepped onto the small boats, and each man was handed two beers. Chugalug. Gone in 60 seconds, and then exit at the back of the boat. After I'd been on the LST long enough to know which guys didn't drink, I figured ways to get their beer. Sometimes, I collected 15 or 20 and drank them all in an hour. Beer calls helped kill any feelings I had about my situation, and for a while at least, I didn't give a crap about what went on around me.

➤ *Numbing with intoxicants was the primary mechanism Dave utilized when he wanted to avoid the anticipatory discomfort of dread. In Vietnam, he continued to employ the same coping mechanisms he had used to escape his fear of his father.*

After three years up the river, the days and weeks ran together in an endless stream of long, hot afternoons and wet, lonely nights. It was a mind-numbing existence, and I no longer cared whether I made it out alive. In time, my focus shifted from the big and ugly to the little discomforts of shipboard life.

I found it nearly impossible to sleep when the *Vernon County* patrolled the Mekong. As they made their circuits, the deck guards threw percussion grenades into the water at random intervals to protect against swimmers. Sometimes every minute, sometimes every 15 minutes, one dammed explosion or another went off and reverberated below decks like a giant gong. Worse, the new guys on guard took potshots all night long at anything that moved. Scared shitless, they believed every old Coke can that floated by was a VC mine. You can't blame them for being spooked and trigger-happy. The VC really did that shit sometimes, and only the second and third tour guys understood they had almost no chance of actually hitting anything. In any case, whether from nervousness or apathy, few slept well while the boat was in the river.

→ *Military psychiatrists and psychologists believed if a combatant knew the time spent in danger was fixed, he would be less prone to psychological escape—mentally fleeing the hazards of battle. In Vietnam, a soldier's exposure to peril was limited to three outcomes: killed in action, seriously wounded and returned to CONUS, or survive the tour and DEROS. However, the recurrent nature of the numerous abbreviated tours that fell to the sailors on Dave's LST bred uncertainty and was itself a stressor.*

Also, drugs entered into the sleep equation. On fire support duty, everyone was awake and on alert for days at a time. No one even tried to sleep, because when the guys on the ground needed help, they needed it right away, and there was no time to roll out of a bunk, fist the sleep from your eyes, take a leak, and then get to your duty station. The ship's crew worked around the clock, and a man was lucky to steal a catnap once or twice a day. My first experience with drugs came during fire support duty, and after a while, the medic became my best friend. Two or three times a day, he dumped a couple pills in my hand, then winked and disappeared. I didn't know what they were, but they sure kept me awake. There were side effects, too, but don't ask.

Hey, I wasn't the only one who took advantage of the available pharmaceuticals. In Vietnam, every boat had a population of speed freaks and potheads. Once, a sailor came to the *Vernon County* from submarine duty in Hawaii. Jimmie had been busted for using large quantities of drugs 500 feet below sea level, and as punishment was sent to Vietnam. A totally committed speed freak, sometimes, Jimmie stayed up 10 or 12 days at a time and ran around the boat jabbering a mile a minute. A complete mental case, the other guys wanted nothing to do with him, so I told them to put Jimmie on my watch. The way I looked at it, the guy was a source of much needed entertainment.

Jimmie obsessed over our position in the river. Every 10 minutes throughout a 12-hour shift, he ran wide-eyed up to my radar screen and gave me some crazy story about why he needed to get a fix and plot it out. Even though Jimmie amused me, I watched him pretty close until I was sure he was harmless. It's not my intention to make a big deal out of the drug thing in Vietnam, but at the time, I'd have bet anything more drugs were consumed every day on the Mekong River than in Haight Ashbury.

→ *More than any previous generation, in Vietnam, American fighting men and women had unprecedented access to alcohol and drugs, and countless thousands embraced these mechanisms for numbing dread.*

During my last tour up river, I was called off the boat and sent on a free trip to Vung Tau, a French resort city on the South China Sea famous for its beaches. Well, an almost-free trip. The navy radar site there had been mortared and several key people killed. Replacement equipment had arrived, and I got the call because I was close and knew how to set it up and operate it.

It only took two weeks to put the site back together and get it running, but the day before I left, another mortar attack came in the night. This time, the VC missed the radar shack and hit my hooch, and I caught some shrapnel in my butt. The medics sewed me up before I returned to my boat. No real harm done, but months later, troublesome cysts formed in the wound, and the doctors in Japan took care of them. I still have a nasty scar from just under my belt down to my ass. My CO wanted to put me in for a Purple Heart, but I told him no. I didn't want to describe to my grandchildren the location of my war wound.

Nearing the end of three years on the *Vernon County*, I burned out. I went about my duties zombie-like, as though under anesthesia. When at sea headed back for the river, I spent nights sitting on the guardrail staring for hours at the phosphorescent glow in the boat's wake. I went there to be alone and not think—make my mind a complete blank, let my eyes glaze over, and block out the world. I had long since stopped communicating with most of my shipmates and hadn't written a letter in over a year. Even now, I hardly remember any details of those weeks and months. A witness to life but no longer a participant, I stuffed my emotions so far down inside me, I became a hollow shell, and things like good and bad, hot and cold, and light and dark no longer had any meaning.

❧ *For much of the remainder of his life, Dave would find no joy or satisfaction in anything, his only emotions being fear and rage.*

Three and a half years after I first stepped aboard the LST *Vernon County*, we steamed into Yokosuka, and she was mothballed. I had good times and bad on board, and I sometimes thought about the thousands of men who served on her between WWII and Vietnam. The bad times I experienced had nothing to do with the boat—it was the mission.

During the time the *Vernon County* sailed the waters of Vietnam, she was awarded a Combat Action Ribbon, a Presidential Unit Citation, four Navy Unit Commendations, five Meritorious Unit Commendations, the RVN Gallantry Cross with Palm, the RVN Civil Action Medal First Class with Palm, the RVN Campaign Medal with 60s device, and the Vietnam Service Medal with 13 Battle Stars.

❧ *Dave's pride in the boat's service record despite the many onerous missions carried out on her decks is perhaps a subconscious attempt on his part to*

reconcile what he witnessed and participated in with his cognitive schema of
absolute right and wrong.

* * *

I had just four months left in the navy. They owed me leave time, so I
hopped a flight to Detroit, where my mother and favorite aunt met me.
The navy had ordered us not to travel in uniform, and when I got home, I
found out why. War protesters were everywhere, and most had mean looks
in their eyes. In those days, Admiral Zumwalt permitted facial hair in the
navy, and I sported a bright red beard. In civilian clothes, I looked like
any other jerk-off, so no one bothered me. Probably a good thing. I was in
no state of mind to listen to someone else's opinions about fighting wars.

When I got off the plane, I spotted Mom and Aunt Bernice right away,
but they didn't recognize me. I could have walked right past them, and
they wouldn't have known it. Did you hear me? My own mother didn't
recognize me! It's a damned cliché! It occurred to me then how much I'd
changed, and for the first time in my life, I understood the true meaning
of the word anonymous.

During the four-hour drive to Champion, I sat in the backseat while my
two favorite ladies chattered endlessly about news from home. Trivial
things mostly, but I felt their need to dispense nervous energy and pretended I hung on every word. Once, during a lull, Aunt Bernice asked
me about the war. "What was it like for you over there, Davey? You're
so thin. Did you get enough to eat?" No one ever accused me of being a
genius, but I was clever enough to know these people—the two who
loved me most in the world—really didn't want to know more,, nor
would they understand if I told them, so I took my aunt's cue and complained about navy food.

The most interesting event during my homecoming was when I saw
my father. I hadn't expected much from him, and he didn't disappoint
me. The ladies and I were in the living room drinking coffee when Dad
came in from work. He put his briefcase on the hall table and stared at
me across the room. His cold eyes told me he recognized me instantly.

He stood half facing me, silent, one foot pointed toward the door.
Finally, Mom said, "Aren't you going to say hello to your son?"

His eyes shifted to her then back to me. "Shave that damned beard. You
look like an idiot." I don't need to tell you I wasn't in the mood for anything like that. I won't go into exactly what I said in response. I'll just
say our clash of wills cast a negative light on the afternoon. After that,
for as long as I was home, Dad tolerated my presence, but only for my
mother's sake.

➤ *Any chance that even a small portion of Dave's emotional and psychological*
  wounds might have been treated by his parents was thwarted by the reception

he received. Even then, his father remained aloof and hostile from his pain, and his mother was detached and disconnected.

The next day, I fired up my old Rambler and drove around town to see what was new and find some of my old buddies. A letdown. I felt like I had been shot through a time warp. Champion was unchanged by the years and unaffected by world events. I swear, those people had no clue what went on in the next county, much less the other side of the world. I tried to check in with old pals, but my closest friends had all gone into the military, and the others only wanted to hear how good the marijuana was in Vietnam. Mostly, I spent time hanging out and doing nothing.

As an experiment, I put on my uniform and went down to Kent, Ohio, to visit friends at the university. We went out to a local tavern for a few beers, and that's when the trouble started. We'd only been in the joint 10 minutes when the local jocks started calling me baby killer and fascist. I'd been waiting for it, and had wondered how long it would take. You might even say I asked for it. Soon, someone threw a beer on me, and that was it. Three years of stored up images of blood and gore rushed out of me in the form of uncontrollable rage. That day, I wasn't proud of myself.

✦ *Dave's early childhood trauma and his wartime traumatic experiences may have had a cumulative effect that aggravated this minor attack on him and became the "straw that broke the camel's back."*

My leave over, I had orders to report to the USS *St. Louis* in Long Beach, California. Eager to get away from home, I left early and spent several lei-surely days on the road driving west. As I traveled America's heartland, my own country seemed strangely foreign to me. I knew I couldn't go home again, but the thought of returning to navy life, even for a few months, repelled me. I believed I fit in somewhere, that I'd find peace of mind if I searched long enough, but just then, I couldn't imagine where.

✦ *Dave experienced more symptoms of PTSD—feelings of detachment or estrangement from others. He knew he was a different person from the one who went to Vietnam, but he was not able to internalize the causes or the meaning for him.*

On board the *St. Louis*, I found myself suddenly back in the real navy among real military-type people. When I reported in, I stood at the end of a line of new recruits just out of boot camp and listened while the ship's executive officer blocked the gangway and threatened them with the brig unless they got haircuts. I looked up the line at two-dozen nearly shaved heads and thought, oh, shit. My beard was longer than their hair, and right away, I figured this stateside XO and I were headed for a collision.

My turn came, and I stood at attention and saluted. The XO's mouth dropped open, and he stared at me like I was a worm in a jar. His face turned three shades of red, and finally, his lips moved, but he couldn't mouth the words. I decided to take him off the hook. Four months left in the navy, I could take anything that asshole dished out. "My hair is short enough, and the beard stays. Admiral Zumwalt said so." I heard a few guys behind me snicker under their breath, and I felt bad about that. I'd no desire to show the man up in front of others, but I wanted to let him know I was no wet-behind-the-ears recruit, and I had no tolerance for stateside bullshit. The XO returned my salute, and I walked away. Nothing came of the little incident, but then again, I was smart enough to stay out of his way for a long time after.

A year earlier, while in the hospital in Japan with my shrapnel wound, I struck up a friendship with the guy in the next bed recovering from some kind of operation. We played cribbage and hung out to pass the time. One day, he mentioned his wife's niece, Yolanda, and a few days later, showed me some family pictures. From her photos, she seemed interesting, so for something to do, I wrote to her. She answered my letter, and our correspondence continued for months.

I met Yolanda for the first time when I arrived at my last duty station in Long Beach. She'd seemed interesting when I saw her photo, and meeting her confirmed it. Interesting and full of surprises. Imagine my dismay when I learned she was still in high school. A child! At 22, I looked, felt, and acted decades older. What could I possibly have in common with this schoolgirl? I hated ice cream and cherry Coke. Would I be her prom date? The whole thing was crazy.

Notwithstanding her tender age, young Yolanda and I were fond of each other from the moment we met, and our evenings were filled with laughter and talk of the future. You think it's strange for a bearded combat veteran to date a girl barely old enough to drive? You bet, but what really mystified and intimidated me was her large Mexican family. Yolanda had grown up in Torrance, California, and had scores of relatives on both sides of the border. Family is everything to a Mexican. I constantly worried I'd say or do the wrong thing, and my fragile ties to this charming person would be severed forever by an overprotective parent. I was always on my best behavior, and my deference and solicitousness to her mother eventually won the day, and I was accepted and welcomed into the family.

Compared to Yolanda, nothing else mattered in my life. During the day, I was a radar operator on a boat that never left the dock, so I went to work and sat around and shot the shit until my shift ended. Nights were for my girl. Four months of doing nothing but bullshit stateside duty flew by, and almost before I knew it, I found myself in civilian clothes descending the quarterdeck boarding ladder for the last time. It was the end of four years in the navy, and hardly anyone noticed me leave. I tossed my things in my car, drove off the base, and never looked back.

One other thing happened almost before I knew it. Yolanda and her mother had planned and organized our wedding, complete with 16 ushers, 16 bridesmaids, two maids of honor, two best men, a ring boy, and a flower girl. Marriage Mexican-style. Yeah!

* * *

Just days after the wedding, Yolanda and I packed the car and moved away from sunny California and her big family. Back in Ohio, the job I found in a steel mill in Warren didn't last long. In 1973, the price of gas sent the country into recession, and new hires at the mill were the first to go.

Besides being laid off a job for the first time in my life, about that time, something else happened to me—something I couldn't understand. I was happy with Yolanda. We never spoke a cross word in our marriage, but that was no longer the case with others in my life. Suddenly, it seemed as though no one and no thing satisfied me. I found no favor in anything that happened around me. Nothing made me smile, and nothing was ever good enough. Most days, I just walked the streets pissed off at everyone.

➤ *Clearly, PTSD symptoms of arousal, avoidance, and restricted range of affect.*

During my last year in the navy, I'd developed stomach ulcers and couldn't drink alcohol, so marijuana became my anesthetic of choice. No other drugs—just reefer, but I smoked every day from morning till night. Now a civilian and stoned 24 hours a day, I was probably not qualified for real work, and certainly, the pot diminished my interest in seeking it. In a matter of months, I developed a huge I-don't-give-a-shit attitude about a career, and I certainly didn't care what anyone else thought of me. That's why I took a job grooming dogs.

I'll bet I groomed every kind of dog there was, and that was just fine with me. I worked in the back of a pet shop, people left me alone, and for months, it was just the three of us—the canines, the marijuana, and me. For me, working with dogs was therapeutic. They didn't ask questions or make judgments. They accepted me, and if I fucked up, they didn't hold grudges. During that dark period in my life, my four-footed companions kept my anger and frustration at a manageable level. Recently, I had experienced powerful and intrusive negative emotions, and frequently, I hallucinated. Somehow, marijuana was the only thing that made my days seem normal.

Who knew what the hell went on in my life? I sure didn't, but just when I thought things couldn't get worse, nightmares came. Night after night, crazy, mixed up jumbles of scenes swam around inside my head, washed sanity away, and left me exhausted. In one recurring dream, I was in my hometown in Ohio, but the low mountains all around were in Vietnam. When I looked out beyond the city streets to the horizon, an army of VC with blood in their eyes crested the hills in swarms looking only for me. In my dream, I always had guns and grenades by my side, ready to fight back, but I fought from my own house. I defended myself from inside my living room. Vietnam, Ohio, gunfights, and my own home—everything was mixed together. I'd try, but I couldn't get away. Finally, panicked at being trapped, I'd wake up, jump from the bed, and then collapse onto the floor, my heart racing and sweat pouring off me.

✦ *Cardinal PTSD symptom— night terrors. However, Dave's dreams differed from those of many other veterans. His sprang not only from the unprocessed trauma of his war experience, but also were intertwined with residual psychological material from his abusive father. Dave relived the horrors of Vietnam and re-fought the battles, but his brain placed him in the setting where he developed his childhood complex trauma—his home and the local environs.*

On other occasions, I fought the bed covers in the middle of the night. I jumped and thrashed and tossed and turned until finally, Yolanda would wake me up. One night during one of these fits, I hit her hard in the middle of the chest. I didn't mean to, of course. I wouldn't even have known I'd done it, but I awoke suddenly to find her gasping for breath. The night terrors came to me two or three times a week for years. To get any rest at all, I stayed really blasted on reefer, because the more marijuana I smoked, the better I slept.

I'd been introduced to marijuana on board my LST in Vietnam. For years, I always said the U.S. government taught me how to smoke, and it's true. The navy had a program then to educate sailors on the evils of drugs. Not unlike the class on gonorrhea, this was a stupid, childish film on the "madness" of drugs, followed by a lecture from somebody who came on board called a Drug Exemption Officer.

He gathered all the ship's lower ranking enlisted men in a room below deck, and after the movie, pulled out a bag of marijuana cigarettes and held it up for us to see. Not to be upstaged by his STD counterpart, during the lecture he told us we were more likely to acquire a venereal disease while using drugs, because people under the influence lost the capacity for circumspect decision-making.

Two hours of typical military nonsense, but this time, the movie and lecture were accompanied by a treat. The guy surprised the hell out of us when he opened the bag of joints, passed it around, and then told us to light up. I guess the idea was for us to try it under controlled circumstances to learn what marijuana was and how stupid we looked and acted when we were high. Hey, no complaint from my side of the table.

I'd never smoked dope before the navy. In my high school, marijuana had not yet arrived on the scene, so all the cool guys drank beer, but on this day, the Drug Exemption Officer's bag went around the room, and as the joints went from man to man, I extinguished several on my tongue and slipped them in my shirt pocket for later. I have no further comments on the wisdom or idiocy of that program or the officer who administered it, but I got stoned silly that first day, stayed high for weeks after, and from then on, I was a dedicated dope smoker.

When Yolanda became pregnant, we lived in a decent apartment, so we welcomed the addition of a child. I stayed stoned all the time and spent evenings watching escapist trash television. Yolanda and I were each happy in our own way, but my bad disposition, grown worse with time, now impacted my family. I'd had several serious blow-ups with my sister—all completely my fault—and my negative feelings toward my father had turned to open hostility.

➤ *Dave was displaying another symptom of avoidance—markedly diminished interest in significant activities. He preferred watching television over interacting with his wife.*

Suddenly being laid off my dog-grooming job took me by surprise and put a huge dent in a household budget already stretched thin by diapers and baby food. I needed to think of something fast. I still had no stomach for a real job, so I applied the navy training I'd received in analog electronics to repairing televisions. I worked out of my home, found my customers through word of mouth, and never paid a dime in taxes. My under-the-table money went unrecorded, and now, with a child in the home, we were eligible for welfare.

It shames me now to think of it. Twenty-five years old, a husband and father of a beautiful little boy named Owen, and I was on welfare, fixing TVs on the side—and selling drugs. Poor white trash was too good a term for me. Yolanda wondered whether I'd ever "grow up," and as for our marriage, she neared the end of her tether. In her mind, we were supposed to be a normal family and live in a decent house, and I was supposed to provide for us like a regular man.

Regular man.

That's what did it. Yolanda's opinion of me had sunk so low, she considered me not a real man, and she told me I needed to straighten out. I got the message loud and clear and immediately contacted the Veterans Administration for help. My subsequent experience with the VA is a long story you don't need to hear. It's enough to say they gave me a battery of tests and eventually decided I had a 10 percent disability from nerve damage I'd received from my shrapnel wounds. Also, they paid tuition for me to go to school and study digital electronics.

Three years later, I received my Bachelor of Science degree in electronic technology.

Getting there wasn't easy. Yolanda and I had no money, I had a family to feed, and I couldn't find an affordable apartment. One day, poking around Champion for a place to live, I ran across a funeral home operator looking for someone to do odd jobs in exchange for rent and utilities on a two-bedroom apartment above the chapel. It sounded crazy at first, but I checked it out and discovered comfortable rooms and a big yard in back for Owen.

It was a comfortable apartment all right, but not entirely removed from the funeral home's daily operations. When they held a service, Yolanda and I found it convenient—okay, necessary—to leave for a few hours while the relatives grieved. After each service, I locked up, vacuumed, and straightened the chairs for the next day. This sounds weird, but the whole funeral home thing fascinated Owen. From the beginning, he wandered unafraid through the gloomy viewing rooms, walked right up to the bodies, and touched them, unconcerned they were dead humans. In the evenings, the chapels and prep rooms were merely extensions of his playroom.

I never asked Yolanda what she thought about life over a funeral home. It was the nicest place we'd ever lived, and she pretended to enjoy it, but I was neither brave nor stupid enough to force the question. Hey, I was doing better with my life. I went to school full time and was finally working toward a career. I believed that at last I lived up to my wife's image of a "regular man." I hoped I did, but there was just one little thing—I still sold drugs.

I finished college near the top of my class. On graduation night, I was celebrating upstairs when two guys came to the door to buy weed. I didn't know them, so I told them to go elsewhere. They wouldn't take no for an answer, begged and pleaded and gave me a whole line of crap about how I had been referred by this guy or that. I was pretty well mashed that night anyway, so I gave them a couple Benadryl Yolanda kept around the house for her allergies. That was all it took. They flashed badges, jumped inside, cuffed me, and took me to jail. I sat in the slammer for the weekend while my poor wife scoured the county for an attorney to get me out.

I was released on bail, but the county prosecutor wanted to make an example of me and talked about multiple years in prison. Yolanda went into full panic mode, and I admit the whole thing scared the hell out of me, too. By the time my court date arrived, I'd landed a job in Chicago, and I was desperate to leave Ohio and start my life over. During the trial, my lawyer argued a man with a family and a college degree just starting a new life in another state deserved leniency and not jail time. Yolanda had chosen well. The lawyer and the judge were related. I paid a 100 dollar fine and obeyed strict instructions to get out of town by sundown. Many years later, when that unpleasant episode came up in conversation, Mother admitted that she and my father had set me up for the cops that night. "I didn't want to, Davey, but your father said it was for your own good."

The trial over, I raced out of the courtroom, grabbed my wife, my son, and my diploma, and headed to Illinois to work at the Fermi National Accelerator Laboratory. The advanced electronics division was on the fifteenth floor, and when the scientists needed a piece of equipment for a particular application, we designed and built it. It was my first real job, and I enjoyed working around clever people and state-of-the-art technology.

Even though surrounded by button-down eggheads, I worked in bib overalls, and I still had my big red beard. I often wondered what old Enrique Fermi would have thought if he could have seen that. However, my choice of wardrobe was not a fashion protest or an attempt to separate myself from others. At the time, I suffered with leg pains, and the nerve damage I'd sustained from the shrapnel wound worsened. The VA doctors traced the condition to a medical screw up in the hospital in Japan, and they recommended the overalls. Good call. Wearing a belt would have been torture. Eventually, the doctors worked through the nerve damage, and I worked through the pain, but not without a ton of marijuana.

I enjoyed my time at Fermi and stayed two and a half years, but the Department of Defense paid only a fraction of what I could earn in the private sector, so in 1980, I took a position at Bell Laboratories in Allentown, Pennsylvania. Also, I hoped the move and extra money would do something to bolster my failing marriage. Yolanda and I fought constantly and were both miserable all the time. Stoned every hour of every day and paralyzed by night terrors, I was so focused on my own problems I didn't realize Yolanda struggled with issues of her own. As a child, two uncles had molested her, and she'd kept it to herself her whole life. Nice, huh? Where did the girl find the strength to keep that bottled up inside?

No matter how you cut it, both of us were a damned mess. For over a year, I'd experienced frequent blackouts and flashbacks, and now they were getting worse. Too afraid to close my eyes, at least three nights a week I got no sleep at all. On good nights, I slept an hour, got up and paced for two, and then repeated the cycle until dawn. Can you understand the deep loneliness attached to lying awake in fear while the rest of the world slumbers? No. Of course you can't.

✤ *Flashbacks and this form of dissociative amnesia are serious re-experience symptoms of PTSD, and can cause anxiety to increase until it becomes disabling because of lack of recuperative sleep, leading to exhaustion.*

The flashbacks hit me hardest when I was upset or angry about something. At the onset of each spell, I felt anger rush through me, and then suddenly, as though someone flipped a switch, instead of being where I was, I'd be right back in Vietnam sorting through mangled bodies on the ship's deck or popping a magazine on some gook sniper in the trees. Sometimes I stayed gone hours, sometimes just minutes. The only certainty was that I had absolutely no control over it. Try as I might, I could not prevent those dark episodes, nor could I will them away.

God love her, it took her a long time, but again Yolanda convinced me to see a doctor and find out what was wrong with me—why I was in such a "bad mood" all the time. I'd been to VA clinics and hospitals several times for medical reasons, but because nobody knew much about post-traumatic stress, their investigations into my unbridled hostility toward the world were mostly just experiments with drug therapy. Over the years, they tried Valium and other derivatives, but nothing did any good. One doctor gave me Tuinal, a barbiturate used to detox heroine addicts, but it was too strong for me, and I found it easier just to smoke dope. This time around, the VA put me through a bullshit relaxation therapy program, but that did no good at all. I was better off at home watching trash TV. I wanted to get well, but despite the VA's good intentions, no one successfully diagnosed and treated the problem. For years, I knocked on the door, but no one answered.

➤ *Dave lived in a world of uncertainty and fear. With no solid diagnosis or effective treatment for PTSD during this period in Dave's life, he and his family struggled with an unnamed and ferocious enemy.*

The job with Bell Laboratories didn't last long. It was strictly a desk position where I shuffled papers all day—too much red tape for my rough sensibilities—and I had no opportunity to work with my hands to design and build something. I tried, but it wasn't in my nature to sit and watch while others made the wheels roll. When I resigned, my supervisor put in my records that I "adapted poorly in team environments." Another armchair psychologist. The world's full of them. The asshole should have worked for the VA.

My next job, in Paso Robles, California, was with army real-time computer programs. I was assigned to the group testing the Apache helicopter and the Humvee, brand new hardware at the time. Interesting work, but two years later, the company lost the army contract, I was laid off, and we left California. The worst aspect of our constant moving was that my son, Owen, was forced so often to change schools. I felt terrible about that, and when we left California, I promised to settle down. Yolanda, bless her soul, endured my faults, hung in there, and kept our family together when any other woman would have taken her child and got the hell away from me forever.

➤ *Dave's episodic employment history is typical of many veterans diagnosed with PTSD. This pattern is associated with several symptoms of avoidance, such as a sense of foreshortened future, feelings of detachment, and diminished interest in significant activities.*

My next job was with General Electric in Columbia, Missouri. They had a contract to service the computers at the university, and determined Owen would finish school there, in 1989 I vowed never to move again. If Columbia would be good for Owen, it would be even better for me. We settled in, I reported to the VA clinic, and the doctor who examined me sent me to a colleague who knew something about PTSD. When he told me what I had, at first I didn't fully understand, but I believed he knew his business, because he described my symptoms exactly. He told me he currently treated several veterans suffering with PTSD, and other VA centers around the country were then becoming aware of it. Together, we experimented with several treatments—drugs (no good), Gestalt therapy (maybe). Sometimes we made progress, sometimes not, but we didn't lose heart, and we didn't give up on each other.

My job turned out perfect for me. When a computer needed repair, I went to the location, got it running, and then went home until I was called again. I'd gone decades without finding true job satisfaction, now, I actually enjoyed working. My commitment to staying in Columbia pleased Yolanda, and the tension in our marriage eased. Funny how things so quickly fell into place. Coincidence? Maybe, but more likely it was because I saw the VA therapist every chance I got, day or night, seven days a week.

Later, when the doctor suggested group therapy, I was skeptical, but I trusted him and was willing to do whatever he said. The first session was strange, but for me a real eye-opener. Those poor bastards in group were really whacked out. Some left the seclusion of their homes only to attend therapy. Others were in ugly, protracted wars with everyone, even their neighbors. These guys had real problems. Almost all had hit bottom, and many were still there. Because of Yolanda, I had never gone through a crisis where my whole world fell down around me. Her persistence, drive, and unfailing support had brought me through everything. As I listened to those veterans speak of their lives and how their spouses had left them or been pushed away, I became petrified with fear that Yolanda might one day leave me and at the same time filled with gratitude she had not. Yolanda's entire make up, her whole mind and heart, had been stronger than that. She knew of the good inside me and refused to let me push her away.

❧ *The power of group therapy for traumatized veterans should not be underesti-mated. In this environment, the soldier can tell his stories of brutality, fear, and bravery and know he will be accepted regardless of how terrible the history is. Letting go of those dark and dangerous secrets is often cathartic and liberating.*

Since then, my doctor and I continue to work on my problems. I am a willing, even eager patient, and he reads everything he can find on the lat-est treatments. Some time ago, he started me on EMDR, Eye Movement Desensitization and Reprocessing therapy. Even though it was new and experimental, I tried it, and it worked. After just one session, I stopped experiencing nightmares. During EMDR, the therapist uses a metronome, the pendulum swinging in one-second intervals. The patient follows the pendulum with his eyes while he tries to recall the details of the traumatic situations he experienced.

In my case, I move my eyes in time to the metronome and visualize the nets full of bodies dropping onto the deck of my ship. Occasionally, my therapist moves his finger in time with the ticking and tells me to pick a place—visualize an interrogation cell—and then pay attention to what my body felt like at the moment. He tells me to concentrate on my imme-diate feelings and thoughts and to bring everything out. I don't know how it works or why, but during EMDR, I have a running dialogue about the darkest moments in my life, and the entire time, I keep my eyes locked onto his finger as it moves back and forth with the ticking metronome.

For me, EMDR therapy has been a miracle. After only one treatment, I felt as though I had emerged from a tunnel. I'd lived in darkness 25 years, and then, suddenly, I saw the world in a new light. Very quickly, I was able to relax, and I started sleeping nights as long as two hours at a time. I felt a new confidence in myself, and I looked forward to every new day just to measure my progress and experience some new feeling of release. EMDR. Who'da thunk it? So simple, and yet so effective.

❧ *Practiced obscurely for 20 years, EMDR therapy has proven to be an effective, if not the most effective treatment for PTSD in combat veterans. Dave was truly blessed when he was linked to this EMDR therapist.*

Now, I treat myself at home whenever I need it. I still take Sertraline, an antidepressant, but in low doses, and it doesn't bother me.

I've been in therapy 10 years now, and I've stopped smoking mari-juana. Also, I no longer experience the red-zone fits of anger that stole from my spirit for so long. I think through situations now and don't make stupid, rash judgments when something unpleasant happens in my life.

My relationship with Yolanda is the best it's ever been. In recent years, we've embarked on a journey to explore our spiritual roots. Together, we've begun to study the Bible and understand its teachings. With Yolan-da's help and encouragement, I've learned to look to God for spiritual support and guidance, and the church has become the focal point of our lives. I don't think I could have continued on the road to wellness with a strictly secular mindset. Today, when I ask myself the larger questions concerning the sanctity of marriage, how to live, and what guidelines to follow when making life decisions, I know the answers are all written in the Bible. Putting it another way, I've discovered if I try to live my life by the Word, everything else takes care of itself.

The church alone would not have been enough for me to get my life straightened out. I needed the PTSD therapy. Likewise, therapy itself would not have been enough. During my treatments, when I started feeling better, the Lord tapped on my shoulder and told me I needed to find Him to fill the void and complete the picture.

Owen is 31 now and a fine young man. For once in my life, I lived up to a promise, and he graduated from high school here in Columbia. The church is in his life, too, and he's been on several missions to Central and South America. He recently graduated from a Bible college in Springfield, and he and his new wife work for an online Bible college. I've apologized to him for his early years. Essentially, he grew up without a father, and that's the saddest part of my life. I can never forget how my father failed me, and it pains me that I committed many of his crimes. Yolanda volunteers with the church and currently works with a program called Open Arms Ministries.

My company lost the service contract with the University of Missouri, but for the past 10 years, I've done the same job for the company that took over. Just five months ago, however, they laid me off, and then retained me as a subcontractor. Now, they call me a "variable work engineer," which means I do the same job for less money and no benefits. I don't like it, but that's way the world's going, and it pays the bills. The VA classified me 60 percent disabled and sends a monthly stipend that helps. Hey, we live modestly, but we get by

After all these years, I've learned the most important thing is a life with God. The trials of this earth are tests to determine where we'll end up in the spiritual world. Everyone's life is important. Good and evil march arm-in-arm in this world, and too many people want to hunker in the gray areas, but they can't. God's word equals peace and harmony, not death and destruction. The joy I've found in my life is rooted in my family and my God. I was lucky. My love for Yolanda and my faith in my Maker have meant the difference between life as it is today and sitting for years in a prison cell.

—Dave Sekol

CHAPTER 4

Sidney Alvin Lee
Louisiana
U.S. Army Airborne Ranger Infantry

My neighborhood was mostly black, but there were Creoles, Indians, and Cajuns, too. You didn't know who was who and what was what. If a kid got pissed at somebody, he might call him cracker or nigger or something else, but he was never sure what name hurt most.

My first real experience with segregation and racism came in the military. In Vietnam, black soldiers rarely served in rear echelon positions. Supply clerks and officers' drivers were always white. Blacks were sent to the field. When it was time for R&R, the white soldiers went first and got the best choices. When a white soldier got wounded with 60 days left in country, they found him a job in the rear. Wounded black soldiers were treated and sent back into the bush. Everybody knew this went on. It was just something we lived with.

I was born Sidney Alvin Lee, Jr. in New Orleans on December 15, 1943. My great-grandfather was from the island of St. Thomas, and my great grandmother was a Cherokee Indian. Add some Creole and Cajun, and I don't know what that makes me. I only know the color of my skin meant a whole lot more to others in this country than to me. That was also true in New Orleans, but I loved my hometown. Now, of course, it is well known multi-racial environments are good for kids, and a great many in New Orleans had known that for generations and lived according to Dr. King's proposition that the color of a man's skin is no more important than the color of his eyes.

I was the eldest of six sisters and one brother, and my first memories of family life are of our old white frame house on five acres below the industrial canal out in Wilderness, USA. Mother had been a city girl her whole life and hated it, but she agreed with my father it was the best place to raise a big family.

I don't know what people know of the backwoods of Louisiana, but below the canal, a good rain turned the whole area into a swamp. If it rained too much, the canal overflowed and sent snakes and other wild critters scurrying for high ground. But rain or no rain, we always had problems with critters—especially snakes. I say it's a wives' tale, but Mother fervently believes snakes smell breast milk and are drawn to homes where babies are present. If what she says is true, then snakes have particularly good noses, because even though we seldom found them inside, they were everywhere else around our house—even in our mailbox.

My father was a mechanic, entrepreneur, and jack-of-all-trades in the fashion of the stereotypical Southern Negro. He died when I was 12, but I have fond memories of the years we spent together before he was taken. Dad was part owner and manager of Avalon Music, a company that provided jukeboxes to bars and diners in the country towns surrounding New Orleans. He also distributed movies and projectors to schools and churches in those same towns. A great many people knew my father, and everybody liked him. He wore his big smile everywhere he went, and people never thought him a mere salesman. A man who treasured exploring backwoods USA could not have had a better occupation.

Often, I traveled those backroad parishes with Dad. He loved to fish and hunt, and when he finished his route, he took me to the Pearl River or elsewhere back in the bayous to hunt alligators, garfish, and turtles. A big man and very strong, Dad could crush the life out of an alligator with his iron grip. A born outdoorsman with a primordial affinity for the natural world, Dad believed his son should learn from doing, and as a child, I trudged through the mud and throttled critters with him, my hands just as dirty as his.

➢ *His father forced Sidney to become a man, perhaps sooner than he liked. At home in the steamy swamplands of lower Louisiana, the wilderness skills Sidney learned as a youth helped him survive his tours of duty in combat, but these same skills would prove useless against the repeated assaults traumatic events and stressors made on his brain*

In the old days, they taught a boy to swim by tossing him into the water and telling him he was on his own. Well, that actually happened to me. Dad took a weekend job with a crew to float a barge sunk in the Pearl River. I was with him and stood on shore watching. When the barge surfaced and the men tied it off, Dad walked casually over to where I stood, picked me up and tossed me in the river. Then, he sat down on a log and lit up a smoke. To a six-year-old, the Pearl was a damned big river and no doubt teeming with sharp-toothed and needle-fanged monsters. I panicked, of course, wailed and screamed like a banshee, but Dad pretended he didn't notice. I beat the surface of the water, clawed at the sky, and begged God or anyone to save me. No good. Finally, I realized no one would come to get me. I was on my own in that river, so I gave up and started swimming. Somehow, I flailed and kicked and fought until I crawled ashore soaked and covered with muddy slime.

➤ *His father's method for teaching a six-year old to swim would be considered emotionally abusive by today's standards. It is also a good example of a caregiver-perpetrated stressor that can predispose an individual to the development of PTSD if exposed to a traumatic stressor later in life.*

In every way, Dad was "old school." He believed a man needed to know how to live off the land, and children did what parents said when the parents said it. No argument about that. Mother was strict too, but that was okay with me. I never broke the rules, because my parents set boundaries and limitations, and I was happy to toe the line.

Throughout my childhood, Father was away on his routes much of the time, and Mother worked as a physician's assistant. In those days, country doctors still made house calls, and Mother traveled the parish to dispense medicine and give injections. At home, there was always plenty of chores, and I stayed busy preparing meals and taking care of my younger brothers and sisters. With no other kids my age to play with, I spent my free time alone in my little world of swamps. I was a skinny little runt and not interested in sports, so between household duties and my solitary sojourns in the swamps, I delivered the weekly paper, and on Wednesdays, *Jet* and *Ebony* magazines.

Religion was a big thing in my family, and I mean big. For generations, the first-born male child in my bloodline had become a minister, but the way my life turned out, I guess I broke that chain. In my youth, Baptist services started early with Sunday school at eight then a two hour morning service at eleven. In the afternoon, Baptist Young Peoples' Union lasted until five, then it was time for evening services. My parents did not force this Sunday routine on their children. There was never any discussion, debate, or argument on the matter. Sunday belonged to the church. Simply put, it was as natural as eating or breathing. On Sunday morning, I woke up early, washed my face, put on my best clothes, and went to church. Thoughts of not going or doing something else never entered my mind. My parents told me fidelity to the church and adherence to its teachings were necessary for getting ahead in life. They called it a sign of diligence in the endless pursuit of self-improvement.

➤ *Sidney remained diligent in the practice of the religion he had been inculcated with as a child until he left home and joined the Army. A symptom associated with Disorders of Extreme Stress Not Otherwise Specified (DESNOS), loss of previously sustaining beliefs, presented before he was traumatized in Vietnam.*

Like most parents, Mom and Dad wanted a better life for their children. Black families in rural Louisiana had struggled for 150 years just to eke out the most meager existence. Hard work and living close to the bone was the norm, and a lifetime of it made my parents tough as shoe leather. Proud, determined, but not dogmatic, they always said if a person has strength and a brain, he can work and obtain the necessities of life. For them, determination and self-reliance were the cardinal virtues.

That was why Dad spent so much time teaching me to hunt and fish. In our family, harvesting wildlife was not mere recreation. Raising kids costs money, and after Dad died, times were lean and food scarce, so I often went into the swamps and brought home a turtle, small alligator, or a couple Poodoo. There was no such thing as a supermarket in our part of the country, and even if one existed, we couldn't afford to shop in it. We just made do with what we had.

After Dad died, Mother and I frequently rode the bus to the French market at night after 11. At that hour, the fishermen had unloaded all their catch earmarked for the commercial outlets, and for a dollar, we bought a bag of 20 or 30 assorted fish. Mom called them the leftovers.

The Gulf is a shallow body of water as oceans go, and the fishermen dragged nets from top to bottom. Mom and I never knew what we'd find in those dollar bags. Now and then, we pulled out a critter so ugly the dog would leave the house, but it was all protein, and as I said, we couldn't afford to be picky. Sometimes, we got lucky and a kind fisherman sold a leftover bucket of shrimp or oysters for 75 cents. Vegetables we didn't grow in our own garden we got from the neighbors, and as Mom had often doctored the children of the foreman at the Sunbeam bakery, he sold her day-old bread out the back door, five loaves for a dollar. She was never embarrassed or afraid of the hands-on, day-to-day business of living and raising a family. This was all part of Mother's concept of self-reliance.

* * *

In 1955, Dad died suddenly of a cerebral hemorrhage, and for the rest of Mother's life, she couldn't decide whether to blame his death on his wild ways or his love for spicy food. I don't know much about Father's wild ways, but I assure you Mom was the best cook in the south. She learned in her mother's restaurant in James Alley next to Parrish Prison in New Orleans, and my whole life, I watched her work Cajun miracles with the food she had available to her.

Dad's death was hard on our family. As the eldest, I knew my father better than my brothers and sisters, and I loved him, but a great many things have happened in my life, and it's difficult now to recall how much pain I felt at his passing. I was acutely aware, however, that Mom now shouldered the responsibility of working and raising six children, and I recognized how difficult rural life and the lack of services had become for her. Therefore, I was not surprised when two years after we buried Dad, Mom moved the family into the city and took an apartment in the Calliope Projects.

✦ *Sidney experienced his first traumatic event in early adolescence with his father's sudden death. Although he does not recall the pain he felt at his father's passing, the unexpected loss of a loving and supporting parent is extremely traumatic and possibly causative for a host of acute and/or chronic mental disorders.*

To help with household finances, I took a weekend job in a print shop. A country boy through and through, I'd wondered how I'd fare in the big city, but I soon discovered lithography. The entire process fascinated me, and I loved every moment I spent working with plate and paper. Later, I took over publication of the high school newspaper. Also, I made extra money printing the school letterhead and business cards, tickets for PTA suppers, and announcement cards for graduating seniors. Being good at lithography got me a full scholarship to Southern University.

I did well in college, earned good grades, made the track team, the *Who's Who* list, and practicing the resolve my parents instilled in me, I lived up to the scholarship I'd been awarded.

During my freshman year, I was selected for a semester-long overseas study program at the University of Mainz. Studying in Germany changed my life. That's where I met and fell in love with the most wonderful woman on the planet, Rose Marie. I'd glimpsed young Rose Marie on campus on several occasions, and one night, I followed her and a girlfriend to a club. I had no idea how to approach this beautiful German girl, and I figured my chances with her were virtually nil, but I stood around for an hour and drank whisky, rehearsed my lines, and waited for the right time. When I finally got enough courage down my throat to ask her to dance, she looked up at me and said, "Nein danke," and that ended it. I didn't see Rose Marie again until a year and a half later.

During my second year at Southern University, I heard Martin Luther King had organized a march and sit-in at the Woolworth store in Baton Rouge. I was curious, but the dean of students had spread the word that anyone caught attending would be expelled. Dr. King was the man I respected most in the world. I kept up with his crusade and watched television coverage of all his marches and demonstrations. When I learned of the Baton Rouge march, I wanted to go, not to participate, but to watch and listen to the speeches. For me, just being there was important. I planned to stay in the background, not get close, and certainly not get involved.

The following morning, I jumped on a bus and rode into Baton Rouge. To my young eyes, the demonstration was an amazing spectacle. Hundreds of brave men and women faced violent retribution from institutional authority and marched unflinchingly for their freedom. Seeing people of color determined to gain for themselves the rights and freedoms other Americans had handed to them profoundly affected me. This was determination and perseverance like I'd never seen before, and more beautifully and magnificently expressed because it was for the good of the many. In my mind, their acts were the very definition of selflessness and altruism.

➻ *The scene that unfolded in Baton Rouge during the civil rights march reinforced in Sidney a sense of duty and self-sacrifice to a noble cause. Deeply moved by the experience, later, he took his deeply held altruism half a world away to fight a war in a place few Americans had even heard of.*

Faithful to my original intentions, I stayed in the background, and I certainly didn't get involved, but how could I know that the television news cameras would pick my big, ugly mug out of the crowd? I made a full-screen appearance on every six o'clock news show in Louisiana.

The next morning, back on campus, the dean called me into his office and expelled me on the spot. Too afraid to go home and tell my mother I'd been kicked out of school, I camped out with a friend for the remainder of the semester. A counterfeit student, for the next two months I went home on weekends and holidays, my laundry under my arm, and dutifully reported how well I was doing.

➻ *Sidney's expulsion from Southern University was directly related to the risk he took when he defied the Dean and attended the civil rights demonstration. Albeit disheartening and embarrassing, that negative consequence was not life threatening. Accordingly, Sidney's brain did not associate the risk he took attending the demonstration with the life-changing consequence that resulted.*

I spent Christmas vacation at home, but when it was time to go back to school, I went to see the army recruiter instead. I'd made up my mind it was safer to go into the army than tell my mother I'd blown my college education. Six months after I joined, I finally found the courage to tell her the truth. That silly confession of mine is still the joke of the family. 40 years later, we still talk about it. The irony was Mom had discovered months earlier what had happened but wanted to see how much time passed before I became man enough to tell her.

* * *

When I joined the army in 1962, they needed infantry cannon fodder for the growing insurgency in Vietnam. Young and gung ho, I applied for every specialized infantry program they offered and got what I most wanted—jump school and ranger training. The military was so completely different from anything I'd experienced it bowled me over at first. Free from the restraints of a conservative university, I was influenced by the wrong people and swept away by women and liquor. I'd grown up physically but not mentally or emotionally. At 20 years old, I was six-feet, 180 pounds of solid muscle, a holy terror willing to try anything.

❖ *Sidney's desire to become an airborne ranger may also be linked to his child-hood abandonment and abuse and demonstrated by behaviors that can be symptoms of DESNOS. Exposing himself to the extreme emotional and physical demands of this specialized training may comprise several DESNOS symptoms: excessive risk taking, modulation of anger, revictimization, victimizing others, and self destructive behavior.*

After basic and advanced infantry training, I transferred to Fort Benning, Georgia, for airborne and ranger training, and then to Fort Bragg, North Carolina, for jumpmaster and pathfinder school. After 13 months of difficult and demanding training, at last I earned the privilege of calling myself an Airborne Ranger, the best of the best, the highest military pedigree.

Imagine my dismay when I received my first operational assignment and found the army years behind in equipment and tactics. Even though Vietnam was heating up, the army still taught European theater tactics, and I was stunned that my long range reconnaissance unit drilled in jeeps equipped with machine guns like in that old television series, *Rat Patrol*. Crazy. Jungle warfare in Southeast Asia was clearly our next challenge, but the army still trained to battle Russian tanks.

You have to understand the whole airborne ranger thing. Imagine the allure. The elite forces of the U.S. Army, airborne rangers were the best trained, most efficient, biggest, and baddest sons-of-bitches around. Men who made it through ranger training were serious, no bullshit, combat-capable fighting men, and the envy of every soldier.

> See that man in the black beret,
> Ask him how he earns his pay.
> See that man in the black beret,
> Killing's how he earns his pay.
> The best the world will ever see,
> He's Airborne Ranger Infantry.

Jumping out of perfectly good airplanes was the stock in trade for the airborne ranger, and I did plenty at Ft. Bragg. Night jumps, water jumps, equipment jumps—probably 200 altogether. In my company, the old saying went that one airborne trooper could kick the hell out of any five straight-legs. Youthful arrogance? Yes. False pride? No. We really were rough and tough, and frequently, we went to town to prove it. It embarrasses me to say it now, but man, if trouble didn't come to us, my buddies and I hit the country and western bars looking for it. Now, of course, I'm amazed the local rednecks never found a way to exercise a little backwoods justice on us. I guess sometimes arrogance can pass for invincibility.

Like everywhere else in the United States, racial tension was high at Fort Bragg. The blacks and whites simply didn't get along. Personally, I had zero tolerance for prejudice. I never once mistreated another because of his race or station in life, and if anyone tried to tell me I wasn't as good as the next man, he was in for a hard time. When my orders came, I was glad to get out of there.

* * *

My first overseas assignment was in mechanized recon with B Company, 503rd Airborne in Mainz, Germany. B Company's mission was to patrol the woods for weeks at a time with troops from other countries, and the duty bored me to tears. Between patrols, I looked forward to getting back to town. Finally fed up with months of repetitive line company duty, I applied for a transfer to the base special police unit that manned the perimeter gates and acted as honor guards at base ceremonies.

Young, dumb, and full of myself and my ranger status, during my stint in Germany, my reputation as a troublemaker grew. I tried to make real the myth of the airborne ranger, the ultimate twentieth century warrior who does anything he wants—soldier hard and play hard. Soon, I was out of control and so full of myself that I couldn't see what an ass I'd become.

➤ *Sidney's transformation from studious lithographer to troublemaker and his self-medicating further illustrates that he was already afflicted with a stress disorder.*

Fortunately, a man in my company took a liking to me. A Korean War veteran with 20 years in the army, he sat me down and asked whether I wanted to end up like him—two decades in the service and still a private. He had held higher rank on many occasions, but each time he sewed a new stripe on his sleeve, he did something stupid and lost it again. Did I really want that life?

Maybe I listened to the old guy because he reminded me of my father, or maybe he was just the first person with the courage to tell me what a jerk I'd become. It took a while, but I finally understood that old soldier was right. My bad behavior proved nothing. If I wanted respect, I'd have to earn it where it counted. With just those few words, that brother veteran changed my life.

One night while on guard duty at the main gate of our installation, I looked up just in time to see Rose Marie walk through, the girl I'd asked to dance a year and a half earlier. Rose Marie! Now, she was even more beautiful than I'd remembered. I knew the girl with her was married to a GI named Richard Greene. As the girl of my dreams approached, my heart raced in my chest, my throat went suddenly dry, and I put on my best smile. She paused, flashed her I.D., and then walked past without a glance.

The next day, I tracked down Richard Greene and pestered him for hours for information on the beautiful German girl. He told me Rose Marie was single and worked at the local hospital. I begged him. I pleaded. I groveled, and finally Richard agreed to arrange a double date.

➤ *Accustomed to achieving what he sought and true to his risk-taking nature, Sidney pursued Rose Marie despite the odds against prevailing.*

Like most good German girls, Rose Marie had been raised to steer clear of Americans in general and GIs in particular. During our first dates, although pleasant and very polite, she shared little of herself. She knew soldiers came and went at the whim of the military, and she wasn't about to give her heart to someone who might not be around next week.

To win Rose Marie's affection, I stepped out of character. I took time, tread carefully, behaved like a gentleman, and finally got the job done. Notwithstanding the army's official policy prohibiting mixed marriages, a year later, I broke the rules and married Rose Marie. Think about it, a beautiful young nursing student and a bright future with a dumb airborne guy like me. Friend, I definitely married above my station.

Rose Marie's father, a Luftwaffe pilot during World War II, was hard as nails and rigid as a board. It was more than just the military thing; he despised me for who I was, and I don't need to tell you why. Interracial marriage, impossible in the United States, was more acceptable in Europe, but he was among the last of a dwindling number in Germany who believed Africans had tails and were unfit to commingle with whites. When we became engaged, it took courage for Rose Marie to face her family and tell them she wanted to spend her life with a black man.

Her father, an executive in the Opal Automobile plant and a respected member of his community, had dreamed of something better for his daughter. It was bad enough she'd chosen a soldier, but a black man—*der Neger*—was beyond credulity. But Rose Marie let him know she would not stand for interference in her affairs. She'd made her choice, and her parents would just have to live with it. Later, I became very fond of my in-laws. They were wonderful people and caring and gentle grandparents.

In January 1965, Rose Marie gave birth our first baby, a boy, Alvien, and at the end of that same year, to our little girl, Torrie Ann. The family enjoyed life in Germany for another year, and then I received a transfer back to Fort Bragg.

Leaving her homeland for the U.S. proved a difficult challenge for Rose Marie. The little English she spoke she picked up from television. In the mid-60s in Fayetteville, North Carolina, a white woman married to a black man found few people with whom to associate, and to make matters more difficult, Vietnam had grown into a full-scale war. I spent weeks at a time in the field and was not much of a husband or father. In mid-1966, when I received orders to Vietnam, we implemented previously made plans, and Rose Marie and the children went to New Orleans to live with my mother.

* * *

The Screaming Eagles, the 101st Airborne, the original Band of Brothers, was headquartered in Long Binh when I arrived in Vietnam.

I reported in, and the CO said they'd just lost a weapons squad leader and needed a replacement. I said, "Yes, sir," and that settled it. I suppose if I'd reported in a week later, somebody else would have gone to weapons, and I'd have filled another dead man's slot. In a combat zone, that's what "rotation of personnel" really meant—put somebody new in the dead man's job.

➤ *A highly skilled and disciplined soldier, Sidney was more prepared to deal with combat than the vast majority of military personnel in his unit, and upon arrival, he got an immediate and morbid picture of what to expect in the 101st. At that moment, Sidney received his first small trauma in the realization his predecessor had not survived the position he was about to assume, a cognitive assault that put his brain in a hypervigilant state to prepare him for the conflicts that lay ahead.*

In Vietnam, airborne companies consisted of three infantry platoons and a weapons platoon. The weapons platoon carried the machine guns and 40 mm mortars that supported the infantry. Airborne in name only, the terrain and style of warfare in Southeast Asia did not lend itself to parachute assaults. More commonly, we transported by truck or helicopter then deployed and did our search and destroy missions.

To find and kill the bad guys, our company swept an area for one to two weeks, and anything that moved got shot or blown up. American forces rarely had trouble killing the enemy. Finding him was the hard part. The mountainous, jungle terrain we frequently patrolled made it difficult even to move, much less locate and kill the enemy.

When not in the field, the company deployed back to a base camp of one kind or another—not permanent installations, but temporary encampments made from sandbags and sheet metal and ringed with barbed wire. Of course, there were bunkers, fairly sophisticated perimeter defenses, and in most cases, an artillery battery to support the ground operations. After two weeks slogging the bush, we welcomed returning to these primitive camps for four or five days of light duty where we stood down, ate hot food, showered, changed clothes, and maybe got a beer. Also, our mail usually caught up with us in camp.

By the time I'd been in country a month, I'd seen a lot of action and knew I'd have to pay attention to business if I were to finish my tour in one piece. In a very short time, I developed a mental toughness, a keen awareness of the bloody nature of the no-holds-barred war we fought. Mental toughness, emotional callousness, call it what you want. I wasn't there to play games.

➤ *Sidney's belief in his own mental toughness was an illusion, albeit one that enabled him to endure his months of almost constant combat.*

Also, I didn't try to make any friends over there. You got friendly with someone, and the next thing you knew, he was wounded, killed, or even worse, his tour was over, and he went home and left you behind. To me, it wasn't worth it. I was older than most and a patrol leader, and I knew people sometimes misused friendship. Sixty to seventy percent of the soldiers in line units were black, and they had this thing about me being a *brother*. According to them, I was supposed to be their *brother* first and a soldier second. Hang out, rap-dap, and get high, but I wasn't into that crap. I wanted to concentrate on not dying in Vietnam, and I turned away from anything that distracted me from survival. For me, going home in one piece came first, and if that meant I had to look a man in the eye and blow his brains out, then so be it.

➤ *During his youth, Sidney maintained a sense of control in the hostile environment of the swamp. He knew what danger to expect, and his father had prepared him to handle any contingency. However, he had never witnessed the ghastly carnage that modern weapons wreak on the human body—had never been in situations where his own physical integrity was so completely compromised.*

One day, battalion sent us out to reinforce a marine unit under heavy fire. There were bad guys everywhere in that particular area around Chu Lai—VC and NVA, and everyone reported high body counts.

They dropped us in the middle of nowhere, and we spread out and began our sweep in steaming midday heat. It is impossible to describe how the choking jungle environment drained strength. Even the toughest man wilted under the combined onslaught of sun, temperature, and humidity. That day, we humped the boonies three hours until finally ordered to stop and take cover. Apparently, we'd arrived at our destination, because the CO spoke to battalion HQ on the radio for several minutes then sent word he wanted us to assault the steep, tree-covered hill to our front and take and hold the high ground. Jesus Christ. How often did an infantry soldier hear that shit? I should have "assault the hill and take and hold the high ground" tattooed on my forehead.

This area of operation was new to us, and no one knew what to expect. The men's faces revealed their uncertainty and trepidation as platoon sergeants spread the company along a line at the base of the hill. The CO ordered the weapons platoon broken into three squads and assigned one to each rifle platoon. Then it began.

Each time we advanced on the hill, the enemy poured heavy fire down on us from all along their line, and they let loose with rocket and mortar fire, too. No one knew how many were up there, but clearly, they were dug in and well-armed. Usually, the VC and NVA hit and ran. Usually, they wouldn't stand and fight against superior American firepower. These guys, however, were determined to hold their ground, and for once, they had hardware as deadly as our own.

We fought for that hill three days and nights. Sometimes, we were hours moving just a few yards. When the fighting became too intense, the CO ordered us back, we did a head count, regrouped, and then started back up again. We paid for that same piece of real estate so many times I lost count.

On the third day, as we worked our way back up, we leapfrogged up the hill, taking cover where we could. The midday sun burned the backs of our hands, and sweat soaked our fatigue jackets and ran in little rivers from crotch to boots. I didn't like it. It was too quiet, too easy to gain ground. The hair stood on the back of my neck, and I smelled adrenaline. When properly set up, you don't see an ambush coming. No matter how many flankers you send out, a well-planned and executed ambush in difficult terrain is deadly, and when it happens, all hell breaks loose, and it seems like the end of the world.

✦ *When overtaken by traumatic events as terrifying as bloody combat, the consequences of the stressors are encoded in the brain and body. Initially, PTSD symptoms such as hypervigilance or exaggerated startle response are defense mechanisms and do not present as problems until the danger is well past, and then this type of defense becomes inappropriate for the circumstances.*

That's the way it was when they opened up on us. The whole world turned to shit in five seconds. It was the perfect ambush. Withering gunfire came at us from all sides, and in only moments, they cut us to ribbons. Everywhere I looked, men returned fire from cover or fell wounded. The awful noise was deafening and the air thick with the acrid tang of cordite.

When ambushed, a soldier is trained to face the enemy and attack—move as quickly as possible out of the kill zone—even if it means hand-to-hand combat. We knew that, of course, and we tried to, but enemy sniper fire from the trees kept us pinned down.

➤ *Sidney's description of this firefight implies more than visual and auditory elements. His olfactory senses were assaulted by the smell of gunpowder, and although he does not mention it, his body and brain would have noticed and recorded vibrations of many kinds. Bullets passing near him at supersonic speed created innumerable pressure waves, and the ground trembled with the detonation of rocket grenades. Also, Sidney's tactile senses were in play, and his brain registered the feel of the ground he lay on.*

Twenty minutes of getting the crap kicked out of us, and the CO finally passed the word to get the hell out of there. My weapons squad was to engage the enemy with machine gun fire until the company got down the hill. Then, they'd cover us while we made our run for it. It was a risky proposition. Three days of heavy artillery fire on the hill had destroyed the vegetation below us, which made getting down easier but exposed retreating troops to enemy fire. Not much of a plan, but we couldn't advance, and we sure as hell couldn't stay there.

My squad set up a gun at each end of the company line and one in the center. Then, we scrambled into whatever holes we could find while bearers brought up extra ammunition and divided it among the three positions. The CO gave the signal, and when the company moved out, we opened up at maximum rate of fire.

My gunners were young but well trained and had nerves of steel. We laid down a wall of covering fire, but when the enemy saw our guys go down the hill, they stood up and charged. I couldn't believe it. Oblivious to our belt-high line of machine gun fire, they just stood up and came at us. I don't know how many we killed before they pulled up and took cover. I was with the center gun crew and had a good view of the terrain below us. When the company reached safety and could provide covering fire for us, I ordered my two flanking guns back. This wasn't like anything you've seen in the movies. My boys didn't stand up with machine guns on their hips and fire at the enemy moving backwards. They crawled on their bellies as fast and as far as they could, and when they reached cover, they got up and ran.

Before they moved out, the two flanking gunners passed their ammo to us. Now, the enemy knew we were the last machine gun on the hill, and they really turned it loose. The sky just over our heads was a blanket of flying lead, and we could do nothing but hug the earth and return fire as best we could. I looked behind and spotted my gun crews work down the hill, a hail of bullets following them. They needed more time to get farther down. Only two of us remained with one machine gun, but we held our ground and fired at anything that moved. You see, we had no choice. This was not any particular act of bravery. I mean that. We were desperate just to stay alive.

✦ *During this violent, life-threatening firefight, Sidney's brain produced large quantities of neurotransmitters such as adrenaline and norepinephrine, which permitted him to function in that paralyzing environment. Neurotransmitters perform a central function in the development of fear and enable a person to turn toward the danger, focus on it, and respond. Additionally, they are responsible for encoding in the Limbic System memories of events that occur during states of arousal and fear.*

The enemy came at us from three sides. I knew we couldn't hold out much longer, but I wanted to try, so I sent my gunner in search of more ammunition. Alone now, I fired to keep their heads down, to give my gunner a chance, but low on ammo, I had to pick and choose targets and fire in short bursts. The enemy knew I was alone on the hill, so imagine my surprise when the shooting stopped, and I heard, "Black G.I., why you fight us? Throw down your weapon. We will not hurt you. They hate you in your country, black G.I., but we do not."

Bullshit. No way did I buy that crap. However, I welcomed the lull in the action and lay still. I wanted to buy time by making them believe I was considering their offer.

Don't ask me how the hell he did it, but a few minutes later, my gunner made it back with several cans of ammunition. He'd been hit and was in bad shape, but even wounded, he'd scrambled around that hill until he got what he went for. The kid was a God damned hero. I can't tell you his name. This is a little off subject and probably sounds crazy to you, but I remember clearly the events of that time, but not the names of people or places. I remember exactly what that gunner looked like. I would recognize him if I saw him on the street today, but I can't remember his name. Hell, I can't even remember the name of that God damned hill he almost died on.

✦ *Studies show that decades after experiencing combat trauma, veterans diagnosed with PTSD maintain high levels of neurochemicals in the neocortex. This firefight and many others that were similar or worse changed forever how Sidney perceived his world. In his mind and body, Sidney Lee never escaped the battlefields of Vietnam.*

When the NVA realized I wouldn't fall for their line of crap, they started in on us again. At that point, I doubted we'd make it out of there, and for the first time since I'd been in country, images of Rose Marie and the children flashed before my eyes.

Stop that shit right now. You have work to do.

My gunner and I returned fire until our gun barrel glowed red. Very quickly, we again found ourselves low on ammo, and then suddenly, we were out. Now at the end of our rope, out of ammunition, and our gun fried, unless we got out right then, our only other choice was to stay and die. Oh, yeah, sometime during the skirmish, I had taken a round in the ankle, but at the time, I didn't realize it.

➤ *This battle for the unnamed hill contained all the stressors Sidney needed to develop PTSD. Faced with a situation that caused intense fear, the enormous threat to his physical integrity was punctuated when he was wounded during the firefight. Sidney's cognitive brain, hard at work to keep him focused on survival amidst the slaughter all around, failed to notice the wound, and it was not stored as a normal memory. Instead, a more primitive part of his brain recorded the assault on his body, and it became a fragmented memory that later presented with his symptoms of PTSD.*

More time passed, and still the CO hadn't signaled a pullback. Who knew what the hell he was doing? Maybe he'd been hit. Maybe the radioman had. Staring certain death in the face, I made the decision myself. My job was to fight for my country, not die senselessly, and besides, I wasn't about to give those Communist bastards the pleasure. My gunner couldn't run, so I picked him up, threw him over my shoulder and headed down the hill.

What happened next changed my life yet again and has bothered me all the years since. Call me a whiner, I don't care. I made it to our lines and got the gunner to the medics. The men were glad to see me, but the CO came over and chewed me out because I'd left the machine gun behind. I stood, a wounded man at my feet, blood and stink on my clothes and death in my hair, and all he said was, "Lee, how could you be so fucking stupid?"

The gun was useless! The barrel had cooked onto the receiver, but that wasn't the point, was it? I knew what that bastard was really telling me, and right then, I wanted to kill him. Right then, I realized where Sidney Lee stood with him and the U.S. government. To that captain, this black man was more expendable than a trashed-out piece of military hardware. In his eyes, I was disposable. The draft board could rake any ghetto and come up with a hundred more like me. Suddenly, a darkness came over me, something I can only describe as madness, and I thought I would explode.

➤ *Sidney paired the trauma of war with his rage at his commander's overt and despicable racism. He'd conquered fear and helplessness on the hill but was unprepared to be berated by his commanding officer for abandoning a useless machine gun. For the rest of Sidney's life, he would relive the rage that overtook his chemically saturated brain and body on that day. The traumatic events of the battle and the verbal thrashing by a white officer imprinted in Sidney's brain and then collided, coalesced, and colluded to drive him to drugs, alcohol, and near insanity in the years to come.*

I'd heard about troops who hated their officers in Vietnam and wanted them dead, and right then I knew why. Three months later, that CO was killed in a firefight, but I was not in the vicinity when it happened. I heard about it later from a friend.

Later that day, someone finally wised up and called the air force. The flyboys worked the place over with 2,000-pound bombs and daisy cutters for 36 hours. After that, the army sent in helicopter gunships. Two more days, and we finally took the hill. You can paint your own picture of what that place looked like. I'll just say hair, teeth, and eyeballs hung from every remaining tree and bush. I don't remember exactly, but we counted at least 200 dead NVA soldiers and another 100 VC. Our company lost 40 men.

I was happy my gunner's wounds got him a trip home. I never knew what happened to him after that, but I often thought about him and always hoped he made it. My own wound wasn't severe enough to get me out of the field. Medics dressed it, and I was back to regular duty in two weeks.

The months wore on and I decided I had to get out of company-sized units. Most of my four years in the military I'd worked recon patrols and scout teams. I had no patience for rifle companies. Too big, too many men, too noisy, and too many line company troops acted like they didn't care. They smoked cigarettes in the field, screwed off, and cracked wise —everything that got soldiers killed, and I'd had enough of it. I looked around for a transfer to a LRP unit or ranger outfit and got lucky. A newly formed South Vietnamese ranger company was ready to go to the field, and they needed American advisors, so I pulled the necessary strings and got the assignment.

Working with ARVNs was good duty. 10-man teams set up ambushes, conducted night raids, located incoming enemy troops, and captured couriers, paymasters, and village chiefs suspected of collaborating with the Communists. The South Vietnamese soldiers taught me to sleep, eat, and move through difficult terrain like a native, and I taught them how to make war like an American. I'd heard South Vietnamese soldiers wouldn't stand and fight, were cowards in the face of the enemy. Bullshit. The ones I knew were as good as any Americans I ever worked with. I advised that ARVN ranger unit until I went home in the summer of 1967.

* * *

After Vietnam, I was assigned back to Fort Bragg to teach infantry procedure. Even though I was happy to be home with Rose Marie and my children, I didn't care for the new duty. The Vietnam build-up was under-way, and the army needed NCOs, so they dreamed up a program for basic trainees with one year of college to take eight weeks infantry train-ing, and then be promoted to sergeant. We called it the "instant shake and bake school" and saw it for what it was, the army's pathetic attempt to half-ass train children for jungle warfare. It was a joke. Naïve adoles-cents were supposed to master land navigation, lead a squad or platoon of other children in combat operations, maneuver under fire, set up ambushes, and work with weapons and aerial artillery in eight weeks? It was a bad joke. Draftees 18 to 20 years old, four months removed from their mothers' teat, were being sent to slaughter.

The kids came to me right from AIT, and I taught them booby traps, ambushes, and explosives Vietnam-style. Ninety-nine percent would be in Vietnam within the year, and I worked hard to drum important infor-mation into those stubbornly indifferent thick heads. Sometimes, I wanted to grab them by the shirt, shake their teeth loose, and scream, "Pay attention! There's a real war going on over there!" It was sad to know that no matter what I said or did, most would only really learn by watching someone else die. I received orders to return to Vietnam in 1969, and by then, I was glad to go.

➤ *Sidney's need to return to Vietnam suggests an attempt to gain mastery over his previous traumas. Persons abused as children and re-victimized as adults learn maladaptive ways of thinking, coping, and relating to others. His post-traumatic symptoms may have predisposed him to be more vulnerable to re-victimization, including what researchers call a biologically-mediated inescap-able shock response upon exposure to danger.*

I didn't know it then, but I was already experiencing symptoms of PTSD. Months of teaching small unit tactics to children had transformed me into a dour, sulking fatalist. When anyone asked me anything, the answer was always "I don't give a damn" or "Who gives a fuck?" My feet seemed mired in the muddy banks of a river of blood and misery, and it was my job to toss boys in and hope they could swim to shore on their own. I couldn't shut my mind to the fact it was only a matter of time before grim reality wiped the childish grins off their faces.

That's why I knew I had to go back. I'd left a whole lot of unfinished business there, and while I didn't like leaving Rose Marie and the kids, somehow that didn't matter. Nor was I concerned about my own safety. My chances of surviving a second tour were much greater than the first. I knew what to expect and what buckets of shit not to step in. I was going back to Vietnam. I had to.

➤ *Sidney had become aware of the first recognizable signs and symptoms of his PTSD, and their effect on his quality of life. He displayed classic avoidance symptoms, such as markedly diminished interest in significant activities, a sense of foreshortened future, and feelings of detachment or estrangement from others.*

* * *

Vietnam looked, felt, tasted, and smelled exactly the same as on my arrival two years earlier. It was as though I'd never left. I stepped off the plane, sniffed the air, listened to the helicopters whopping in the distance, and my U.S. ties were instantly severed. It occurred to me then Fort Bragg, North Carolina, now had become foreign. Vietnam was home.

The 199th Light Infantry Brigade in Bien Hoa needed someone to give in-country orientation training to new replacements. The CO knew I'd taught that in the States and snatched me from a nasty field assignment. Fine with me. Light duty in Bien Hoa, a secure area where I could shower every day and sleep in a bed, looked damned good to me.

Teaching in-country orientation *was* good duty, but only lasted two weeks. Prior to my arrival, the 199th had taken a pounding and needed men everywhere. Their recon company commander and a platoon sergeant were both killed in the same week, so I volunteered to fill in until they got somebody else. A mistake. I *knew* what would come of that decision. Humping the bush during my second tour aggravated old injuries that put me in this wheelchair today.

Yeah. I know. You don't need to say it. I was dumb and thought myself bulletproof, but I really didn't care about Sidney Lee's problems. I'd seen too many American boys killed and wounded. Was I just supposed to forget about them? Did their sacrifices mean nothing? In my mind, I belonged in the field. A bad parachute drop and an enemy bullet during my first tour had left my leg in bad shape, and I figured I'd suffer in the long run, but no problem. I knew about pain, and I knew about methadone and Demerol.

→ *With drugs, Sidney developed new neural pathways to associate relief from pain. When a person experiences physical or emotional pain, which is subsequently relieved by an ingested chemical or by the brain's own endogenous opioid system, that information is stored. When a second episode of pain occurs, and relief is gained through the use of a substance, this reinforces the first drug use, and the brain expands the initial neural pathways into something akin to an unpaved country road. After repeated episodes of pain and drug-induced relief, the brain builds a superhighway. To alleviate the pain in his leg, Sidney built his own neural interstate.*

I joined a recon company that conducted operations from Hue to Saigon. For a while, we worked for a Vietnamese ranger company. Later, we went to Chu Lai when the marines got hit hard there. My team, however, had a specialized mission.

We called them "suicide ambush patrols." Usually, recon operated with five to seven-man teams and avoided contact, but our entire platoon went to the field as one team, and we *tried* to make contact. We didn't just count heads and make lists or hit and run. Our job was to find the enemy, make contact, and maintain it until reinforcements arrived. We *knew* we were going out to step into the shit, and that's why we called them suicide ambush patrols.

We were all business in the field. We traveled light and moved fast. In the bush, we only carried things that went boom or bang. Typically, offensive operations lasted five to seven days, then we returned to base camp, where I drilled the men constantly. We had lots of do's and don'ts on my team, and we spent hours dissecting booby traps, diagramming ambushes, and studying how to get into and out of an area in one piece. Then, we rested, re-supplied, and went out again.

For an infantryman in Vietnam, recon was the glam assignment, and it attracted young officers fresh from the states who thought they knew it all because they'd attended West Point. Trouble was, they didn't, and usually, they didn't last long. The first platoon leader we lost after I joined recon was killed on a mission during the first month of his tour. I liked the young man. Serious-minded and a hard worker, he was different from other officers, and his actions in and out of the field told us he cared about his job, and he cared about us. The patrol that killed him almost killed us all. We were sweeping a section of the Ho Chi Minh trail crawling with NVA. We'd worked there before and made significant contact every time.

At sundown, we dug in just off a narrow trail and set up an ambush. The bad guys moved in food and weapons at night, and frequently, propaganda officers and paymasters accompanied them. The terrain was thick, triple canopy jungle. To insure an escape route if needed, I ordered the guys to line a corridor through the underbrush with claymores. If things got too hot, on my signal they'd blow the claymores in succession, clear the path in front of us, and we'd follow them out.

Just after midnight, we heard the enemy moving, and moments later, we saw them—NVA regulars wearing canvas uniforms and helmets of woven bamboo. We hunkered down and held our breath while they walked right past our noses. I counted 127. Our patrol could do nothing against a force that size, so we lay still and prayed they wouldn't discover us.

To this day, I don't know how they saw us, but they did, and both sides opened up at the same time. It was chaos. Outnumbered 10 to 1, we were definitely in the shit and had no choice but to fight. Our only chance of survival was to lay down serious lead and hope they didn't get behind us.

Two things were in our favor: we'd taken them by surprise, and we were dug in and fired from concealment. They were exposed, couldn't find cover, and couldn't pinpoint our position in the dark. The lieutenant got on the radio and called for air support. I'd gone over coordinates with him earlier, so I wasn't worried about getting hit by our own ordinance, but at that point, it didn't seem to matter how we bought it. These soldiers were seasoned NVA troops, not a ragtag band of poorly trained VC. We had definitely bitten off more than we could chew.

The enemy quickly recovered from their surprise and went to work on us in earnest. Impressive the way they regrouped, broke into platoon-sized formations, and spread out. Then, they played a little fire and move-ment game they'd probably learned from some Chinese infantry training manual, and it worked, because they flanked us, zeroed in, and we started taking hits. At that point, I was pretty sure the last thing I'd see on this earth was a green tracer ripping through black jungle headed straight for my heart.

➤ *Sidney describes an almost universal visual traumatic stressor for Vietnam veterans. Green Communist block tracer ammunition moving towards him at supersonic speed became an integral part of Sidney's PTSD.*

I don't know how long we fought. It seemed like a year, but when the choppers arrived on the scene, things changed. The first to arrive put down rockets and 40 mm grenades in front of us. Then, two more joined in. While the chopper pilots pounded the area, we broke contact and got the hell out of there. Remember lining an escape route with claymores? That was exactly why I always took the time and trouble to do that.

Back at the rendezvous point, we regrouped and took inventory. Three men had been hit, but only one needed transport. The lieutenant reported what we'd seen and gave coordinates. A short time later, the air force arrived and conducted air strikes all along that trail, and I napped an hour listening to the comforting sound of 500-pound bombs finishing our job for us.

The next morning, we went back into the area and found the NVA base camp. Spooky to walk out of the jungle into a deserted camp and see cook fires still smoldering and half-eaten tins of rice scattered about. The NVA had dropped everything and left the area right after we broke contact the night before, because they knew air strikes would follow. The air force had bombed the whole trail. I don't know how they missed the camp. Walking between the raindrops?

Judging by size and condition, that camp had been there a while. A half dozen thatched-roof hooches contained baskets of rice, onions, and other vegetables, and another had been a command headquarters. I ordered the men to spread out and clear the area but watch for booby traps. In five minutes, we found a spider hole that led to a maze of tunnels connecting the hooches. We cleared those and found a large cache of weapons, medical supplies, uniforms, sandals, and more food.

I knew when the NVA abandoned a camp, they booby-trapped everything—discarded weapons, the entrances to the hooches, rice bags, even the bodies of their comrades. Time dragged as twelve cautious GIs moved slowly through the camp and cleared one hut at a time.

In the mid-afternoon, the lieutenant called me over to the NVA command hooch, and we entered together to search for maps or other paperwork Intel could use to identify the units operating in the area. Two sleeping mats on the floor, a chair and a wooden table against the far wall, the place was sweltering and smelled of Cosmoline and body odor. A Chinese Communist army pistol lay on the edge of the little table.

In training, that lieutenant had been told a hundred times not to pick up something without first checking for booby traps. He knew better, I knew he knew better, and who knows how this shit happens, but I turned just in time to watch him sit down and reach for a souvenir. There was nothing I could do. He had his hand on it before I could stop him. I hit the ground and covered as the blast passed over me and blew the roof off the hooch.

When the dust cleared and I regained my senses, I was pretty sure my eardrums were blown from the concussion, but that's not what bothered me. Even now, 36 years later, at this very moment, I remember every detail of what was left of that young officer lying in a twisted, bloody lump on the mud floor. By the time I crawled out of the hooch, the whole team had gathered outside and stood in a semi-circle staring at me. They knew what had happened, and it hit them hard, too. They had liked the lieutenant as much as I. He knew better, God dammit! One little mental lapse, one little break in concentration for one little second cost him his life. Senseless and wasteful. The rest of the day was tough on all of us.

You know what? People died senseless and needless deaths in Vietnam every day, but that didn't change the fact we still had a job to do. With the lieutenant gone, I became the ranking man on the team. I didn't want the men to dwell on his ugly death, so I quickly ordered them back to work inside the tunnels. Before day's end, we completed the sweep and destroyed the base camp.

➤ *From prolonged exposure to terrifying and shocking events, Sidney's brain learned to avoid and numb his feelings. His comment about the lieutenant's death is an example of how he had learned to detach from normal reactions to a dreadful stressor. In a relatively normal brain, reactions to this terrible occurrence might range from sadness to rage, but to avoid pain, Sidney compartmentalized, and subsequently, this and all the other terrors of Vietnam were never integrated into his normal memory system. Instead, they became*

Sidney's own mental and emotional booby traps that would explode on him after his war was over.

Later, Dust Off took the lieutenant's body out, and towards evening the CO radioed and told me to stay out there and poke around the NVA trail for more treasure. Great. Everything we'd seen told us we were in the wrong area at the wrong time, but the company commander hadn't asked my opinion, and I was pretty sure the matter wasn't open to debate.

The next day, I split the team into two six-man squads to reconnoiter. We marched all day but didn't get far through the thick vegetation. Late afternoon, we came across a clearing bordered on one side by rocks that jutted out from a hillside protecting the entrances to several small caves. The area had been heavily trafficked recently, so we set up in concealed positions and waited.

As we expected, when darkness fell, the NVA started moving. This time, we made sure we kept our heads down and avoided contact. As the night wore on, the place became like Grand Central Station. I couldn't believe how many North Vietnamese carried weapons and supplies in and out of those caves. They laughed and joked among themselves and generally acted like they were the only people on the planet. This time, there really was nothing to do but watch, count, and make lists. Toward morning, the hustle and bustle died down, and just before dawn, while their comrades disappeared into the jungle, a squad remained behind to clean up the area and camouflage the entrances and openings.

Recon teams are outnumbered every time they encounter the enemy. That was always the case, so that wasn't the problem. The problem was, the bad guys knew we were there, and they knew why. Tough to win a hand when all your cards are dealt face up, but I had my orders, and I wasn't about radio in and say, "Sir, I think we should reconsider this," or "We're feeling a little nervous and exposed. Maybe we should come in and talk things over." The CO wanted information, and sometimes a soldier has no choice, so two hours after sunup, I moved team two into position to provide covering fire, and then my team moved in.

People always say if you want to hide something, put it in plain sight. If that's so, what better place for an enemy supply depot than a sun-drenched hillside in the middle of a clearing? Let me tell you, none of us liked the idea of going in there. We spread out, crossed the clearing, and came upon a dozen thatched-roof lean-tos covering mounds of little canvas bags filled with rice and corn. Then, we moved under the rock face of the hill and took cover. It was eerily quiet, nothing moved in the clearing, and I knew the men were spooked. We literally smelled trouble.

After 10 minutes silence, I signaled the second team to join up, but just when they moved, the enemy opened fire. Of course, they'd waited for us. We knew they would. We returned fire immediately, but team two was stalled and couldn't close the distance. In seconds, the NVA had us pinned down on either side of the clearing. I don't know whether I have the words to describe what happened next. This *was* like the movies. Snipers in the trees with automatic weapons fired at us from three directions, and rifle fire and grenade shrapnel split the air over our heads.

I needed to do something fast, so I got on the radio and called for artillery. I'd plotted our coordinates the night before, so I signaled the men to find a hole and told arty to dump it right on us and fire for effect. The enemy knew there were only a dozen of us, and when the artillery came in, they did what I would have done. They charged.

NVA soldiers dashed through a hail of bullets and shrapnel screaming like madmen. My guys screamed back and threw everything they had. I don't know how long this went on. Time has no meaning in a firefight. I recall thinking, how strange, a face-to-face shootout in the middle of the day. Funny what comes to mind when the shit flies. The artillery walked the heat right up to us, the sky turned black, and the earth shook under my belly. Then, another thought came to mind. With the lieutenant gone, I alone was responsible for every man that died that day. What a bunch of crap that was.

In the middle of it all, battalion called and said they didn't want to fire any closer to our position and asked for instructions. I told them I didn't want them to fire any closer to our position, either, but there was no other choice. The next rounds alternated between high explosive and white phosphorous, 50 meters to our front. Good. We were making progress. I told artillery to keep bringing it and drop 10 meters with every six-round volley. Sometime during that period, two helicopter gunships called and asked us to mark our position. We fired pen flares up through the trees, and in 10 seconds, they opened fire with rockets and mini-guns.

Every man sees combat from his own perspective. Someone else might tell this story differently. I only know the next 20 minutes were hell on earth. Unless you've been there, you can't imagine the noise and heat and savage insanity. Faced with imminent destruction, even well trained men will abandon their humanity, and sometimes, things happen they don't want to talk about later. I won't go into that right now with you or anyone else. Each man deserves to tell his own story. I'll only say that finally, the NVA broke contact, and we spent the next hours taking stock and licking our wounds.

Later that night, we moved back 200 meters, dug in, and set up a makeshift perimeter. There was too much enemy activity in the vicinity for the choppers even to get our wounded, so we knew we weren't going anywhere. I ordered claymores placed 360 degrees around our position, and we settled in and hoped to be alive when morning came. A sleepless but otherwise quiet night passed slowly, and just after sunup, we went back to the clearing for extraction. While we waited, we destroyed the weapons we found and counted 60 dead NVA. Midday, the choppers came in and lifted us out.

➤ *Sidney alludes to conduct during this fierce firefight he will not describe. This could be related to both DESNOS shame-based feelings and PTSD, efforts to avoid thoughts, feelings, or conversations associated with the trauma.*

Our recon platoon was always in the middle of some kind of shit—the suicide ambush patrols lived up to their name. It seemed we were always in over our heads and screaming for help. After a while, calling artillery on our own position became routine.

A few months later, toward the end of my second tour, we traveled the claymore highway one more time. We dug in to the military crest of a hillside along a known VC supply trail, set up an ambush, made ourselves invisible, and waited for nightfall. At midnight, the VC moved into the area on parallel trails, and we were caught in the middle. We opened up on what we thought was the main group but instead was an advance patrol, and when the firing started, the main body of the VC charged us from the other trail.

In five minutes, we were so completely outnumbered, outflanked, and outgunned, I believed no amount of artillery or close air support could save our sorry asses. This was the most intense fighting I'd seen in my Vietnam experience, and I was certain I'd lose my entire patrol. With clearly no way to win, I fired a signal flare to tell the team get out of there. Once again, we'd left two men behind our position with claymores to blow a path out, and once again it was a good thing we did, because that's what saved our lives. On my signal, they blew the claymores in front of us as we ran. When we went back the following morning, the area we blew with the claymores was littered with VC bodies. In blowing our escape route, we killed more VC behind us than in front. So, my friend, if you ever find yourself in the jungle surrounded by people who want to kill you, before you dig in to fight, remember to set up your claymore escape route.

In a way, it saddens me to tell you the other things we did in Vietnam. At the time, it was okay, but I'm older now, and from hindsight, I see it as a piss-poor way to wage war. When enemy activity slowed and the commander decided he didn't have enough kills for the week, he sent us out to see what we could stir up. These were purposeless missions to make senseless contact with the enemy. We had no plan, occupied no real estate, and did no real damage to the enemy's capacity to wage war—a waste of lives on both sides. Sometimes, they loaded us into helicopters and flew low and slow through an area trying to draw fire from the ground. If the bad guys stuck their heads up, the gunships rolled in with rockets and mini-guns. Then, they dropped us in to mop up.

Sometimes, they sent us on patrol, and we'd find a little clearing, spread out, and sit down. After a while, every other man got up and walked into the bush, and then stopped. Then, the remaining men just sat there and waited for the enemy to attack. The idea was to make the enemy think the patrol was only half as strong. Dumb, but it was what we did at the whim of a commander who longed to see his face on television news.

I carried a rifle into the field until my last day in country. I even went on patrol the night before the morning I got on the plane to come home. By the time my second tour was over, I was exhausted, spent, and disillusioned. I was ready to go home, but I regretted parting with my team. I felt guilty for leaving them and knew I had left a big piece of me behind. I was emotionally and mentally drained, and I knew things would not get better in Vietnam. Nothing good would ever come from all the fighting and dying. Politicians ran that war, not generals, and a great many people died because of it.

I also knew I had only myself to blame for serving a second tour in Vietnam. Deep inside me, I had wanted to go back. Something inside had pushed me. During my first tour, I'd seen so many young men die needlessly, killed by inexperience, and every dead American boy broke my heart because chances are, with proper training and leadership, he didn't have to die. The newcomers—the guys with little training and no experience in combat—were always first to find a bullet. You know what? The whole God damned war was a God damned mess.

I had once believed the Vietnamese people wanted us there, but now I wasn't sure anymore. Over and over again, we were told the Vietnamese loved us because we'd save them from Communism. By the end of my second tour, that line of crap carried no more weight than the line the NVA tried to sell to me on that hill two years earlier. I never met a Vietnamese peasant who wanted anything but the safety of his children and enough rice to feed his family between harvests. After two years of combat, I finally understood why Vietnamese children sold bottles of soda to Americans with ground glass inside and why prostitutes put razor blades in their vaginas. I knew why if you left a jeep unguarded, you risked getting a grenade in the gas tank with tape around the handle that blew an hour later when the gasoline dissolved the adhesive. I knew why women pushed baby carriages packed with explosives into American compounds. No matter what our leaders told us, I knew above all else, the Vietnamese people wanted the foreign invaders gone from their land.

It was bad enough brave young men had to put up with all that, but worse, when they came back to the States, their fellow Americans at home called them murderers and baby-killers. To this day, I can't fully understand that. People walked around safe on the streets in the United States and called us monsters and killers. Sure, women and children got killed in Vietnam. It was war, God dammit! Right or wrong, our government put us there, and I guarantee the only thing a soldier in combat wanted was to get home in one piece.

➤ *Perhaps unconsciously, Sidney employs one of Sigmund Freud's defense mechanisms—displacement, a redirecting of emotions to a substitute target—in this case, the government. In distorting reality, Sidney's change in perception allowed for a lessening of his anxiety and guilt.*

* * *

After Vietnam, the army sent me to Michigan to advise an airborne ranger National Guard unit. As the senior enlisted advisor, my job was to make sure the unit kept up with training and stayed qualified.

My leg was pretty messed up after my second tour, so I went to Fort Benjamin Harrison for corrective surgery. Six months later, still hobbling around in pain, a civilian doctor told me the army surgeons had left bone fragments and spurs in my foot. The army doctors offered to operate a second time, but I wouldn't let them. I wanted a civilian specialist to do the procedure right. Of course, the army wouldn't authorize that. If I wanted care outside their system, I had to pay for it.

Another six months passed, and discouraged and disgusted with the military, I made the decision to get out. 10 years in the army and a sergeant first class, I'd had my fill. It was unheard of for someone with that much time invested just to walk away, and my commander didn't think I'd do it, but in late 1972, with my leg still in a cast, I turned in my gear, cleared post, and never looked back.

➤ *The medical treatment Sidney received for the wounds to his leg did not relieve his continuous, crippling pain, and true to the counterintuitive compulsions that develop with the symptoms of PTSD, he attempted escape by resigning from the army. This act set in motion many years of dysfunctional feelings and behavior that destroyed any chance he had at a normal life.*

* * *

If what I tell you next—the rest of my story—sounds vague or disjointed, it's because that's how I remember it. Twenty years of my life is buried somewhere I can't get to, can't bring into focus. Controlled by anger and crippled by pain, drugs and alcohol dominated my existence, and I spent two decades swimming against the current in a murky sea of dark urges and bad choices. Now, as I relate the events of that period, I hope you will believe me when I say I had no power to act any other way.

➤ *Sidney's description of his inability to recall much about two decades of his life is clearly the PTSD symptom of an inability to recall an aspect of the trauma.*

It is also a compelling depiction of how traumatic memory is fragmented and improperly stored in the brain.

I underwent three more corrective surgeries on my leg in three years. I wore a cast to night school and trained in computer programming. Companies needed programmers in the 1980s, so the first employer I applied to, Chrysler Corporation, hired me. Can you picture me in a corporate environment wearing slacks, a white shirt, and a tie? I couldn't, either. It didn't matter that I was good at what I did—I didn't fit in with my coworkers, so I didn't last long. A black man had no chance of gaining entry into their closed club. After a few months, I gave up trying.

➤ *Sidney had paired racism with rage in Vietnam, and the alcohol he used to escape his pain began to have a negative impact on his ability to stay employed.*

I earned a small monthly salary from weekend Guard duty (yes, even with my bum leg, I'd joined the National Guard and started jumping again), and Rose Marie's nursing job paid well. We had enough to get by, but one day, an opportunity presented itself, and I grabbed it. My Guard unit had been detailed to teach scaling and repelling procedures to members of the Michigan State Police Swat Team. As the months went by, I became friendly with the commander, and needing minorities to fill his affirmative action quotas, he asked me to apply.

I passed the entrance exams, dodged the physical, aced the rookie school, and four months later, I was out on the road as a Michigan State Trooper. If they'd known how much alcohol I drank around the clock in those days, I would have been fired on the spot, but I hid my vices, worked hard, and enjoyed being there. Six months later, however, yet another leg operation brought my law enforcement career to an end.

While I recovered, I tested for the FAA, and then went back to school and qualified as an air traffic controller. At that point in my life, the PTSD symptoms really kicked in. Prior to working as an air traffic controller, I'd declared a guarded truce with my anger, excessive drinking, and running from job to job. I believed I was the cause of my problems, and bitter disillusionment was somehow native to my personality. But now, being closed in a radar room for hours looking at little green lights on a screen presented a whole new set of problems. Flashbacks.

Sitting before a screen in a darkened room gave me the jitters, and I found it difficult to maintain concentration. Two hours into my shifts, I heard the sounds of combat in my headset, and when I talked to an airline pilot, I flashed back to talking on the radio in Vietnam. Sometimes, I believed I was calling in artillery or guiding a medivac chopper into an LZ. Then, I found myself concentrating more on the imaginary communication than on the aircraft flying through my airspace. The red lights on the walls and the green lights on the screen reminded me of red and green tracers, and I fixated on them. As time went on, I had memory problems and struggled to keep track of the aircraft in my sector. On many occasions, I made repeat calls to pilots and sometimes gave conflicting instructions.

➤ *The closed-door environment of Sidney's new job was filled with an assortment of auditory and visual stimuli that for a man with PTSD was like walking through a minefield. Each time he communicated over the radio and experienced auditory flashbacks, figuratively, he stepped on a mine, and the lighting in his work environment triggered visual flashbacks.*

Of course, I couldn't discuss these problems with anyone. Rose Marie had tried on numerous occasions to speak to me about my erratic behavior, but I blew her off. My drinking now reached levels that surprised even me. I awoke each morning with a bottle and went to bed every night with a different one. Because of my leg, I'd convinced the doctors to give me mega-doses of Darvon tablets, which I bought in big jars and stashed around the house, my car, and at work. Determined to stop the pain by taking pills and drinking booze, I was killing myself, but at that point, I didn't care.

➤ *Sidney's attempt at self-medication is common behavior in veterans with PTSD. His psychological pain, shame, and guilt were more powerful than his will to live.*

I don't need to tell you I didn't last long in air traffic control. The FAA had calculated the average burnout point for controllers at five years, and I had only three when my problems rendered me unfit for the job. With no chance for a transfer within the FAA, I landed a full time position as a recruiter with my Guard unit.

As a recruiter, I traveled the back roads and visited small towns where black men in uniform weren't welcome. At least that's how I justified packing a weapon with me everywhere I went. Carrying a firearm anywhere stateside is stupid enough, but if I was in the wrong mood and any little bad thing happened, I pulled my gun and blasted away. One night at a club, a guy asked Rose Marie to dance, and I wigged out. If she hadn't stopped me, I'd have killed him where he stood. As it was, I shot up the place and everyone dove for cover. Now, I realize how dangerously unstable I was, but at the time, I believed my behavior appropriate for an airborne ranger Vietnam combat vet. The good Lord takes care of babies and fools. I was so bad for so long, I'm lucky to be alive.

➤ *As the years progressed, Sidney presented with more debilitating and dangerous PTSD symptoms. He experienced intense psychological distress at any cues that symbolized his traumatic events, and he became hypervigilant. During his career as a recruiter in the national guard, the rage and racism his brain had paired in Vietnam exploded in violence. Stuck in his role as an airborne ranger, his response to perceived threats was wildly inappropriate for the circumstances that triggered the symptoms. Now, he was a danger to himself and society at large.*

Over the next years, I routinely shut down my recruiting office in the early afternoon, hit the bar on post, and stayed until it closed for the night. At her wit's end, Rose Marie tried to talk to me, tried to get through to me, but I wanted none of it. To this day, I don't know how or why she put up with me through 30 years of hell. My children had grown up, and I barely knew them. I had been no part of their lives. I am ashamed to say this, but years later, they told me when I came home from work, they watched to determine my mood, and they checked how I parked the car to see how much I'd drunk that night. They had learned by the signals I gave whether to try to engage their father in meaningful conversation or steer clear of a drunken, unpredictable hothead.

All through the 1980s, I slept with weapons beside the bed and under my pillow, and nightmares haunted me every night. Horrific terrors, they were always violent but not always centered in Vietnam. I rarely saw faces, but I always saw fighting. Many nights, too petrified to move, I lay still and sneaked my eyes open, afraid whatever was out there would see me move and kill me. Sometimes, I caught a dream just when it started and forced myself awake. Then, I got up and walked around the house awhile, but inevitably, when I lay back down, the dream started again, right where it had ended. It was like being forced to watch a violent, bloody video game with a hateful, malevolent operator at the controls.

➤ *Posttraumatic stress disorder had reduced Sidney Lee, airborne ranger and veteran of two bloody combat tours, to a man too afraid to open his eyes in the safety of his own bed.*

Daytime was little better. If I drove past a park or glimpsed a billboard that depicted greenery, I was immediately whisked back to Vietnam. In a way, the flashbacks were worse than the night terrors. When a nightmare ended, at least I woke up in bed. During the day, I could not account for the missing time I spent flashing back. Frequently, I'd "come to" after a flashback in my car or in a restaurant and not have a clue how I got there, what I did, or whom I encountered while away.

➤ *Sidney now experienced perhaps the most frightening PTSD symptom, dissociative flashbacks. Imagine living in a world where you find yourself lost to bygone horrors simply by viewing a billboard. For combat veterans with PTSD, visual triggers are everywhere, and if untreated, render them unable to navigate successfully in society.*

In 1990, I retired from the National Guard. Six months earlier, I'd been diagnosed with sarcoidosis by doctors at the veterans hospital in Washington, D.C. In my case, it had attacked my lungs and nervous system and caused me to lose control temporarily of my hands and legs. Not much was known about the disease at the time, but the people in D.C. told me about specialists practicing at the VA hospital in Tacoma, Washington, and recommended I see them.

The Tacoma doctors conducted physical and psychological examinations then immediately put me into a PTSD program and assigned a counselor. The treatment for sarcoidosis was Prednisone, so I took heavy doses, and I saw the PTSD counselor three hours a day, three times a week for two years. I wanted to get better, so I stopped drinking and quit taking all pain medication.

➤ *Sidney's success in stopping his substances abuse without chemical dependence counseling speaks to the reality of his self-medicating for PTSD and not alcoholism or drug addiction.*

Today, I'm still in PTSD counseling. I liked the Pacific Northwest, so I took permanent residency in Tacoma. The nightmares mostly have gone away but come back now and then. My sarcoidosis is still with me, and I've lost the use of my legs. If I have to, I can get around on crutches, but mostly I rely on this wheelchair.

I wish I could finish this story by telling you the U.S. government was generous and forthcoming with my requests for care and disability, but I can't. Talk about a throwaway. Uncle Sam was happy enough to call me *brother* when I did his dirty work for him. As long as I pulled the trigger, he liked me enough to award me a Silver Star and 13 Bronze Stars for Valor, but when time came to help with the physical and mental injuries I'd sustained in his service, he acted like I didn't exist. The government's official policy for disability claims is to accept the word of a decorated combat veteran—that's in the regulations—but even to this day, they do not.

I fought for years for my disability rights. Ultimately, I wrote the President of the United States, the Chairman of the Veterans Committee for Funding, and the Secretary of Veterans Affairs. I sent copies of my records and all supporting documentation. It took years, but I finally succeeded in getting them to acknowledge my disability.

With that mission accomplished, I realized how difficult the procedure must be for a person of color with an even greater disability than mine, or a person with fewer resources or perhaps less education. How would that veteran wade through the government's bureaucratic tangle of arsenic and red tape? How many others were out there in the cold struggling with dark forces they did not understand? If our government made getting help so difficult, I decided the best thing I could do was everything I could, and I began by helping veteran friends file claims.

Three months later, I met Clarence Slaughter, Deputy Regional Director for Veterans Affairs. He told me a group of black veterans in Tacoma needed help getting organized and asked whether I would be interested. He said they met Saturdays to discuss issues facing black veterans and encouraged me to attend. To me, this seemed a worthwhile cause. An organized group has a better chance of helping others than a loose collection of concerned individuals. Also, the senator from my state told me congressional groups often work in partnership with non-governmental veterans organizations to get things done that neither can accomplish on its own.

I met with the group and found good men whose interests and passions paralleled mine, so I set to work filing charters, applying for tax free status—things an organization needs to be formally recognized. We call ourselves the African American PTSD Association, and I am president. Since our founding, the members have worked together to secure the necessary legal and educational accreditation from the State, the Department of Veterans Affairs, and Congress. Also, we've acquired the individual training to serve as Veterans Service Officers.

The African American PTSD Association has done marvelous work over the years, but we are badly under funded. I have paid for a large percentage of the association's activities from my personal savings, and I petition the State of Washington constantly for funding to continue our work. Currently, we are attempting to expand to other states. In Washington, we now process 150 to 200 veterans a month, but receive only $60,000 a year from the State—30 dollars per veteran, not enough even to cover paperwork expenses. Our staff is composed entirely of volunteers, and if we never paid a staff member, never hired a single minimum wage employee, we'd still need four times the amount the State gives us to continue providing services according to demand.

I always thought I'd like to be repaid someday for the money I've spent keeping AAPTSD afloat, but now, I don't expect to see any of it. I continue to support the group with my own money, but my savings are nearly depleted, and I don't know how much longer I can keep going. The future of the organization is very much in doubt. Will political leaders ever learn that wars cost a society a whole hell of a lot more than just bombs and bullets?

—Sidney Alvin Lee

CHAPTER 5

Lance Johnson
Hawaii
U.S. Army Artillery

✤ *Under threat, higher animals experience an immediate physiological reaction commonly referred to as the fight or flight phenomenon. However, the brain can trigger a third action to protect the animal and preserve life—the freeze response. Akin to the other responses to threat of imminent danger, all three are generated in the brain's limbic system, specifically the amygdala. A tiny, almond-shaped neurostructure, the amygdala regulates the emotions associated with fear and anxiety. The amygdala can be associated with the emotion of pleasure but also at the opposite end of the spectrum, the pleasure derived from aggression. Studies show the larger the amygdala, the more aggressive the species.*

As I look back on my life, the foremost thing I remember after Vietnam was my seething rage at our government for getting us into that mess in Southeast Asia. It took a long time and a great deal of professional help for me to finally come to the conclusion that pure anger was eating me up inside. I'll tell anyone who wants to listen. Powerful people—men who wouldn't have the guts to get near a battlefield—misused our generation for a shameful purpose, and to this day, society pays the price.

I've found peace of mind—not complete and not all the time—but I'm better now. I live in Hawaii with a woman who loves me, and I've reunited with my son. I still go to counseling, and the doctors adjust my medication when the Prozac quits working. Jesus, man, it's time I experience a little joy. I'm 66 years old, and I've spent half my life in an emotional wilderness.

I don't know why posttraumatic stress hits some guys harder than others. A great many combat veterans aren't bothered by their wartime experiences, but I can't account for them. I can only tell you about the paths I felt compelled to travel in life. A few years ago, I found a way to tell my story to my son. I think he understands his father now, and I believe he's forgiven me. Maybe, another veteran's son or daughter will read this and gain insight or develop a level of empathy, perhaps even forbearance for the father who was never there. Maybe, I can help that way.

* * *

My whole life, I never considered myself special or anything but ordinary. I entered the army by way of the ROTC program at the University of Idaho. That was okay with me. You see, the Vietnam build-up hadn't started yet, and public opinion of the armed services was still positive.

We lived in a different nation then. The post-WWII glow still fueled our sense of moral superiority, and Cold War fears fired our patriotism. Right or wrong, Americans believed in the institutions of America, and if you had doubts, John Wayne, Gary Cooper, and Randolph Scott would set you straight. In those days, a young man swore his allegiance to God and Country with pride. All that came naturally to me, and I enjoyed the ROTC drills, the uniforms, and the camaraderie. I received my college degree and was commissioned as a second lieutenant in the U.S. Army on the same day. What could be bad about that?

My earliest memories are of my father, the classic, old-fashioned military man. He went on active duty the day of the attack on Pearl Harbor and served six years as an infantry officer and military policeman. Dad wasn't a big man, but he stood ramrod straight, carried himself with authority, and people listened when he spoke. As a youngster, I recall he seemed always in his pinks and greens and Sam Browne belt and always in charge. To my young eyes, my father looked 10 feet tall.

➤ *Lance describes his father in terms that present not so much a close, nurturing paternal figure but an officer with a rigid military bearing, often absent for extended periods of time. Lance likely did not have the intensity and extent of paternal involvement necessary for optimum personality development. This dearth of paternal role modeling and support may have rendered Lance less emotionally resilient in later years.*

Mother and I couldn't travel with Dad on all his assignments, but when we did, we rode trains, a mode of transportation almost completely in America's past. In a way it's too bad. Modern air travel lacks the style of passenger trains and the potential for adventure. In addition to her many other talents, Mother was an excellent seamstress. To show support for the war effort, she cut down to tyke-size one of Dad's old uniforms, and

I wore it when we traveled. The trains were full of service men shipping out for overseas, and I spent hours walking from car to car showing off for the real soldiers. I was a hit. The servicemen gave me thumbs up and trinkets and good luck charms. The little-boy soldier in the spotlight and the center of attention—for a five-year-old, it didn't get any better.

Dad's last military assignment was commanding the Italian POW stockade at Camp Weingarten, Missouri, a place that later achieved notoriety, not for anything the prisoners did, but because for a while, Art Moilanan was stationed there, the Boogie Woogie Bugle Boy of Company B.

Sometimes, I accompanied my father to the prison. Weingarten was a huge camp ringed by wire and watched over by soldiers in 12 guard towers equipped with .50 caliber machine guns. The first time Dad and I pulled up to the big front gates, I remember thinking it was like a sprawling summer camp for young men. Indeed, many of the prisoners were very young—some only 15. For the Italians, life at the camp was generally uneventful. Many worked on local farms for 80 cents a day, welcome employment that provided a break in the monotony. The prisoners always told me to imitate them and save the money I earned to help my family.

I never met a German POW, so I had only a few vague stereotypes for comparison, but even as a child, I believed the Italians were more easygoing and quicker to laugh. They organized soccer leagues, camp orchestras, and theater groups, and tried to make Missouri seem like Italy. Also, in keeping with the Italian love of art, many talented prisoners painted, sculpted, and wrote poetry. Once, a trustee in Dad's office carved a battleship and a submarine out of hardwood and presented them to my father. They were beautiful works of art, and we kept them around our house for years. Later, Dad gave a photo to a prisoner who did a pencil drawing of me at age six. We still have that sketch in the family.

❧ *In his youth, Lance discovered the "enemy" was just like him, and this knowledge would have a major impact on the formation of his guilt for his dealings with the enemy decades later in Vietnam.*

At Camp Weingarten, we lived in the civilian community because the army hadn't yet constructed living quarters for dependent families. A rural area of Southern Missouri, St. Genevieve County clung to the best and worst of the Old South—friendly people, family values, and racism and xenophobia. Our family employed what the locals called a "black Mammy." A large woman overflowing with kindness and good will, Sarah took me with her shopping and seemed always to look over my shoulder with a smile on her big, round face. I realize now the poor woman was in a socioeconomic trap and no doubt yearned for a better life, but things were different then, and as a youngster, all I knew for sure was she really cared about me. When we left Camp Weingarten, Sarah gave me a little black doll, which I kept for many years.

* * *

After WWII, we settled in Idaho Falls, and Dad took a job selling stocks and bonds, which required travel to service clients. Mother ran the household when he was away. Of German-Dutch heritage, she was a blend of angelic mother-dear and the aloof but sensitive love-you-from-afar type. By today's standards, she might appear frigid, but inside, that was not the case at all. She rarely spoke of love and eschewed overt displays of affection, but that was okay with me. I didn't need a lot of hugging and kissing to know she loved me.

➥ *Lance described his father as ramrod straight and always in charge—observations illustrative of an emotionally unavailable and rigid parental figure. For much of his childhood, Lance was with his mother, whom he also portrays as rather emotionally closed. She offered young Lance little of the intimate, physical contact a developing child requires to feel physically safe and psychologically resilient.*

Mom was exceedingly talented. I remember sitting with my grandparents by the radio on Saturday nights listening to her sing. An accomplished opera singer, she traveled with a professional company, but when they performed close by, Dad took me to the theater, we sat in the front row, and I was amazed by the lavish costumes and live orchestra, and in the middle of it all, my mother. Quite a site for an eight-year-old. Later, Mother took charge of the community concert series, where various well-known singers traveled to perform in small towns. After the performances, the artists frequently came to our house for dinner and conversation. One night, I sat at the table wide-eyed and speechless next to Mario Lanza, a huge thrill for a young boy. Mom still sings. She's 93 now and complains she can't hit the notes she used to, but I think her voice is as beautiful as ever.

Since I'm telling you all this, I guess I should tell you about my grandparents. They lived only a half-mile away, and when Mother traveled, they watched over me. I spent a great deal of time with them, and as their only grandchild, they lavished me with love and attention.

Granddad had moved to Idaho from New York in the 20s and invested in potatoes. When the war started, the market went crazy, and he made a pile of money. During the spring and summer months, Grandfather played baseball with me in the vacant lot across the street, and in winter, he flooded the backyard with water and taught me to ice skate. A natural athlete, as a young man in New York, he played hockey with a semi-pro team. As a child, I spent countless nights spellbound while my grandmother held me in her lap, and we listened to stories about how Granddad's team traveled from town to town in horse-drawn sleighs and racked up season after season of hard-fought victories. I don't give advice, but if I did, I'd tell every parent to make sure his kids get to know their grandparents.

➤ *The happy childhood Lance remembers was largely the result of the relationship he had with his grandparents. A loving, dependable male role model, his grandfather gave Lance much of the paternal nurturing his own father was unable to provide.*

I already told you I never considered myself special. Like most other boys, I was mediocre in school and crazy for sports. Today, when we think of kids getting into mischief, we think of drugs, petty theft, graffiti, and rejection of parental authority. Believe it or not, the mischief I made as a boy included tipping over outhouses, throwing snowballs, and playing hooky—Mark Twain stuff.

Our town had few organized school sports, but everyone skied. The local radio station organized a ski club for high school students, and on Saturday mornings, we all loaded into a bus and headed up the mountain. We skied all day, and then rode the bus back down the mountain after dark. By the time I finished school, the club had three buses, and I had become an advanced instructor.

In high school, I dated the class secretary, a pretty girl with red hair and an outgoing personality. Cindy could have been class president, except she wore glasses, an outward symbol of genetic imperfection in the days before contact lenses. Worse, hers had red plastic frames that curled up and came to points at the top. In those days, that little accoutrement automatically placed her in the category of *smart*, and smart girls only got elected to positions nobody else wanted. Cindy was among the most popular girls in school, but poor eyesight dictated the duties she was deemed suited for.

I don't know what Cindy saw in a tall, skinny introvert, but somehow, out of the white noise that was her social life, she decided I was all right and picked me out of the herd. Cindy ran with the class elite, people who'd never dream of throwing a snowball or tipping over an outhouse. When I hung with that crowd, I stayed pretty much in the background. I didn't really have much to say to the school swells, and they were not at all interested in me. They considered Cindy's fondness for me just another hiccup in her genetic assembly. Once, at a school dance, the class president noticed me leaning against the wall while Cindy flitted around the room. He walked over, looked me up and down, and then asked me how things were in the chemistry club. I knew the guy was being an asshole, but all I did was stammer something stupid and walk away. Later, I heard him repeat that story to a crowd of his smirking buddies. Whatever the reasons, like most other high school infatuations, Cindy's interest in me eventually waned, we drifted apart, and I never saw her again.

On my own, I was more comfortable with the crowd that hung out in the school parking lot, smoked cigarettes, and talked cars. In time, my adolescent social life became like a carnival house of mirrors. Each way I turned, I was somebody different, and I developed methods for moving unnoticed between the groups. I never knew whether I was truly accepted by any of those disparate people, nor did I care.

➻ *The skill of managing interpersonal relations served Lance well in his role as an army officer but eventually symbolized a terrible deceit in which he played the lead actor and which haunted him for the rest of his life.*

I went to the University of Idaho because both my parents went there. My father had a degree in business, so that looked like the way for me to go, too. Although only an average student, I was good in math and had a passing interest in chemical engineering. College life was good for me, and the years passed quickly. When I graduated, my parents came to the ceremonies. After four years of ROTC, I'd earned my reserve officer commission, and I remember the lump in my throat when my folks pinned the shiny gold lieutenant's bars on my shoulders. Winter, 1963, I had my degree in business, and I wore the uniform of the U.S. Army. I had become my father.

* * *

During college, I dated a girl from Idaho Falls, and three weeks after graduation, Joan and I married and moved to Missoula, Montana. I had six months before I reported for active duty, so we took a small apartment, and I worked as a fireman on the Northern Pacific Railroad. Firemen rode on the left side of the engine car, provided an extra set of eyes for the engineer, and monitored the instrument board for blown fuses. Our route took us from Missoula over the Continental Divide into Idaho. It was like stepping back in time—long nights pushing through frozen wilderness, and when weather came, heavy gray clouds blanketed the hillsides, and then opened and filled the valleys with snow. Early on, the engineers had told me of a strange, hypnotic flicker vertigo induced by the headlamp shining through blowing snow. I experienced this first-hand when, during a particularly heavy storm, the plough on the front of our engine threw snow and ice 50 feet on either side, and for hours, the night sky was alive with millions of flashing points of light streaking past. Hypnotic, indeed.

Time came to go on active duty, so Joan and I packed our little apartment and moved to Fort Sill, Oklahoma, a big training center for the army and marines, where I spent six months learning basic artillery. I'd been commissioned in that branch after ROTC, but never had any real, hands-on training, and I found it fascinating.

Artillery is indirect fire. A rifleman points at what he wants to hit, but the big guns fire in an arc, like shooting a basketball. The coordinates came in over the radio from a forward observer on the ground actually looking at the target. The fire direction control center used a table of formulas (or sometimes a slide rule) to turn that information into deflection and elevation settings. Also, depending on the gun, they calculated how many powder bags to place into each round. Those numbers then went to the gun crews who applied the settings to the artillery piece and fired the round. The lieutenant's job was make sure all this happened properly. There's a lot at stake when you give an order to fire, and you'd better make sure you've done it right.

We drilled with 105s, 155s, 175s, and 8 inch guns. As an officer, I showed up for work in the morning and went home in the afternoon. We'd rented an apartment in Lawton, Joan taught school, we had a large circle of friends, and we were happy.

After training, my first regular duty assignment was with a newly formed battalion at Fort Sill equipped with M-107s, the latest self-propelled 175mm guns. Originally designed to move around the battlefield and provide a long-range umbrella of protection and destruction, M-107s looked like tanks but were fast and fired a 120-pound projectile 33 kilometers. Our unit consisted of three firing batteries, a headquarters battery, and a logistics and supply battery. Each firing battery consisted of four platoons of 25 men and one 175mm gun. I commanded four guns and 100 men.

After several months training, the entire battalion deployed to a huge Army installation in Bamberg, Germany. Joan and I welcomed this change of scenery, and we quickly started enjoying life in another culture.

Thirty miles north of Nuremberg, Bamberg had been a troop garrison for 1,000 years. In 1964, its function was to stop a Russian invasion of Germany through Czechoslovakia. Our daily routine consisted of endless battle simulations and maneuver operations. Weekends, Joan and I toured the countryside, hung out at the officers club, and enjoyed the company of friends.

Change being the only constant in military service, in just over two years, I received orders back to the United States to join a newly formed air defense unit at Fort Bliss, Texas. Nicknamed "Dusters," our weapons were 1940s-era 40mm guns mounted on open tanks. Originally designed to shoot strafing airplanes in WWII and Korea, the Duster's new role in Vietnam would be perimeter defense, convoy support, and sometimes, if absolutely necessary, direct-fire cannons on the skirmish line. Highly mobile and with a crew of six, Dusters were equipped with twin 40mm cannons that fired 120 self-detonating rounds per minute to a range of 10,000 meters. This was a real close-infantry support weapon, and we trained not in conventional, European theater tactics, but for guerilla warfare in jungle terrain, and for the first time, I saw myself eventually assigned to fight in Vietnam. Our Duster unit was formed, equipped, and ready, and then, don't ask me why, but in its infinite wisdom, the army decommissioned the battalion two months before deployment.

Joan and I knew I would have to serve a tour in Vietnam before I left the army, so we talked about it and decided then was a good time to get it over with. I wasn't getting any younger and didn't care to put off the inevitable any longer, so we talked the whole thing out, and I requested a transfer.

* * *

In 1967, when I arrived in Vietnam, I was already a captain. After my in-country orientation, I received orders to liaison with the Riverine Force, a joint army-navy operation in the Mekong Delta. I was assigned to an artillery battalion equipped with 105 Howitzers mounted on barges designed for towing up and down the rivers behind the armored boats of the brown-water navy. When the navy ran into something messy and needed artillery support, they tied the nearest barge to the shore and let the army blast away. Although officially headquartered in Dong Tam, I spent all my time running up and down the Mekong River on an LST.

My job was to coordinate the artillery barges to make sure the troops had fire support where and when needed. I worked with a naval communications officer, and after operational planning sessions, we coordinated the call signs and frequencies. I enjoyed my job, and navy food definitely was better than army. Unfortunately, it only lasted six weeks. Much to my chagrin, my old battalion commander from the 40mm unit in Fort Bliss discovered I was in country and commandeered me. He commanded the Fifth Battalion, 2nd Artillery, a Duster unit headquartered just outside Bien Hoa, and was on the lookout for officers familiar with the machinery. I don't know what strings he pulled, but in two days, I said goodbye to my cushy navy duty and was on my way to the field.

5th Battalion was headquarted in relatively civilized Bien Hoa, but all four firing batteries were deployed out in support of various division artilleries. I was given command of a battery supporting the 25th Infantry Division at Cu Chi, two hours west of Bien Hoa, halfway to Cambodia. Because of its mobility, mechanized artillery provided convoy support, perimeter defense, and skirmish line direct fire. In short, we did anything the 25th Infantry Division asked of us.

In addition to the 16 Dusters in my battery, I also commanded a detachment of 12 quad 50s mounted on five-ton trucks. Better suited for operating in heavily vegetated areas, the quads were often airlifted into jungle terrain for firebase support. Also, we had eight jeep-mounted search-lights. My augmented battery consisted of 36 fighting vehicles, six lieutenants, and just over 200 men; however, we never fought as a unit. The 25th had troops all over western III Corps, and we often found ourselves split into platoons of four Dusters each assigned to various far-flung firebases.

Cu Chi, home to one of the largest army installations in Vietnam, was 75 kilometers northwest of Saigon, adjacent to what they called War Zone C, the heart of VC and North Vietnamese controlled territory. In the early 60s, when the army built the base camp, the goal was to place American troops in the path of the enemy and interdict forces that may gather and move against Saigon. I don't think the army knew it at the time, but they built the entire installation on top of a huge enemy tunnel complex—an underground city serviced by hundreds of kilometers of tunnels stretching all the way to the Cambodian border. Ho Chi Minh's guerilla forces had begun constructing the tunnels in the early 1940s during the Japanese occupation and expanded the network over the following two decades.

Think of the tunnels as a web—a complex of interconnected service and supply stations along a grid of byways—underground towns more than mere tunnels. Dug with primitive hand tools, the tunnels had technologies like underwater trap doors, fresh air ventilation, and ingeniously concealed exhaust vents to disperse cooking smoke. The network reached several stories deep and was home to 10,000 people, many who went years without seeing daylight and came out only at night to tend crops and gather supplies. The tunnels included first-aid posts and surgical hospitals, huge chambers for weapons and ammunition, food storage, kitchens, dorms, classrooms, and even small theatres. Countless Vietnamese couples married, reared their children, and grew old underground.

Because of my battery's tremendous firepower, the 25th positioned us on the perimeter facing the Cu Chi tunnels. Enemy ground assaults and rocket attacks came from that direction, and our job was to lay down the heavy metal.

The 40mm Duster was put-together from a WWII Walker Bulldog tank with the turret removed and replaced with an open, tub-shaped structure made of steel. Its cannons loaded from the top, so nothing could be overhead that might restrict movement. As a result, helmets were the crew's only armor protection. Each Duster carried two 40mm cannons, and each gun fired 120 rounds per minute. Also, a .50 caliber machine gun was mounted on the tub, and the gunner traversed a full 360 degrees. In open terrain, the Duster traveled at 45 miles per hour and carried a vehicle commander, two loaders, a gunner, and driver. A formidable weapon for its day. In that environment, the Duster brought a lot of firepower to the party.

Duster platoons spent most of their time in the field supporting infantry units. Sometimes, my battery was scattered around seven or eight different locations in the division's area of operations. When the infantry was on the move, we interspersed throughout the convoy and provided ambush protection. When they set up camp, we deployed at the perimeter corners.

As battery commander, I needed to monitor activities, so three times a week, I was allocated a helicopter to get around and see the troops. My NCOs were the best in the business and did just fine without me, but I think they were glad to see the CO out in the field with the troops, even for only a few hours every other day. I always brought soda, beer, and mail, so the guys were usually happy to see me. After I'd been on the job a few weeks, an enemy RPG hit one of our Dusters, and the battery received a replacement. Later, the motor sergeant repaired the damage and converted it into a command track, and that became my ground transportation for the rest of my tour.

My battery's first major campaign was Operation Yellowstone. Begun in December 1967, Yellowstone was a massive offensive into an area known as the Parrot's Beak in Tay Ninh province. Within sight of Cambodia, the North Vietnamese army staged fresh troops there and stored huge amounts of weapons, ammunition, and other war supplies. We convoyed with elements of the 25th Division into the area and set up a base camp on a little rise overlooking the border.

A couple days after we arrived, I received orders to take a platoon of Dusters to a Special Forces firebase located right on the border. En route, I wasn't sure what to expect or even what to do when we got there. I assumed they expected trouble and wanted our big guns for perimeter defense. We arrived on station two hours before sundown, and a squad of ARVN soldiers came out to lead us through the wire.

That camp was the strangest place I ever saw. Star-shaped and much smaller than I expected, it was a maze of trenches and sandbagged bunkers covered with canvas tarps or sheets of corrugated tin and surrounded by a little ocean of concertina wire studded with claymore mines and trip flares. In the center of the firebase, two 105-howitzers had been lowered into holes and ringed with sandbags.

When we entered, Vietnamese people—men, women, and children, some dressed in rags, others in uniform—emerged from the bunkers, leaned on their M-16s, and stared while we struggled to maneuver our heavy machinery in the confined space. As we shut down, an American wearing a green beret stood up on a pile of sandbags and waved.

It was more like a Wild West town on the edge of Indian country than a military installation. I was shocked to find the Americans not dressed in camouflaged fatigues or wearing rank insignia—unheard of in a combat situation. Three Special Forces guys, Vietnamese girlfriends on their arms, lived in a bunker, empty booze bottles floor to ceiling and only a ragtag band of Vietnamese paramilitary between them and the Cambodian border. If you saw it in a movie, you wouldn't believe it. What were they doing there? Surely the enemy could take out that camp anytime they wanted.

The team commander, a captain with thin blonde hair and a perpetual smile, told me they'd patrolled there several months, but with Operation Yellowstone underway, they expected things to close in on them very soon. They wanted to break camp the next day, and asked for cover getting out.

The following morning, I took the captain aside, told him my battery would be back working that area soon, and asked him what he knew about enemy locations and where to look for ambushes. He unfolded my map and wrote out 10-digit coordinates. "A huge tree stands alongside the road here," he said, "two kilometers outside this camp. On the days you escort convoys through that area, send a patrol ahead and drop a case of scotch and a couple cases of beer behind that tree. Do that, and I guarantee you'll not get hit."

For the rest of Operation Yellowstone, every time we convoyed that road, I took that Special Forces captain's advice, and we were never once ambushed. To me, this was the ultimate irony—in a huge battle for control of a strategically important area, men fought and died every day, and yet we bought safety with 100 dollars worth of booze. I wondered why we fought at all. Why not just sit down with the Communists and get drunk together?

Yellowstone lasted months. American ground forces were restricted from entering Cambodia at the time, so the NVA attacked, and then easily retreated to safety on the other side of the border. My battery sustained a number of casualties. Night after night, the enemy fired rockets and mortars with pinpoint accuracy from close range then followed up with infantry assaults on the perimeter. Later, we found out many of the defensive positions the Americans occupied in that area had been used before in prior engagements as far back as the French occupation. The enemy had pre-plotted coordinates and could walk the mortars right in. There were lots of casualties, and too many young men on both sides died.

Once, I was with one of my platoons in a forward camp typical of the temporary artillery firebases of the time. Concertina wire encircled a no-man's land of claymore mines and trip flares. Just inside, listening posts ringed the perimeter every 40 meters, and inside that, more wire, bunkers, and sandbags. A Duster was positioned at each corner of the perimeter. The infantry frequently conducted search and destroy missions that lasted five to ten days, and when they were out on patrol, the remaining artillery personnel were responsible for providing fire support and defending the base camp. I don't remember the exact date—sometime in February, I think—the infantry was on patrol when, in the middle of the night, a battalion-sized unit of the North Vietnamese army hit us.

Better trained and supplied than the VC, they outnumbered us three to one, and they'd clearly done their homework. They must have done chalkboard rehearsals for days, because when they hit us, they assaulted the outer wire at all the places we had the least firepower. Once inside the wire, they rotated into position and charged. From atop my Duster parked in the center of the camp, I saw exactly how they did it, and for me, it was like a movie playing out before my eyes.

We threw everything we had, but they kept coming, and it didn't take long for things to get serious. Flares popped, cast an eerie, yellow aura over the camp, and illuminated an ugly picture—hundreds of Communist troops advancing on our inner perimeter. Enemy mortars thudded from close range, fell straight down from high overhead, and exploded upon impact. Huge jagged shards of shrapnel whined through the air and ripped into sandbags and earthen berms. Rockets and RPGs flew everywhere. The NVA were winning, and everyone in camp knew we were in deep trouble. When the situation got really nasty, the 105 crews lowered gun barrels to zero-elevation and fired Flechette rounds. My dusters poured out 40 mm cannon rounds at maximum rate, and we fired our .50s until the barrels glowed red. Just after midnight, the NVA breeched the inner wire.

Now, the whole situation became very unstable, so I moved my Duster to the edge of the perimeter. My big guns were inoperative, but I hoped to do some damage with my .50. Surreal, fascinating, mesmerizing to watch the NVA in gray uniforms and African safari hats swarm through our line, firing on the move. Funny, as I think back on that moment, what I remember most is my surprise at how much bigger they were than their VC cousins, and I thought it curious to see women ammo bearers follow the men through the wire.

I rotated the turret toward the biggest hole in our perimeter and fired my .50 at anything that moved. Hard to say how long the fighting went on. I fired hundreds of rounds. The NVA were everywhere, and one must have moved in behind me, because when his RPG hit my Duster, it blew me out of the tub, and I landed on my belly in the mud 50 feet away.

Dazed and in shock, my ears rang, and I couldn't move. I could not will my body to do anything. Face pressed into the mud, I looked up, and when my eyes focused, I saw them run past me, saw their black sandals made from old truck tires, uniform pants muddy and stained, saw them fire their AK-47s, and then move on. In the heat of the battle, they thought

I was dead. Sometime later, our guys got the upper hand and finally pushed them back through the wire. I don't remember any of that, but it was still dark when they found me and called for a medic.

➤ *The phenomena of fight, flight, or freeze are part of what has been termed the "general-purpose defense response control network," and react in response to signs of danger encoded in unpleasant sights, sensations, or smells. Anger, avoidance, and defensiveness are emotions activated by the amygdala, and all three are primary symptoms of PTSD. It is believed the origin and function of the amygdala began with the early fishes and activated ancestral signs of distress to facilitate rapid choices for action. Lance experienced a major traumatic event that night on the Cambodian border, and his reaction was automatic and self-preserving.*

This is the really strange part. When I came to, I found I wasn't seriously hurt. A piece of track from the RPG explosion had landed on my leg and bruised it pretty badly, but that was it. Who knows how that shit can happen to a guy, and he comes away without a scratch? I was lucky. A whole lot of men got hurt that night.

➤ *Lance was wrong in his belief he had not been seriously wounded. The bruises on his leg paled in insignificance compared to the injury his brain suffered during the ferocious battle for the camp. During that late night horror, he met the first criteria for a diagnosis of PTSD—the threatened death of self—and he reacted with helplessness. The evolutionary survival mechanism of freezing saved his life. Had his brain chosen one of the other two options—fight or flight—most likely, Lance would have been killed.*

The next morning, we went out to mop up, get a body count, and re-fortify our perimeter. You see enough action and after a while, you can tell by how the bodies are bunched which were killed by the 105 Flechette rounds and which got hit by the Dusters. Using the 40mm cannons in direct fire, gunners aimed at the ground in front of the advancing troops to achieve maximum shrapnel spread after detonation. Invariably, when 40mm hit the enemy, we found only pieces—part of a leg sticking out of boot, an arm, or the occasional skull. That morning, we saw firsthand the killing power of our M-107 Dusters, and we spent the whole day outside the perimeter cleaning up the mess.

➤ *Even though his conscious mind saw only dismembered and defiled NVA bodies, Lance was further traumatically stressed by the implied threat to his own physical integrity. The mess he speaks of so nonchalantly might well have been his own scattered remains, and while sorting through the carnage, his brain faithfully recorded the images and his own bodily sensations.*

* * *

Originally designed to shoot down strafing aircraft, the Duster fired a 40mm cannon round designed to detonate at 2800 meters. When used in a direct fire role, high-velocity, low-trajectory rounds sometimes skipped off the surface of the ground and detonated far beyond the target—like skipping a stone over a pond. Sometimes, rounds traveled twice as far as the gunner intended, ploughed into villages, destroyed hooches, and killed and wounded civilians.

I'm going to tell you something you're not going to believe, but I swear it's true. The army came up with a program to pay money to Vietnamese civilians for loss of life, limb, or property resulting from American operations near their village. The brass called them "salation payments." I guess they thought bribes would win the hearts and minds of the Vietnamese people. As battery commander, it was my job to deliver the cash.

In Vietnam, when a village took a stray round, we heard about it several days later, after the Vietnamese inventoried their victims and reported up through the province chiefs. Then, I got into a jeep with a Vietnamese translator and a bag of money, traveled out to the village, and paid off the parents or loved ones for their losses.

The army gave the province chiefs a menu—a list of prices we paid in local currency. For example, destroyed hooches were the equivalent of $25. If someone lost an arm or leg, the price was double that. Most expensive was the death of a child, $100 for a boy, and $200 for a girl.

On the appointed day, the village elders gathered in the road to greet me. The translator, an ARVN usually from the same province and often known by the villagers, offered a few pleasantries, and then dispensed the usual dogma about VC terrorists and how patriotic Vietnamese did not support their evil. That done, one at a time, the elders presented me to the families with claims.

This part is really strange, and I never got used to it. The people treated me like a visiting dignitary. Even when torn by grief, the Vietnamese peasant farmers invited me into their hooches, where we sat on bamboo mats or rickety old chairs while they served tea and cookies and chatted about the weather or the rice harvest. Very often, the injured family member lay bandaged in a corner staring silently at me, the 500-pound gorilla in the room.

❖ *This grotesque situation stripped away any psychological defense Lance could have maintained against the guilt he felt for the senseless killing of noncombatants—a dichotomy of the Vietnam War that contributed to his later psychological and emotional disintegration. Destroying the very people they fought to protect pained American soldiers like Lance.*

It was always the same—we sipped tea, and they smiled. I carried a speech provided to me by headquarters, which I then read aloud, apologizing on behalf of the governments of the Republic of Vietnam and the United States and expressing regret for the losses the family suffered. Then, I produced an envelope, which, without making eye contact, the family accepted and discreetly put away.

Can you imagine? Can you imagine sipping tea in a man's living room while you pay him for killing his child? More money than those Vietnamese peasants had ever seen? Sure, but try to imagine the situation reversed. What's the life of your child worth? What's adequate remuneration for a loving spouse blown to bits by a 40mm cannon round?

➤ *Lance's military duty and his childhood involvement with the Italian prisoners caused him to question the war and his role in it.*

How could I know what they felt inside? I couldn't even get hold of my own feelings. I had caused the problem. I aimed the gun and pulled the trigger, and now I was at the crime scene trying to do something for the survivors. I felt like an actor in a play written by Satan. A sad, strange, and confusing experience for me, it was by far the most ugly and unpleasant part of my job as battery commander, and I still haven't justified it in my mind or heart. I still wonder whether the Vietnamese believed the money I gave them was fair exchange for their children. They never showed any animosity toward the American invader who'd shattered the sanctity of their families, their tiny parcels of land, and their God. How they welcomed me with open arms in the face of personal tragedy is a mystery that's haunted me 35 years. For me, making salation payments all day ended in an all night drinking session in the officers club.

➤ *Now, Lance presented with the classic PTSD symptom of avoidance by drinking to dull the images and numb his thoughts. Too psychologically healthy to accept this barbaric band-aid and not be deeply wounded by the gross injustice of the activity his government required him to undertake, too good a man for such vile duty, he needed something to make the revulsion go away. In time, however, he became enveloped by a deep and profound remorse that would plague him for life. When Lance assumed the role of salation payment officer after a round-skipping incident, his morality—indeed, his basic belief system —was challenged and ultimately stretched to the breaking point.*

Under my command, my battery sustained no more casualties than any other in the battalion, but most occurred in one firefight. Just before the 1968 Tet offensive, one of my Duster platoons was called out to support a 101st Airborne operation engaged in search and destroy missions 10 kilometers east of Cu Chi. The infantry unit had only been in country a few weeks, and everyone, including the CO, was green. Their base camp lay behind a low hill—tactically not the best spot for a defensive perimeter. An experienced officer would have chosen more easily defended terrain.

The second day of the operation, the infantry went out a half mile to search a tree line and took four Dusters along for close fire support. I've already told you about the miles of tunnels that crisscrossed the Province and made that area so damned dangerous. Through them, the enemy moved men and supplies into a fight, and then disengaged and disappeared whenever they wanted. That day, the airborne guys ran into all kinds of hell. The night before, a battalion of North Vietnamese had moved into the tree line, dug trenches, and by dawn sat waiting for them.

What ensued was the most intense firefight I'd ever seen or heard of. I was at battery headquarters when second platoon radioed in for more ammunition, the lieutenant in charge shouting over the roar of .50 caliber and 40mm fire. I checked my watch—07:00— they had to be in serious trouble to expend that much ammo so soon after sunup. Something was wrong, so I hopped into my Duster and escorted the re-supply vehicles to the field.

I arrived on scene 15 minutes later and immediately saw the problem— a blind spot in the American artillery coverage. Blocked by the little hill next to the base camp, the tree line was in the one place the infantry's 105s couldn't cover. With no heavy gun support, the troops couldn't move and were taking a real beating. The four Dusters had moved in front of the men on the ground and pounded the enemy positions, but their old cannons weren't designed for sustained maximum-rate fire. My gunners and loaders were well-trained, seasoned combat veterans, but on this day, asked to accomplish the impossible, even they struggled to stay in the fight.

I moved my Duster to the line and joined in the firing. Five Dusters put out a combined thousand rounds per minute, softened the enemy position, and after what seemed an eternity, began gaining ground. I cursed the airborne commander for his stupidity in misplacing his artillery. He must have slept through his infantry training classes. Besides, we'd been in contact with the enemy over an hour. Where the hell was air support? Who the hell was running that mess?

We moved forward by inches. Finally, I saw the infantry fall back—a good thing, because both my 40s suddenly jammed at the same time.

Only 20 meters from the tree line, I opened up with my .50 caliber. Then, I heard the other Dusters crank up their .50s and figured they were jammed or out of ammo, too. The .50 caliber machine gun is a popgun compared to the 40mm, and I knew it was past time for us to get the hell out of there. I gave the signal to withdraw, but I stayed to cover the others as they backed away. Determined to leave nothing in the jar, I fired until I overheated the barrel of my machine gun, and it jammed, too.

Then, a really crazy thing happened. I can't remember every detail of the incident, but I can't forget it, either. When my gun fell silent, an NVA soldier popped out of a spider hole to my front and leveled an RPG right at my Duster. I don't know what fraction of a second it took for me to draw my .45 and fire. It happened so fast, I hardly remember doing it at all. Like a scene in a bad war movie, I pulled the trigger, and the guy slumped dead into his hole. I say this was crazy because in my life, I'd never been good with a pistol—I barely qualified with it in ROTC—but at that moment, when it really counted, I pulled it out and put a bullet square in the middle of that man's forehead.

➥ *When face-to-face with instant annihilation, Lance reacted instinctively to save his life, but this time, he chose fight over flight or freeze, and the bullet hole in the enemy's forehead punctuated the final blow to Lance Johnson's ability to cope with traumatic stress.*

Finally, the air force showed up, and napalm and high explosives finished the job while we made it back to the perimeter and spent the afternoon licking our wounds. I don't know how many infantrymen got hit that day, but our own casualties were bad enough. We lost a platoon leader, an NCO, and five enlisted men. Later, when things settled down, the events of the day hit home, and the men were pretty low. They didn't have to be rocket scientists to figure out their comrades died that day because of bad decisions by an incompetent infantry officer.

For years, I blamed myself for the deaths of my men. I had attended the pre-mission briefing, and I could have refused then to let a green commander use my Dusters as tanks in support of infantry. For years, I believed my men died because I didn't have what it took to stand up to a lieutenant colonel.

I spent the day after the firefight writing letters to the mens' families, a commander's most odious job. I agonized over the task. The army had a manual of sample letters to choose from, but none sounded like me or conveyed the depth of sorrow I felt, so I composed my own. You better hope you never have to write grieving loved ones and tell them their son or husband has been killed in pursuit of a worthy cause when you know—you *know*—it is not.

➥ *When Lance wrote letters to the families of men who'd died in his unit, he felt he contributed to the hypocrisy and futility of the situation.*

Three days later, we held a memorial service at battery headquarters. Two hundred soldiers attended. First Sergeant Mendez placed seven pairs of boots side-by-side, and behind them, seven M-16s with bayonets stuck into the ground. I lost it when he placed the men's helmets over the rifle stocks, and the hot afternoon wind sprinkled them with red Chu Chi dust. It was a tough, hard time for everyone, and for me, nothing was the same after that.

➤ *Lance's guilt over the loss of his men can be viewed as a major stressor in PTSD, as each man killed or wounded posed an oblique threat to his own physical integrity.*

I didn't know my combat fatigue showed while in Vietnam, but I must have worn it on my sleeve for everyone to see, because during a visit to battalion headquarters, the commanding general stopped me and said he thought I needed a transfer out of the field. At first, I jumped at the invitation, and he seemed pleased, but at the same moment, I worried about leaving my men and was reluctant to accept any transfer until I was sure my replacement was up to the job. I tried to articulate my thoughts, tried to make him understand, but to no avail. The general did not take opinion surveys from junior officers. He told me my replacement was his responsibility, and I should pack my bag.

The next morning, I cleared my office and packed a few personal items. The men were all in the field, so I said goodbye to the first sergeant and company clerk and then walked alone to the chopper pad to await my ride out. An unceremonious departure? For many, that's how it happened in Vietnam. One day, you fought, lived, and died with a group of guys, and the next day, you were gone. As I stood in the blistering noon heat looking back at my battery headquarters, I thought of T.S. Elliot's poem, "The Hollow Men," and recalled the last two lines: "This is the way the world ends. Not with a bang but a whimper."

➤ *Taken out of context, many would interpret these statements as a description of being killed, not merely transferred to another assignment. Of all Lance's unseen wounds, his feelings of solitary abandonment weighed most heavily on his psyche.*

The last two months of my tour in Vietnam, I served out of harm's way at a big officers club near Long Binh, supervising the creation of gin and tonics and vodka martinis for rear area staffers who never in their lives fired a shot in anger, who spent their 365 days shuffling papers and carrying General Westmoreland's water, and who wanted to go home as badly as anyone else.

* * *

Many of the planes carrying returning soldiers landed at Travis Air Force Base, California, and I'll never forget the huge crowd of people there to greet us at the airport. In those days, anyone could walk out onto the tarmac and meet an incoming plane, and as we taxied to our parking ramp, I counted over 100. A sea of faces, but far from a welcoming committee, these people were war protesters, outraged at the return of the government's little criminals. So strange to see the long hair, beards, facial jewelry, tie-died clothes, and leather sandals, as though they all shopped at the same store and if asked, would drink the same kool-aid. To my eyes, they looked like automatons, vaguely human but certainly not American, and it suddenly occurred to me they thought the same about us.

As we stepped off the plane and descended the stairs, their angry voices filled the air, and they waved signs and banners in our faces and chanted peace slogans. Still in my jungle fatigues and boots, I carried an old Chinese rifle—a war trophy souvenir from my days with the Duster battery. When the crowd got a look at that weapon and me, it was like deflating a tire. The air went out of them, and for several moments, I heard only hushed whispers and uncertain expressions of dismay and expectation. For them a terrible and frightening epiphany, the mentally deranged, blood-guzzling, baby-killing Vietnam war veteran of their worst nightmares now stood in their midst—armed. When I reached the tarmac, everyone's eyes remained glued to the weapon, and several silent moments passed before someone in the rear of the crowd found courage, and the chanting resumed.

➤ *At the time unaware he fit any portion of that unflattering description, symptoms of his PTSD would soon present Lance with harsh reality.*

My parents came to the airport to welcome me home, but in all the commotion, I walked right past them. Funny, they didn't recognize me, either. However, we found each other at last, and Mom cried. Dad told me how proud he was, and I shed a tear of my own. They told me Joan had been too busy and couldn't make it up from Los Angeles to greet me. Five days later, I was discharged from the U.S. Army.

My homecoming reunion with Joan was strained and sad. We'd last seen each other in Hawaii on R&R six months earlier, and things hadn't gone well. I thought she'd changed from the person I married, and she thought I had. I know now, of course, the truth lay somewhere in between. Like two people who casually meet and never dream of exchanging intimacies, Joan and I were strangers to each other. She'd long since quit wearing her wedding ring, and I guessed she'd been fooling around for months. Two hours after I arrived, we looked at each other across her kitchen table and knew our marriage was over. Nothing more to do or say, I just got the hell out of there and never looked back. For me, that part of my life was finished.

➤ *Two of the most frequently experienced avoidance symptoms of PTSD among veterans returning from Vietnam were feelings of detachment or estrangement from others and a restricted range of affect, the inability to have loving feelings.*

Lance, like thousands of other soldiers, came home fundamentally changed, and their domestic relationships crumbled.

I wanted to look for work in San Francisco but first took a month off and visited relatives and friends in Idaho. Strange to see old friends at home. They'd had such different life experiences, it seemed we no longer had anything in common. Around them, I felt like an outsider, somehow out of the mainstream. Our conversations were filtered, awkwardly contrived, and everyone stepped gingerly around discussion of the war in general and my experiences in particular. My closest friends no longer related to me on any meaningful level, didn't know what to say, and were fearful of saying the wrong thing. In short, they didn't know me anymore. The Lance Johnson in their midst was different from the one who'd gone away just a few years earlier. When I finished that trip home, I was done with the people from my earlier life. The experiences that had bound us together in the past were utterly meaningless. Now, I embraced different values.

✦ *Everything in Lance's world had changed. The connections to his family and his pre-war life that might have helped to ameliorate his PTSD not available to him, he was unable to lock back into a condition of normalcy.*

In San Francisco, I stayed with an army buddy until I found my own apartment. I had decided to go into finance, so I purchased civilian business attire, wrote a resume, and went door-to-door looking for work.

✦ *In a subconscious effort to regain some portion of his previous life, Lance followed in his father's footsteps and worked in the financial field.*

It was like pounding my head against a wall. Months went by with no luck. I applied at three dozen finance and mortgage companies and stock brokerages. Finally, in frustration, I consulted a company that polished resumes. The solution was simple, they said. Remove any mention of Vietnam service from my resume. Potential employers immediately disqualified me because, at the least, I supported the military and the illegal war in Asia, and at worst, I might be crazy from serving in Vietnam. I amended my resume to show I served that year in Germany, and immediately, doors opened for me.

✦ *To be deemed acceptable for the job he wanted, Lance repudiated his valorous service and denied his sacrifice and that of his comrades.*

My first civilian job was with Bank of America. They sent me to their in-house school of international banking, a 10-month course where I learned about letters of credit, money exchange, and anything to do with moving financial instruments around the globe. At the time, Bank of America had financial ties to almost every major bank in the world, and

I considered myself fortunate to be with a company that offered so much career potential.

After training, I went to work in the department responsible for business development in middle-east countries. I interacted with foreign banks, read the English language newspapers from Lebanon, Jordan, and Egypt, and studied world events from a different perspective. Dave, my immediate supervisor, was a navy veteran, and we hit it off right away. We made a good team at the office and were equally comfortable side by side at the local watering hole after the workday ended.

Dave was the first person to tell me I didn't respond to the world like other people. Long before anyone else had spoken of PTSD, Dave told me my strange behavior might be related to my experience in Vietnam. I was skeptical. What the hell? Who wouldn't be a little rough around the edges after what I'd been through? I had a few readjustments to make, that's all. I wasn't about to call it quits and check myself into a loony bin just because good old Dave said I should.

➤ *Another PTSD symptom—estrangement from others.*

I'm an ordinary guy, somebody people don't give a second look. I never did anything for attention, and I never wanted the spotlight. Dave knew that and saw something in me completely foreign to my nature—anger. In a change so gradual I didn't notice, during the year and a half since I returned from Vietnam, I developed a mighty short fuse. I became hopelessly impatient with the slightest inconvenience, became furious standing in line at the supermarket, blew up at the boy who washed my car and missed a spot. I road-raged at innocent motorists and school crossing guards. I argued with my supervisors at work. It seemed I was happiest when angry, and that wasn't the way I was brought up. Nor was I that way while serving in Vietnam.

➤ *The DSM-IV manual types these symptoms of PTSD as irritability or outbursts of anger. However defined, it was foreign and uncomfortable behavior for Lance. Because Lance's amygdala was impaired, he experienced difficulty adapting to social life, a condition that occurs because a healthy amygdala not only regulates emotions like fear and aggression but also models and quickly recognizes the presence of these emotions in others.*

Along with the anger—maybe because of it—I began having nightmares. They didn't come every night and didn't follow any pattern. When I lay down to sleep, I never knew whether I'd get a good night's rest or be drawn back to some forgotten firefight, sentenced to relive the details, the whistle of flying steel, the chatter of machine guns, the stink of bloated bodies when we mopped up after. The night terrors visited me three, four nights a week, and for me, they were more real and more immediate than actual combat. I saw every detail of every moment. Every sound was amplified, every odor enhanced in a way I knew not possible when I lived through it. It was a cruel and horrible joke, a dispiriting mockery. My subconscious intensified action, exaggerated sensory input, heightened awareness, but did nothing to augment my ability to cope, gave me no tool to wind down the subsequent effect. Awakening was like climbing out of a well. Afterwards, I lay trembling for hours, sweat soaked and exhausted.

➤ *Lance believed his dreams magnified the reality of what he actually experienced, but that may not be the case. When a person is traumatized, by definition, the traumatic event's composition is fragmented and improperly processed by the brain.*

My most recurring dream was making salation payments to the village families who'd lost loved ones at my hands. The same each time, that dream troubled me most:

I see myself from the perspective of the fourth wall, in a jeep, a bag of money on my lap. My driver concentrates on the narrow road between rice paddies. The translator is dressed in army fatigues, his hat pulled down over mirrored dark glasses. Sullen and suspicious, he doesn't like this duty any better than I. Ahead, a little knot of village elders and Province dignitaries wait at the entrance to the village. Three minutes of formalities, the usual Vietnamese exchange of pleasantries and their oaths of allegiance to democracy and the American Way.

Flash forward to the entrance of a village hut. The elders peel off, and my translator and I step in. Papasan and Mamasan stand against the back wall, as though surrendering their entire home to me. They smile through broken, betel nut-stained teeth, bow, and beckon us inside. My eyes adjust to the suddenly dim light, and I see a small child, a girl sitting on a low palate silently peering at me through bandages that cover half her face. An empty palate beside her, she glances at it, and then turns her gaze back to me.

The translator speaks the usual greeting, but this time, he adds a brief, shopworn prayer to everyone's revered ancestors. Smiling, Mamasan steps forward holding a tray on which are four tiny cups of a thin, green tea. She bows, extends the tray, smiles again, but will not look me in the eye. I'm the first to take a cup. Mamasan then repeats this ritual until everyone is served. We squat and sip tea. Soon, the translator rattles off something in his strange, duck quack language. Papasan smiles and bows, but he looks me in the eye when he speaks. "Two female children," the translator points to the little girl in the corner. "That one has lost an ear. Her father implores you to not trouble yourself with her other injuries. She will heal, and her scars will be barely noticed."

Papasan then places his hand on his forehead, as though to convey great worry and concern. His eyes dart back and forth between the translator and me. At the end of a short soliloquy, he takes a breath, smiles again, and nods. He's said his piece, and he leaves the matter in my hands. "The other child, Doi, a girl of twelve, is in the Province hospital. Fate has taken one of her legs, and circumstance a hand." The translator indicates the empty palate. I see my own image reflected in his mirrored glasses. "Her parents and sister pray she will recover and return soon to her home."

I read from my script: The American government and the government of the Republic of Vietnam deeply regret . . . All the while, Papasan and Mamasan smile, nod their heads, and bow as though every word I utter is holy.

I open the bag, remove a freshly minted stack of Vietnamese Piasters, and begin counting. One hundred, two hundred. I search the faces of the Vietnamese people squatted in front of me. The bills hit the tray, and as the little stack grows, they become transfixed, mesmerized by the sight of more money than they have ever before seen. The translator's jaw slackens, and his breath comes in short, quick gasps.

I finish counting. The government-prescribed salation is delivered. Mamasan scoops the cash and like an amateur magician turns her back and makes it disappear.

We stand. The Vietnamese couple bow and smile and bow again. Papasan shakes my hand, and then extends his to the translator, who turns his back and walks out. I back out behind him. Appropriately obsequious, I return the bows and smiles until the burlap flap falls shut. Outside, the sun blazes down from directly overhead and hits me like freight train. The translator turns to me, and again, I see my reflection in his glasses. This time, however, something about me is different. My face is blurred, my features less distinct, like seeing a painting of a reflection. He glances up at the sun then consults his wristwatch. "Three more," he says. "This whole day is wasted."

➼ *This dream is different from his other nightmares. Lance is an observer, a person who might pass judgment on the participants. Recurrent and the same in every detail, the unprocessed material in these dreams alludes to his sense of shame and guilt.*

In addition to the mood swings and bad dreams, I began having problems staying focused, which of course reflected on my job performance. My mind wandered, and I often felt like a schoolboy trapped in a classroom on a spring afternoon. I began to resent my coworkers' successes and distanced myself from them. On numerous occasions, Dave took me aside and told me to lighten up and think about what I did around the office. Now and then, he made an oblique reference to posttraumatic stress, and even though I wasn't ready to hear that, I paid attention to everything else he said. Dave was the only friend I had left at the bank, and I didn't argue with him.

➼ *No longer in Vietnam and in a state of constant alert, Lance's brain attempted to sort out the tangle of horrific images it had recorded during the war. In the brain, the hippocampus is associated with episodic memories—memories of experienced events and their associated emotions—and damage to Lance's hippocampus resulted in his inability to form new long-term episodic memories. In simpler terms, Lance Johnson experienced lifelong difficulty forming new episodic memories not associated with the traumas he suffered in Vietnam.*

In 1972, I transferred to the Vietnamese desk, which was a surprise, because I didn't know any American bank did business in Vietnam. We were at war, for Christ's sake. Shows you now naïve I was. The planners at Bank of America knew the war would end someday and were greatly interested in the economic future of the region.

One day, after six months in the department, the bank president sent me a personal letter encouraging me to support the American oil companies' bids on offshore drilling rights. A map accompanied the letter showing the drill sites already awarded throughout Southeast Asia, and I saw the void around Vietnam that, with bank support, would be filled by American companies.

What a joke. Twenty years, millions dead, and for what? To stoke the fire in the belly of big business. I'd already tired of working at the bank for too little pay and too little spiritual reward. That letter was too much for me. After three years with Bank of America, my letter of resignation was accepted without comment.

➤ *Lance may not have been cognizant of the similarity between the bank president's request for his support in gaining access to Vietnamese oil and his onerous duty as salation payment officer while in Vietnam, but nonetheless, his PTSD was triggered. Lance went to the extreme of resigning his position to avoid any activity that aroused recollections of his trauma.*

San Francisco was great place to live in the 70s. I had a downtown apartment, a new car, and I found pretty women everywhere I went. Two months after leaving the bank, I passed the NASD and SEC exams and went to work for a mutual fund company. Ironically, I found a sales job like my father's with a subsidiary company of the one he worked for. Behind a desk and on the phone all day was okay with me. I was an independent contractor and my own boss. As the years went by, I always exceeded my quotas and made good money. I still wrestled with anger, but I considered it a side to my personality I needed to control—like talking too much or laughing too loud. The nightmares stayed with me, too, but like my bad temper, I saw them as just another set of bags I'd have to tote as I got older.

A good thing happened in 1975. I met Lucille. Like my first wife, she was beautiful and a schoolteacher. Lucille was a great girl, the first person I'd met in a long time with whom I believed I could build a lasting relationship. After dating a little less than a year, I popped the question, she said yes, and we married in the spring.

At 37, I lived in a great town, had a good job, and was married to a wonderful woman. What could be wrong? Already, I'd done more, traveled farther, and lived better than I ever imagined. A person would have to be crazy to muck up the good deal I had, but maybe crazy was the right word for me.

How did it happen? It's difficult to describe. Even now, I'm not sure I have the words. I couldn't point to anything wrong in my life. The sun shined all day, and things just fell into place. Misfortune visited others, but not me. The problem was, I felt like my good times were happening to someone else. I witnessed happiness and contentment but was not a participant. I felt on the outside of life. I didn't live in the world, but moved alongside it. Like in my nightmare, I was the fourth wall in a stage play. It was the best seat in the house, but I couldn't influence the action. Worse, I couldn't shake the sense of impending doom that huddled in the back of my mind and forced me to keep my real emotions in reserve.

➤ *The psychological wounds Lance suffered in battle were invisible to everyone but him. The impending doom he speaks of is the PTSD symptom of foreshortened future.*

On the outside, at least for a few years, everything was great, but eventually, the demons inside me won out. Now, I had real trouble sleeping, and fatigue fueled the anger I was less and less able to control. For a while, Lucille and I were relatively happy together, but as time passed, we argued—about little things, mostly—and our relationship was constantly strained. At her suggestion, we saw a succession of marriage counselors, but to me, they talked nonsense, and eventually, I refused to go back. In spite of our deteriorating marriage and much to my surprise and delight, in 1980, Lucille announced she was pregnant. I was immediately excited about becoming a father, and I hoped having a child would motivate Lucille and me to work through our problems and rebuild our relationship. October 1, 1980, the day my son Marsh was born, was the happiest day of my life.

The joys of fatherhood notwithstanding, I simply couldn't keep my life together, could not control the dark moods that came out of nowhere and took over. The same familiar patterns repeated on the job as well. I became angry with clients when I thought they failed fully to appreciate the value of my financial expertise, or worse, when they took my advice, and then invested with someone else. Of course, my supervisors saw my changing behavior, and in keeping with the corporate philosophy of the day, they ordered me to counseling.

Strange, now that I look back on that time. So many hours sitting across from trained professionals, and not one convinced me anything was wrong with me. In those days, the buzz phrase was *Type A*. An aggressive or assertive person had a *Type A* personality. Counselors looked at the world through that lens, and because I had none of the substance addictions generally associated with neurotic behavior, they concluded I only needed to find and employ the right tools to manage my *Type A* personality. The subject of Vietnam never came up in any counseling sessions I ever attended.

➤ *The lack of effective therapy for Vietnam Veterans was a tragedy in itself. During the war years and the decades following, there was little understanding of how trauma could be effectively treated. Until the publication of the DSM III in 1980, there was no diagnosis for and little understanding of the debilitating psychological disorder afflicting thousands of veterans. The nature of the fragmented memories, the arousal of the limbic system, and body memory of the traumatic events were seemingly immune to conventional psychotherapy.*

As time went by, the pressure of commissioned sales finally defeated me. My interest in the financial markets had flagged years earlier, and now, I couldn't even force myself to read the *Wall Street Journal*, much less sell stocks. I had to will myself into the office each morning, and I didn't care whether I ever talked to another client. 10 years in the industry, and I was at a dead end. One particularly busy morning, I ignored the insistent ringing of my phone, boxed my few personal items, and walked out. I don't think anyone even noticed me leave. Shades of Vietnam. Not with a bang but a whimper.

➤ *Beginning to loose the battle with his disorder and the pressure building, Lance attempted escape by abruptly walking away from his job, and in his mind, connected this departure with leaving his unit in Vietnam.*

In 1985, while working in the trust department of a small Marin County bank, I ran across an old army buddy. A medical doctor, he worked in veterans care. Over lunch, he suggested I put in a claim with the Veterans Administration—not for posttraumatic stress, but for a continuing psoriasis-like problem I'd had since Vietnam. Also, my hearing had begun to fail. My friend advised me to apply then in the event I ever needed future medical care to treat my service-related conditions. I thought that was a good idea, so I ploughed through all the government red tape, and eventually, the VA awarded me a 10 percent disability. That was my first experience in the VA system.

A year later, a financial conglomerate purchased the bank I worked for, and my position went away. Suddenly unemployed and housebound all day, I was like a caged tiger, which of course only compounded the problems between Lucille and me. Soon, we were constantly at each other's throats. We wanted to hold on to our marriage, to keep the family together for Marsh's sake, and we tried, but I couldn't control my dark side, and Lucille never gave an inch.

For months, I traveled all over the state looking for work, but no one wanted anything to do with me. Ultimately, I realized my VA disability was a matter of record, and everywhere I applied, the prospective employer uncovered it. No one wanted to take on a potentially crazy Vietnam vet who files disability claims.

* * *

In 1989, I was at home babysitting Marsh when the big San Francisco earthquake struck. Even in Marin County, I felt the strong tremors, so I snapped on the television to see what happened in the city. News cameras showed panicked people screaming and running for cover. Rescue personnel loaded crushed and broken victims into waiting ambulances, firefighters battled block-wide blazes, and over it all, groomed and manicured announcers, hungry for more drama, warned of aftershocks.

I sat on my couch, a cup of coffee in my hand, watching those scenes of fire and destruction, and something happened inside me. A switch tripped in my head, and instantly, I was back in Vietnam. In my mind, the concept of time suddenly meant nothing, and I traveled through a wormhole in space from San Francisco to 20 years earlier in Southeast Asia. Panic. I didn't know what to do. This was far more than a simple hallucination. I felt trapped between two realities, two dimensions, and I was unsure which would win the tug of war for my consciousness.

➥ *Now, Lance experiences the most frightening of all PTSD symptoms—dissociative flashback.*

Physically paralyzed and helpless, I fly down the rabbit hole and stand in the dim light, the bag of money under my arm, while Mamasan forces a cup of tea into my hand. Behind me, arms around each other's shoulders, staring, grinning, and bowing, Papasan and my translator block the only exit. I hand Mamasan an envelope stuffed with bills. Her eyes widen, she puts her face close to mine, looks deep into my eyes, and smiles, her betel nut-stained teeth the color of old blood. Then, grinning like fools, the three gather around me and point to the crumpled body in the corner of the hut. What the hell do they want? I know their child is dead. I killed him, for Christ's sake! They aren't telling me anything new. I reach into my pocket and take out the script the army provided for me: The American government and the government of the Republic of Vietnam deeply regret...

Now, they laugh at me. I don't believe it. What do those people think is so funny? I try to read my canned speech, but consumed with laughter, they don't listen to a word I say. Mamasan laughs so hard, she doesn't even bother to cover her mouth, a serious breech of etiquette for a Vietnamese woman. Behind his mirrored glasses, tears run down the translator's cheeks. I'm suddenly furious. I stop reading and shout, "WHAT THE HELL IS WRONG WITH YOU PEO-PLE? WHAT'S SO DAMNED FUNNY? I KILLED YOUR KID! I'M A MUR-DERER, AND YOU'RE LAUGHING ABOUT IT!

At the mention of their child, Mamasan and Papasan explode in a new fit of laughter, point to the body, bow and nod, and indicate they want me to view the corpse. Soon, the translator joins in, using both hands for emphasis. Mamasan thinks this hysterical, clutches her ribs, and horselaughs.

No, I don't want to do it! I don't want to look at your dead child! The three move in, seize my elbows, and march me across the room. Reluctantly, I look down at the corpse, a boy in peasant garb. A conical straw hat covers his face. The translator bends over, slaps both knees, and chokes on his own expressions of glee. I look again at the body. Papasan reaches down and removes the straw hat, and I see the pale, dead face of my son, Marsh, staring up at me, his cold, cadaverous blue eyes open wide, like staring through a hole in the clouds. Sudden silence in the hut. Grim-faced now, the three Vietnamese glare at me. Mamasan's lip curls in a hateful sneer. I hear the clucking of chickens just outside the hut, and I run. I run as fast as I can, but the man and woman chase me. I am much bigger and run much faster but can't gain any ground. I run until I think my heart will burst.

Then nothing.

➤ *Lance reels at the horror of the juxtaposition of the victims and the accusatory faces of the other players in the tragedy. These shocking images more than Lance can handle, he blacks out, his only defense against a complete psychotic break.*

The next day, I drove to the VA hospital and started PTSD counseling.

Weeks went by, and even though in therapy three hours a day, I found little relief. My nerves were frazzled, and I couldn't hold a thought. Some-times, I'd sit semiconscious, staring at a wall, then a few moments later, look at a clock and discover four hours had passed. A few days after the earthquake, I drove by an area of North Bay where the immigrant Viet-namese went to fish. As I passed, I saw them hunkered down by the water's edge smoking cigarettes and talking, and I lost it again. I don't remember what I did that day or how I got home.

Lucille never put much stock in the notion of posttraumatic stress. I don't mean to be unkind, but I don't think she ever took it seriously. In her mind, I should put those issues behind me and move on. She believed not being in absolute control a weakness responsible people overcome quickly, and then get back to the serious business of life. I tried, she tried, but after a while, she lost patience with me and wrote me off. Our separa-tion was the lowest period in my life. I'd lost my wife, my son, my job, and my home. At that point, not much left of my dignity, I felt I had to get out. I needed a change of scenery, so I moved to Sonoma County.

✦ *Fleeing again. Lance experienced all three reactions—fight, freeze, and flight.*

At first, my PTSD therapy consisted of one-on-one counseling with a fine man who worked at the local veterans clinic. As the months went by, he taught me—and made me believe—I wasn't crazy, that nearly all my behavioral traits sprang from trauma. After all the years, I finally viewed my life in perspective and saw the motivation behind so many of my bad choices. In addition to therapy, the counselor recommended vocational rehabilitation. He told me the last thing a person with PTSD needed was a job in sales. Of course, he was correct. In hindsight, now I know I merely played a role in my sales career. I acted a part and never really considered my own sense of truth, purpose, or fulfillment, and just contemplating leaving the demanding and spiritually unrewarding field of sales excited me. I felt the weight of the world lifted from my shoulders, and for the first time since my college days, I looked forward to tomorrow.

Later, I participated in group counseling to augment my one-on-one sessions. Soon, I attended therapy three full days a week and took daily 60mg doses of Prozac. The medication bothered me at first. I'd never used drugs in my life, but I trusted the VA doctors and followed their direction.

This is what I want you to understand—the treatment worked. I opened myself to the people trying to help, and slowly, the fog in my brain started to clear. Each day, I found myself more able to deal with the circumstances of life. For me, it was a miracle. Think for a moment where I was when I surrendered myself to PTSD therapy—middle aged, separated from wife and son, unemployed, and friendless. I'd sunk as low as a man could, but damn it, the treatment worked, and I felt better and began living again.

In 1990, my newfound energy and sense of purpose led me to apply through a VA vocational rehabilitation program to a commercial dive school in Seattle. I'd scuba dived often in my life and always felt comfortable in the water. Potentially a perfect career, commercial diving offered a work environment away from the things I resented about the outside world. I could work alone and, at the end of the day, physically measure the progress I made.

It was a good decision and a great experience. I had no problem with the school. I learned underwater construction, demolition and salvage, hazardous materials disposal, and photography. There was no problem with the training, but I was twice the age of the other students, and upon graduation, no one wanted to hire me. With nothing else to do, I started my own dive service. I bought an underwater ROV—a remotely operated vehicle used for observation—and contracted for underwater photography, body searches, and treasure hunts. When I couldn't find work for the ROV, I made expenses scraping hulls, cleaning propellers, and changing zincs.

Being a self-employed diver worked for me. I still went to regular counseling and still tussled with the occasional nightmare, but I was relatively happy, in good physical condition, and living healthy. One night, even though I wasn't much of a drinker, I decided to go to a neighborhood club for a beer.

I was in the joint only 30 seconds when I saw her sitting with friends across the room. Thirty seconds more, and I worked up the courage to ask her to dance. A social worker, Erica was attractive, forthcoming, and easy to talk to. We hit it off right away. It took me a while to open up to her about my life, but when I did, she listened and didn't judge—for me, a welcome breath of fresh air. She was an angel.

After that first night, Erica and I became fast friends. She owned a small sailboat, and as the months passed, we spent time together cruising Puget Sound and the San Juan Islands. She was everything I needed in my life. By nature a caring person, Erica understood my difficult moments and helped me through them. She didn't think me weak or flawed or damaged goods. To her, Lance Johnson was an ordinary guy whose good qualities outshone the bad.

To this day, I am as much in love with Erica as the first moment we met. Eventually, we bought a house in Seattle and lived happily for eight years. Can you believe it? At my age, a normal life? I still took Prozac, of course, and attended counseling. Sometimes, the nightmares came back, and I went through occasional spells of depression the drugs couldn't handle, but compared to that other existence, I was in paradise.

Erica retired in 2001, and we moved to Hawaii. Together, we built a modest home and live within our means. My son, Marsh, is a man now and visits twice a year. Not long ago, I was finally able to talk to him about my life experiences. I felt he had the right to know why his dad was the way he was. Not easy for me to do, it was a difficult moment for both of us, but I believe Marsh understood, and his expressions of empathy were sincere. He is a good, caring young man, and I'm very proud of him.

I still attend counseling, and the doctors occasionally adjust my medication to fill the gaps when the Prozac quits working. Now, I realize there are two Lance Johnsons—the person I was before Vietnam and the person I am since. Two very different people, and I struggle to embrace them both. The Lance Johnson I am now is committed to the sanctity of life. It is his new church, and there is no longer a place for organized religion in his life. This Lance Johnson will attend a funeral or wedding, appreciate the ceremony, and enjoy the music as much as anyone, but when he hears a politician or preacher talk about God and the culture of life and then come out pro-guns, pro-death penalty, and pro-war, he gets sick to his stomach. If God is for all that, then He doesn't need this Lance Johnson.

I'm 66 now. As I look back on my life, the foremost thing I remember after Vietnam was my seething rage at our government for getting us into that mess in Southeast Asia. It took a long time and a great deal of professional help for me to finally come to the conclusion that pure anger was eating me up inside. I'll tell anyone who wants to listen. Powerful people—men who wouldn't have the guts to get near a battlefield—misused our generation for shameful purpose, and to this day, society pays the price.

—Lance Johnson

The Science of PTSD

As early as 1900 B.C., Egyptian physicians depicted hysterical psychological reactions in soldiers exposed to traumatic events in battle. Greek philosophers and historians have recounted hysteria in individuals after being exposed to traumatic stressors. Many months after the event, a survivor of the great fire of London in the 1600s recalled in his diary, "strange to think how to this very day I cannot sleep at night without great terrors of the fire."[1] During the American Civil War, the symptoms of posttraumatic stress disorder (PTSD) were known as irritable heart or soldier's heart. Then, it was believed the reactions were primarily physiological and affected the cardiovascular system. Later in the nineteenth century, the effects of trauma were first addressed in the civilian population. For example, persons who developed somatic and psychological symptoms after being involved in occurrences such as train accidents were diagnosed with what was called "railway spine."[2]

In the later decades of the nineteenth century, French and German physicians began seriously to study the disorder known for centuries as hysteria. The accepted belief of the time was that hysteria was a disease of incoherent and incomprehensible symptoms most commonly found in women and originating in the uterus—thus the name, hysteria. French neurologist Jean-Martin Charcot, father of the study of hysteria, practiced and lectured at the Salpetriere, Paris, asylum for the poor and insane. Other notable doctors such as Sigmund Freud, William James, and Pierre Janet were among those who traveled to Paris to attend Charcot's lectures. Charcot called hysteria "the Great Neurosis," and he became its first taxonomist by careful observation, description, and classification of the disorder.[3] As he progressed through his research, Charcot became interested in the symptoms of hysteria that most resembled neurological damage and impairment such as sensory losses, convulsions, motor paralyses, and amnesia, and by artificially inducing and relieving the symptoms through hypnosis, he proved them psychological in nature.

Sigmund Freud and Pierre Janet advanced Charcot's work with hysterical subjects by interviewing hundreds of patients over a period of years and forming the hypothesis that hysteria was the result of psychological trauma. Freud and Janet hypothesized the somatic symptoms exhibited by hysterical patients masked the representations of extremely stressful events which had been cast out of memory. Janet described his hysterical patients as "ruled by subconscious fixed ideas."

Janet labeled the hysterical emotional reactions to trauma "dissociation." During the 1890s, he labored meticulously with his patients to work back through more recent traumas to earlier childhood traumatic events. He stated, "By removing the superficial layer of delusions, I favored the appearance of old and tenacious fixed ideas which dwelt still at the bottom of the mind. The latter disappeared in turn, thus bringing forth a great improvement."[4]

Freud and his associate, Joseph Breuer, termed these unbearable emotional reactions to traumatic events "double consciousness."[5] They believed these stressors caused an altered state of consciousness that in turn created the somatic, hysterical symptoms. Breuer and Freud postulated that hysterical patients suffered from reminiscences or memories of early childhood psychological and physical assault, which led them to explore the adult and childhood lives of the patients. What they discovered shocked them. The patients repeatedly told of incest, physical abuse, and sexual assault suffered during childhood.

In 1896, Freud declared he had discovered the reasons for the development of hysteria in women. In *The Aetiology of Hysteria*, published that same year, he stated, "I therefore put forward the thesis that at the bottom of every case of hysteria there are one or more occurrences of premature sexual experience, occurrences which belong to the earliest years of childhood, but which can be reproduced through the work of psycho-analysis in spite of the intervening decades. I believe this an important finding, the discovery of a *caput Nili*,the root cause, in neuropathology." In essence, Freud had given the world an avenue to walk toward discovery of how to relieve the suffering of terribly traumatized women. However, societal prejudice prevailed, and the publication of his paper was the last research undertaken in this field for almost a century.[6]

If his patients' stories were true, Freud would have to accept the premise that exploitive and assaultive acts against children were commonplace in all levels of society, including respected upper class families. Although credible, for Freud, this idea proved too controversial and potentially fatal to his practice in Vienna. Not wishing to promulgate such a damning theory, ruin his reputation, and end his career, he abandoned the theory that sexual and physical trauma could be factors in the development of hysteria. Despite pressures from without, Freud continued to believe his patients had been sexually exploited in childhood, but to mollify elite sectors of Viennese society, he shifted his focus to the investigation of the patient's own feelings of erotic stimulation as a result of the sexual abuse and eventually repudiated his earlier thesis as stated in his 1925 autobiography, "I was at last obliged to recognize that these scenes of seduction had never taken place, that they were only fantasies, which my patients had made up."[7]

Thus ended the study of psychological trauma and any attempts to alleviate its debilitating symptoms. That pursuit of knowledge of the disease of hysteria was largely forsaken is unimaginably unfortunate for millions of men and women who have suffered and died as a result of this abandonment of clinical research. What if Freud had held to his early theory and not abandoned it in favor of one more socially acceptable to the patriarchal Western European culture to which Freud and his contemporaries belonged? How many millions have suffered as a result of wartime traumatic events, both directly as a combatant and indirectly as one close to the traumatized veteran? Today, we can only look back and wish Freud had stayed the course so others could have followed more quickly in his footsteps.

World War I resulted in the battlefield deaths of over eight million men and produced countless millions of other victims, many suffering psychologically. One estimate of British losses stated 40 percent of U.K. casualties were the result of mental breakdown. In the war to end all wars, soldiers were subjected to constant threat of terrible death, witnessed the mutilation and extinction of their comrades, and were helpless to protect themselves from similar fates. The record shows that under the pressure of untold carnage, once strong and resilient men eventually behaved in the same manner as the hysterical women Janet and Freud studied. They wept, screamed, and became mute and psychologically paralyzed. Amnesia was common, and stricken soldiers lost their ability to feel emotion for themselves and others.[8]

Known by many names during WWI including battle or operational fatigue, combat exhaustion and war neurosis, at first, PTSD was called shell shock—the condition ascribed to the constant artillery bombardments to which the average soldier in the trenches was subjected. As with the patients Freud studied, the actual etiology of these soldiers' disability was ignored and another less sympathetic cause for shell shock was put forth. British psychiatrist Lewis Yelland published a paper in 1918 in which he declared stricken soldiers suffered merely from laziness and cowardice and subsequently based his treatment on shame, threats, and punishment—much the same treatment hysterical women had been subjected to in earlier times. Not different from hysteria discounted and forgotten in women, soon after the war, the medical establishment ignored the thousands of men egregiously suffering from the trauma of their war experiences.

In 1920, having recently returned to New York from a yearlong personal psychoanalysis with Sigmund Freud, a young American psychiatrist, Abram Kardiner, began working with WWI veterans in the psychiatric clinic of the Veterans Bureau. Kardiner related well to patients suffering from war neurosis because his own childhood trauma included his mother's untimely death, poverty, neglect, hunger, and domestic violence. As his work progressed, in addition to the psychological symptoms his patients exhibited, Kardiner observed physiologic abnormalities such as extreme startle reactions to unexpected loud noises. The young doctor helped many troubled soldiers but was unable to develop a theory of war trauma that worked within the framework of psychoanalytic theory. After three years, he gave up the effort until 1939.

During the intervening period, Kardiner became interested in anthropology and, with Cora du Bois, co-authored an anthropological text, *The Individual and His Society*. Kardiner's intellectual grounding in anthropological conceptualization allowed him to recognize the impact of social reality and enabled him to better understand psychological trauma. In 1941, he published a comprehensive clinical and theoretical study, *The Neurosis of War*, in which he deplored the lack of continuous professional interest in the study of war neurosis. The theoretical and clinical outlines of traumatic syndromes known today are based on Kardiner's pioneering work with the shell-shocked veterans of World War I.[9]

The Second World War brought about a revival of medical interest in war neurosis, then called combat fatigue. Once again, large numbers of soldiers became casualties of psychological trauma and were deemed unfit for duty on the lines. During this period, psychiatrists began to remove the stigma of the stress-related debilitations experienced by these soldiers. At last, medical professionals began to realize any man might become psychologically wounded if exposed to severe traumatic events in combat. In collaboration with Herbert Spiegel, a psychiatrist with considerable experience treating soldiers with combat fatigue still in the theater of war, in 1947, Kardiner revised his theory. Spiegel contributed to Kardiner's theory by suggesting men who had the strongest ties to their leaders and fighting units were the most resilient in the face of overwhelming terror.

Wartime psychiatrists implemented treatments to mitigate the psychological effects of combat-induced trauma, including hypnosis and what was then termed narcosynthesis, the use of sodium amytal. Doctors applied both techniques to induce an altered state of consciousness that facilitated a cathartic reliving of the traumatic memories, which could then be processed and relieved, methods which proved effective in the rapid reduction of symptoms in large numbers of troops afflicted with acute stress. Records show up to 80 percent of these soldiers returned to some form of duty within one week, and 30 percent eventually returned to combat duty.

However, in the aftermath of the war, little was done in the way of longitudinal research on the lasting effects of the treatment or the traumatic stress itself. Notwithstanding, many psychiatrists understood treatment would not be successful in the long term if the memories retrieved under hypnosis were not integrated into the soldier's consciousness. They stated the psychological effect of combat is not like "writing on a slate that can be erased, leaving the slate clean as it was before. Combat leaves a lasting impression on men's minds, changing them as radically as any crucial experience through which they live."[10]

The first edition of the Diagnostic and Statistical Manual (DSM-I), published by the American Psychiatric Association in 1952, included a diagnosis of "gross stress reaction" for trauma cases that involved exposure to "severe, physical demands or extreme stress, such as in combat or civilian catastrophe." In 1968, the second edition of the manual, DSM-II, was published, and the diagnosis for PTSD was watered down and called "transient situational disturbance." DSM-II postulated that even though the nature of the stressor was overwhelming, "transient fear associated with military combat and manifested by trembling, running and hiding" was an acute condition that would resolve itself naturally. The concept of a long-term chronic disorder suddenly cut from the psychiatric lexicon, the new language clearly reflected a restructuring of thinking motivated by the political and financial ramifications of thousands of traumatized veterans returning from the war in Vietnam.

Not until the late 1970s, after the development of "rape trauma syndrome" and "battered women syndrome," did the generalizability of life-threatening stressors begin to apply to veterans of the Vietnam War. Finally, in 1980, DSM-III presented Posttraumatic Stress Disorder as an anxiety disorder, its causes and symptoms delineated and categorized, and for the first time, the nature of combat-induced stressors were given an approbatory definition—"generally beyond the realm of normal human experience that would evoke significant symptoms of distress in most people." Published in 1994, DSM-IV went further and required the traumatized individual to have had an "overwhelming emotional reaction, defined as intense fear, helplessness or horror" when confronted by an extremely stressful experience.[11]

So what became of the surviving Cro-Magnon hunters who returned to their tribe changed men? No diagnosis of PTSD for them, no understanding, treatment, or comfort. How did they manage their symptoms? Could they understand what had happened to them? Sadly, ignorance of combat-induced stress has been a reality for traumatized soldiers and civilians for millennia. Hopefully, the fighting men and women returning from the horrors of today and tomorrow's wars will receive better care than their predecessors.

Now we know something of how a person develops PTSD and some of its history. Let's delve deeper. What is PTSD? What does it look like, and most importantly, what does it feel like to those affected by its symptomology and their family and friends?

In his book, *Incubated in Terror*, Bruce D. Perry, M.D., Ph.D., one of the world's foremost scientists studying and writing on the impact of trauma and abuse on the human brain, describes how the brain developed in an environment dominated by violence:

> 250,000 years ago, a few thousand Homo sapiens (our first genetically-equivalent ancestors) migrated out of Africa, began the long process of inhabiting and ultimately dominating the rest of the natural world (Leakey, 1994), a fragile process aided by a great deal of luck and the remarkable potential of the human brain to allow non-genetic, transgenerational transmission of information (sociocultural evolution). For thousands of generations, life was characterized by danger—omnipresent threat and perverse intra and inter species violence. Humankind and our current sociocultural practices evolved in—and therefore, reflect—a brutal, violent and unpredictable world. The evolution of complex cultures and civilization has not protected millions from the brutality, which characterized the ascent of humankind. While civilization has decreased our vulnerability to non-human predators, it has done little to decrease intraspecies violence (Keegan). Indeed, modern history is characterized by increasingly efficient, systematic and institutionalized violence (e.g., the inquisition, slavery, the Holocaust, the Trail of Tears). Men were, and men remain, the major predators of vulnerable humans (typically women and children). The profound impact of domestic violence, community violence, physical and sexual abuse and other forms of predatory or impulsive assault cannot be overestimated. Violence impacts the victims, the witnesses—and ultimately, us all. Understanding and modifying our violent nature will determine, in large part, the degree to which we will successfully adapt to the challenges of the future—the degree to which future generations of human beings can actually experience humanity.[12]

NOTES

1. *Diary of Samuel Pepys*, 1633-1703

2. Harrington, R. *Journal of the Society for the Social History of Medicine.*

3. Herman, J. (1992). *Trauma and Recovery.* United States, Harper-Collins.

4. Janet, P. "Etude Sur Un Cas D'Aboulie et D'Idees Fixes." *Revue Philosophique* 31 (1891). Translated by H. Ellenberger in *The Discovery of the Unconscious.* New York: Basic Books, (1970). In *Trauma and Recovery.* J. Hermaned. 12-13. United States: Harper-Collins, 1992.

5. Herman, J. (1992). *Trauma and Recovery.* United States: Harper-Collins.

6. Freud, S. (1896). "The Aetiology of Hysteria." Translated by J. Strachey in *Standard Edition*, 203, n. 3. London, Hogarth Press (1962).

7. Freud, S. "An Autobiographical Study." Translated by J. Strachey in *Standard Edition*, 34, n. 20. London, Hogarth Press, 1959.

8. Showalter, E. "The Female Malady: Women, Madness, and English Culture." New York: Pantheon, 1985. In *Trauma and Recovery*, ed. J. Herman. United States: Harper-Collins, 1992: 12-13.

9. Abram Kardiner, A., and H. Spiegel. (1947)."War, Stress, and Neurotic Illness." *The Traumatic Neurosis of War.* New York, Hoeber.

10. Grinker, R. and J. Spiegel. (1945). *Men Under Stress.* Philadelphia, Blakeston.

11. Diagnostic and Statistical Manual of Mental Disorders Fourth Edition (Text Revision): American Psychiatric Publishing, 2000.

12. Perry, B. (1997). "Incubated in Terror: Neurodevelopmental Factors in the 'Cycle of Violence.'" In *Children, Youth and Violence: The Search for Solutions.* Ed. J. Osofsky. New York, Guilford Press.

Glossary of Military Terms and Nomenclature

.50 Caliber Machine Gun: A heavy machine gun firing 12.7mm rounds at a rate of 550 rounds per minute.

40mm Grenades: Mounted in the nose of gunship helicopters, the 40mm grenade launcher fires high explosive rounds at the rate of 300 per minute.

105 Howitzer: High trajectory cannon firing a 105mm exploding shell to a distance of 25-30 kilometers.

155 Howitzer: High trajectory cannon firing a 155mm exploding shell to a distance of 25-30 kilometers.

175mm gun: A field gun firing a 174-pound high explosive projectile up to 33 kilometers.

AIT: Advanced infantry training.

AK-47: Russian made standard issue infantry rifle firing a 7.62mm round at 600 rounds per minute.

ARVN: Army of the Republic of Vietnam—South Vietnamese soldiers.

AWOL : Absent Without Leave.

BC scope: A sighting device used in controlling machine gun or artillery fire.

Bush: Slang term meaning enemy territory.

BX: Base Exchange.

C-7: Caribou. A twin-engine turboprop light, tactical transport aircraft designed to operate in primitive conditions.

C-118: Liftmaster. A four-engine aircraft used widely in military and civilian roles.

C-123: Provider. A twin-engine turboprop transport aircraft known for its rugged reliability.

C-130: Hercules. A four-engine turboprop transport plane valued for its versatility.

Charley: Vietcong (Victor Charley).

Claymore mine: Remotely detonated anti-personnel mine.

CO: Commanding officer.

Concertina wire: Razor wire in large coils designed to expand like a concertina.

Cong: Vietcong.

CONUS: Continental United States.

Cordite: A smokeless, explosive propellant commonly used in firearms.

Corpsman: An enlisted soldier with training in basic first aid.

Cosmoline: A yellowish or light-amber ointment similar to Vaseline used to prevent rust of metal objects.

CP: Command post.

Cs: C rations.

Daisy Cutter: BLU-82 bomb sometimes used for clearing terrain such as landing fields.

DEROS: Date of expected return from overseas.

D.I.: Drill instructor.

Dust Off: Army aero-medical battlefield evacuation in Vietnam.

Eight-inch gun: Track mounted field gun firing 8″ diameter exploding projectiles up to 17,000 meters.

FAC: Forward air controller.

Flechette Round: An exploding anti-personnel projectile containing hundreds of darts or small arrows.

FNG: Fucking new guy.

GI cans: Usually five-gallon containers.

Gook: Pejorative term for Vietnamese.

GP tent: General purpose.

Greenie: A soldier newly arrived on station in Vietnam.

GRO: Graves registration office.

Gunny: Marine gunnery sergeant.

Hmongs: the eighth largest ethnic group in Vietnam.

Ho Chi Minh Trail: A network of roads and trails used by Communist forces beginning in North Vietnam and crossing into Laos and Cambodia en route to South Vietnam.

Hooch: Slang term applied to American and Vietnamese living quarters.

ICU: Intensive Care Unit.

In country: Term commonly used by military personnel to describe actually being in Vietnam.

KIA: Killed in action.

Klicks: Kilometers.

LP: Listening post.

LRP: Long-range reconnaissance patrol.

LST: Landing ship tank.

LZ: Landing zone.

M-16: Standard issue infantry rifle firing 5.56mm round at the rate of 750 rounds per minute.

M-60 Machine Gun: Offensive and defensive weapon firing a 7.62mm round at the rate of 550 rounds per minute.

M-79 Grenade Launcher: A large bore, break-down, shoulder-fired weapon firing a 40mm explosive projectile at the rate of five to seven rounds per minute.

MACV: Military Assistance Command, Vietnam.

M.A.S.H.: Mobile army surgical hospital.

Medivac: Medical evacuation of wounded from a battle zone by air.

Military crest: The area just below the crest of any hill through which infantry soldiers can move and not be silhouetted.

Montagnards: a mountain-dwelling ethnic minority living in Central Vietnam.

MOS: Military occupational specialty.

MP: Military Policeman.

Napalm: Gasoline-based incendiary bomb.

NCO: Non-commissioned officer.

NVA: North Vietnamese army.

OP: Observation post.

POGE: Slang. See REMF.

POW: Prisoner of war.

PT: Physical Training.

PZ: Pick up zone.

R&R: Rest and relaxation. Usually one to two weeks away from the war zone.

REMFs: Rear Area Mother Fuckers.

Remington raiders: Typists.

ROTC: Reserve Officer Training Corps, a college program for students who choose to trade tuition assistance for military service.

RPG: Rocket propelled grenade.

Sam Browne Belt: Associated with a military or police uniform, it is a wide leather belt usually supported by a strap over the right shoulder.

SEATAC: Seattle/Tacoma Airport.

Straight legs: Non-jump rated soldier.

TAOR: Tactical area of operation.

Tet: Vietnamese new year holiday.

Tracer round: Cartridges that glow when fired permitting the shooter to follow their trajectories.

VC: Viet Cong. Members of the National Liberation Front who fought against the American occupation of Vietnam.

About the Authors

WILLIAM SCHRODER is a writer, businessman, past helicopter pilot infantry officer, and Vietnam veteran. He is an auxiliary cadre member of Warriors, Inc., a Hollywood film industry military technical advisory company. His own PTSD symptoms and their decades-long effects on his spouse, children, and loved ones compelled him to begin a deeper exploration of the disorder.

RONALD DAWE is a licensed Mental Health Counselor in Florida and currently Executive Director of The Palm Beach Institute in West Palm Beach. His special interest is the link between early, complex trauma and substance abuse or dependence in later life. His clinical focus is on treating the underlying psychological causes of chemical dependency and other addictive behaviors. Dawe is also a Certified Clinical Sexologist and a Diplomat of the American Board of Sexology. He served as a helicopter pilot in Vietnam and subsequently struggled three decades with PTSD.